Privatiz

Privatization in Practice

*Reports on Trends, Cases
and Debates in Public Service
by Business and Nonprofits*

Edited by
Joaquin Jay Gonzalez III *and*
Roger L. Kemp

McFarland & Company, Inc., Publishers
Jefferson, North Carolina

LIBRARY OF CONGRESS CATALOGUING-IN-PUBLICATION DATA

Names: Gonzalez, Joaquin Jay, editor. | Kemp, Roger L., editor.
Title: Privatization in practice : reports on trends, cases and
debates in public service by business and nonprofits /
edited by Joaquin Jay Gonzalez III and Roger L. Kemp.
Description: Jefferson, North Carolina : McFarland & Company, Inc.,
Publishers, 2016. | Revised edition of Privatization, 2007. |
Includes bibliographical references and index.
Identifiers: LCCN 2016026041 | ISBN 9780786476770
(softcover : acid free paper) ∞
Subjects: LCSH: Municipal services—United States. |
Privatization—United States.
Classification: LCC HD4605 .P745 2016 | DDC 338.9/25—dc23
LC record available at https://lccn.loc.gov/2016026041

BRITISH LIBRARY CATALOGUING DATA ARE AVAILABLE

ISBN (print) 978-0-7864-7677-0
ISBN (ebook) 978-1-4766-2568-3

Front cover inset images *top to bottom*: school bus, prison,
and emergency room; *background* road construction
(all images © 2016 iStock)

Printed in the United States of America

McFarland & Company, Inc., Publishers
Box 611, Jefferson, North Carolina 28640
www.mcfarlandpub.com

Jay:
To my wife, Michelle,
and daughters, Elise and Coral

———⚬⚬⚬———

Roger:
To my granddaughter, Anika,
the best and the brightest

Acknowledgments

We are grateful for the financial support of the Mayor George Christopher Professorship and the Russell T. Sharpe Professorship at Golden Gate University. We appreciate the encouragement from Dean Paul Fouts and our wonderful colleagues at the GGU Edward S. Ageno School of Business, the Department of Public Administration, and the Executive MPA Program.

Our heartfelt thanks go to the contributors listed in About the Editors and Contributors in the back of the book and the organizations and publishers below for granting permission to reprint the material in this volume. Most waived or reduced fees as an expression of their support for practical research and information sharing that benefits our community.

Alliance for Innovation
American City & County
American Planning Association
American Prospect
Baker Tilly
City of Carrollton, Texas
e.Republic
Firehouse Magazine
Governing
Government Finance Officers Association
Huffington Post
Institute for Local Government, California
International City/County Management Association
John Geyman
League of Women Voters
NACo County News
National League of Cities
New York Times
PA Times
Planning Magazine
PM Magazine
Responsible Hospitality Institute
Stanford Social Innovation Review
Thomas Guilfoy

Table of Contents

Part III. Discussions and Debates

Appendices

Preface

The first edition, *Privatization: The Provision of Public Services by the Private Sector*, was released in 1991. Initiatives covered were propelled by the Reagan-Thatcher privatization push of the 1980s. In that compilation, privatization practices were in their relative start-up stages—most being tried and tested for the first time. As government coffers dried up and bureaucrats found traditional reorganization as not an adequate solution to balancing budgets, new and radical changes were necessary. Many political leaders believed that the best approach to government reform was to mimic private sector thinking and doing, including outsourcing operations. The ultimate goal was efficiency or simply increasing revenue and reserves.

Since the publication of the 1991 edition, a lot of privatization experimentation, implementation, and evaluation have transpired, not just in the United States but globally. Millions of Request for Proposals (RFPs) have been issued and a commensurate number of Memorandum of Understandings (MOUs) have been signed. In 1992, Osborne and Gaebler's *Reinventing Government* unleashed privatization version 2.0. Then the turn of the century brought 9/11 and the addition of security and intelligence to privatization efforts before the Great Recession ushered in massive government belt tightening efforts. Federal spending for infrastructure projects (especially highways and bridges) were increased to spur economic recovery and

thus more private contracts were outsourced to create jobs. At cities and counties, privatization efforts slowed down for these speed bumps but then surged forward again once the rear wheels went over the last hurdle. Privatization gained speed in both scope and magnitude. Going from contracting out to shared services, from garbage collection to parking services.

As professors who worked decades in public and community service, we feel that we have the "duty" to reveal what has happened after the publication of the first edition in this new compilation. Why? Primarily because in our view although there have been many successful programs, there were also failed attempts. Revenue and savings were not always achieved. Sometimes, the service was cheap only in the beginning but then gradually became more and more expensive as the years went by. Market forces sometimes made public services more costly and unaffordable especially to residents who did not have high incomes. Thus, we pose caveats and caution.

Consequently, the lessons learned from the successes and failures gave birth to a new aspiration—effectiveness. Effectiveness is measured in terms of accountable results and sustained high performance. In other words, government managers should not only be contented with the budget savings. They should also be satisfied with the quality of the private contractor's work output and ultimately the happiness of citizens.

Thus, this second edition answers these

questions: How was effectiveness achieved? What adjustments were incorporated into current trends and practices? Are there examples of good cases and applications? What are the lingering discussions and debates?

Additionally, the earlier book helped concerned citizens, communities, businesses, government officials, and students of public service who were in search of possibilities, inspiration, or concrete examples. This one seeks to continue that same tradition but with better results and performance in mind.

Part I: Trends and Practices

As stated in the previous section, in the 1980s, the ultimate goal of privatization was efficiency. Efficiency brought cost savings, increased revenue, balanced budgets, and fiscal prudence. During the 1990s and beyond, privatization shifted to effectiveness. Thus in Part I, we gathered together fifteen lucid chapters demonstrating the continuing and contemporary privatization trends and practices and how they made public services more effective.

Prior to 1991, privatization of public services was driven mainly by the private sector. But during the years beyond, saw the rise of nonprofits (or non-governmental organizations) as a capable public service delivery alternative to or partner with government and/or business. Many have become a more cost-efficient substitute to pricey private contractors. After all, nonprofits are not supposed to be focused on profits and shareholders but service and stakeholders.

The effectiveness of nonprofits is amplified in the writings of Professors John Carroll (Chapter 1), Alicia Schatteman (Chapter 2), and Henry Mintzberg (Chapter 3). Carroll points out that in trying to reduce personnel cost and increase effectiveness, governments have gone to nonprofits or shared services as the cheaper alternative

to expensive private contractors. To reinforce this point, Schatteman underscores the recent addition of nonprofit providers as an important alternative service delivery option especially amongst municipalities dealing with fiscal stress. While agreeing that its significance has grown over the years, Mintzberg argues against the use of labels such as "nonprofit" or "third sector" or even "nongovernmental organizations." Rather, he proclaims the rise of the "plural sector."

According to Joaquin Jay Gonzalez III (Chapter 4), David Swindell and Cheryll Hilvert (Chapter 5) and Monte Mercer (Chapter 6), partnership and collaboration are trendy practices that almost always gets the nod when mentioned in tandem with privatization during city hall meetings. Professor-practitioner Gonzalez elaborates on the mechanics of how the "plural sector" aligns with public and private sector stakeholders to form "public interest partnerships." Professor Swindell and ICMA Director Hilvert add that another successful concept to consider is "collaboration" which has proven to be an effective tool for jurisdictions to join with others. While based on their experiences at the North Central Texas Council of Governments, Deputy Executive Director Mercer recommends customizing collaborative arrangements for effective shared services relationships.

For privatization to be effective and not just efficient, Cathy Lazarus and Ted Volskay (Chapter 7), Amanda M. Girth and Jocelyn M. Johnston (Chapter 8), and Jonas Prager and John Flint (Chapter 9) allude to the critical importance of not just focusing on the cost savings but to also carefully overseeing the contracting process from selection to evaluation. Lazarus and Volskay provides tips for effective contract selection, from determining if privatization of the service is the best route to negotiating the agreement. Based on their National League of Cities supported survey, Girth and Johnston found that municipal managers feel that their job does not end when the contract has been awarded. It is still essential to track and monitor contractors to ensure the best performance and results. A majority of U.S. cities have less than 100,000 residents, using the case of Weston, Florida, Professor Prager and City Manager Flint reveal contract management issues and lessons from small municipal governments.

After cautioning that public-private partnership (P3) are evolving, Justin Marlowe, William Rivenbark, and A. John Vogt reveal the full range of best practices available to municipalities (Chapter 10). Using the case of Sandy Springs, Georgia—another small U.S. city, Amy Davis illustrates why they chose a global engineering firm to handle virtually all of their citizens' needs and how they creatively enhanced their revenue streams (Chapter 11). While scholar Bob Bland discusses ongoing trends in third-party agreements and diversifying financial risks (Chapter 12).

The final three chapters of Part I delves into the latest "trends and practices" using innovation, competition, and liquidation. County Manager Katy Singlaub shares some thoughts on the meaning and place of innovation for effective local governance particularly in a continuing era of privatization (Chapter 13). While Director of Competition Tom Guilfoy expounds on the nationally-recognized experience of using managed competition among city agencies instead of outsourcing in Carrollton, Texas (Chapter 14). This section ends with Pew Project Director Christopher Swope's discussion of Chicago's much-touted asset liquidation approach which helped pay down huge sums of debt and raise the city's credit rating (Chapter 15).

Part II: Cases and Applications

The collection of twenty-three cases and applications we assembled for the midsec-

tion of the book demonstrate good practices on the move from privatization efficiency to privatization effectiveness. Armed with lessons from past practices, mayors, city managers, local councils, citizen committees, and municipal departments initiated customized privatization programs and services grounded on achieving results and high performance. Patterns of similarities existed but most were different depending on each of their unique circumstances and needs.

After 1991, privatization efforts in order to improve effectiveness saw movement from single industry or area to integrated development and multi-stakeholder approaches. This is illustrated in the first six chapters dealing with applications of business improvement zones and cases of mixed use development.

The next three chapters look at methods of effectively improving a city's economic development. Jim Peters and Alicia Scholer look at how downtown San Jose, California, businesses shared in an effective nightlife policing costs (Chapter 16). Lawrence Houstoun discusses how utilizing mainly non-profit corporations, 1000 U.S. cities adopted a Business Improvement District (BID) approach, including at Maplewood, NJ, Jacksonville, FL, Denver, CO, Hollywood, CA (Chapter 17). While Ken Pulskamp elaborates on how in Santa Clarita, California, the local government partnered with private firms to lay down the groundwork for a successful business retention strategy (Chapter 18).

The next four chapters offer colorful examples of how successful mixed used development areas are run and managed. Jennifer Grzeskowiak writes about government, business, and non-governmental organizations coming together to form a public interest partnership (PIP) in New York City's Local Initiatives Support Corporation, San Francisco's Neighborhood Marketplace Initiative, Indianapolis' Focusing

Commercial Urban Strategies, and the Main Street Milwaukee Program (Chapter 19). While Helen S. McIlvaine discusses how in Alexandria, Virginia, Potomac Yard Development converted a former regional rail yard into a successful mixed use development via a public, private, and nonprofit collaboration (Chapter 20). Craig Chavez looks at how a unique public interest partnership between the city of Ann Arbor, Washtenaw County, other local communities, Eastern Michigan University, the University of Michigan, Washtenaw Community College, and the private sector, created the Ann Arbor SPARK to help in integrated mixed use regional development (Chapter 21). Greg Beato takes a look at San Francisco, where the Presidio Trust and the city banked on anchor tenant Lucasfilm to draw in other firms and eventually raise the funds to spruce up a historic military base into trendy mixed use commercial, technology, community, and recreational spaces (Chapter 22).

Thereafter, we delve into good "hardware" practices in solid waste management, green initiatives, renewable energy, public works, utilities, technology, parking, and building inspections. Some good environmental privatization practices are provided by Ed Brock's description of how Austin, Texas officials hired Loomis, Calif.–based Gary Liss & Associates to help the city reduce the amount of waste going to its landfill by 20 percent in 2012 and 100 percent by 2040 (Chapter 23). While Connie Kuranko shares two outsourcing case studies (Chapter 24). One on how Seattle, Washington introduced a Green Purchasing Program to promote goods, materials, services and capital improvements that help reduce greenhouse gas emissions. And another on elaborating on Hennepin County, Minnesota's Environmentally Preferable Purchasing and Waste Reduction Resolution.

On energy, Anna Read writes about a unique relationship under the Solar America Communities Outreach Partnership involving the Department of Energy, ICMA, and ICLEI-USA who are working to increase the use and integration of solar energy technologies in local governments across the country through a multiyear outreach effort (Chapter 25). While on health and sanitation, Ted Volskay pens the case of Franklin, Ohio which became the first municipality in the nation to privatize a publicly owned water treatment plant that had been constructed with federal grant funds (Chapter 26). While Steve Klepper and City Manager's Office Team shares how they streamlined Corpus Christi's utility and public works operations by implementing a computerized work and asset management system (Chapter 27). At Centennial, Colorado, Robert Barkin writes on how they trusted global engineering company CH2M Hill to run all their public works functions from water and wastewater system optimization and operation to community development and public works administration (Chapter 28).

On the technology end, Kevin Fitchard's *American City & County* piece discusses how Philadelphia saw its poorest residents being passed by the broadband revolution and decided to bridge the digital divide between the rich and Internet savvy and the poor and unconnected based on the free WiFi successes in Boston, Austin, Vail, and Corpus Christi (Chapter 29). While the City of Chicago, Illinois considered the benefits and disadvantages of privatizing parking and decided to lease both its 36,000 metered spaces and four municipal garages with commendable results according to David Taxman's assessment (Chapter 30). *Government Finance Review* contributor Kyle Steitz documents how in Troy, Michigan a private firm effectively manages the daily operations of the building department, which includes performing inspections, planning reviews, staffing the front counter, archiving city records, and working with city officials on departmental budget (Chapter 31).

From the hardware, we shift to good "software" applications and cases in arts, senior and human services, library, public safety, and education. Beginning with Wichita, Kansas, which *PM Magazine* contributor Robert Lynch reveals participated in the Americans for the Arts' Arts & Economic Prosperity program and eventually generated millions in economic activity and much-needed jobs using public interest partnerships (Chapter 32). While Christen Smith pens how cities that provide a high quality of life, including broad-based, innovative park and recreation opportunities for their residents age 50-plus, are attracting seniors to relocate to their communities for retirement, and these migrating seniors are providing a significant stimulus to their local economies (Chapter 33).

NACo County News staff writer Charles Taylor shares how Santa Clara County, California and Cuyahoga County, Ohio became the first counties in the nation to explore a new financing model—social impact of bonds—to address some of their thorniest human services problems (Chapter 34). While Muriel Strand expounds on the successful outsourcing of patron services to Library Systems & Services, LLC at public libraries in Jackson County, Oregon and Santa Clarita, California (Chapter 35). *Governing* staff writer John Buntin writes about Redlands, California ambitious efforts to integrate public safety volunteers—Citizen Volunteer Patrol (CVP) unit—into the workings of local government (Chapter 36). Using another approach, Tom Guilfoy illustrates the Carrollton, Texas approach to public safety privatization using managed competition (Chapter 37). Finally, education administrator Frank Woodward expounds on the Western Governors University–Tennessee State public-private educational partnership seeking to raise the

percentage of Tennessee residents with at least a two-year degree or certification to 55 percent by 2025 (Chapter 38).

Part III: *Discussions and Debates*

After reading the good practices in Part II, we may have painted a picture of an abundant garden in your mind. But we would like to remind you that weeds will always find a way to grow in between the beautiful flowers. Thus, we conclude this new *Privatization* edition with thirteen thoughtful pieces on the lingering discussions and debates. We hope citizens, leaders, and analysts remember them as caveats as they improve and refine not just the efficiency but also the effectiveness of future versions of privatization in their communities.

Kicking off this concluding section are important ethics discussion and debate. First, former City Manager Michael Abels talks about whether America's communities have sacrificed the public interest in the name of revenue generation (Chapter 39). Second, American Planning Association CEO Paul Farmer asks his fellow planners to reexamine their core values vis-a-vis larger questions of social equity and morality as they get more involved in privatization (Chapter 40). Third, the Institute for Local Government shares an interesting "question and answer" exchange on the best deal, fair process, avoiding favoritism, and trust (Chapter 41).

Adding to these ethical concerns are skeptical assessments about placing public services in the hands of for-profits by: Dennis Compton (Chapter 42) on public safety and emergency services; John Geyman (Chapter 43) on Medicare and health; as well as Ann Hagedorn (Chapter 44) on defense and prisons. These ethical discussions are followed by two-side exchanges on the "argument for and risks" by the

Chicago Council on Global Affairs Emerging Class of 2008 (Chapter 45); "wows and woes" are considered by Rachel Burstein and Edward Shikada (Chapter 46); "pros and cons" discussed by Russell Nichols (Chapter 47); "benefits and downsides" by Stephanie Rozsa and Caitlin Geary (Chapter 48), and "claims and concerns" by Nora Leech (Chapter 49).

Macroeconomic factors adversely affect the effectiveness of privatization efforts. The 2008 financial crisis put a damper on privatization gains and reduced both state and federal support for local governments. We share two opinions on the debates and discussion that transpired during this dire period. First, Christine Smith and Shelley Fulla writes-up a summary from a survey their firm, Baker Tilly LLP, administered documenting how the situation necessitated a scramble for budget solutions that would appease both taxpayers and public employees—which is not an easy task (Chapter 50). Second, former Indianapolis Mayor Stephen Goldsmith elaborates on his suggestion to exercise prudence and provides principles which might help guide the debate in Chapter 51.

Appendices

We append useful documents, including the League of Women Voters' Privatization Glossary; Washoe County, Nevada's Managed Competition Guidelines; League of Women Voters' "Privatization Position," and the International City/County Management Association's "Steps to Effective Privatization."

Privatization in Practice builds on the classic 1991 Compilation with an updated collection highlighting what has transpired since it was printed. Written by practitioners, reformers, scholars, and journalists just like the 1991 edition, this book is easy to read as well. It is incisive and thought-provoking. The experiences cover the East Coast to the West Coast, from New York to San Francisco as well as the North to the South, from Hennepin County, Minnesota to Corpus Christi, Texas. As you could see from the acknowledgements, the reputable publications from a broad political spectrum make for a colorful tapestry of ideas and opinions representing America's diversity and democracy.

We hope you have an insightful read.

1. Private Delivery of Public Services, 20 Years On

John Carroll

It has been a little over 20 years since Osborne and Gaebler rocked the public sector with "Reinventing Government." In those early years of the Clinton administration, all levels of American government looked in the mirror to think about how we could do it better. In describing their models of government, the delivery of public services through contract with private entities played a substantive role. The book did incredibly well and I remember at least some academics quietly murmuring their displeasure at the time that practitioners had taken the lead in this area (probably more like envy at the success).

Since the reinventing movement of the 1990s, government performance has shifted from the emphasis on efficiency to effectiveness. It still makes me crazy when the terms "effectiveness" and "efficiency" are used interchangeably in conversation or writing—as if they were the same thing. They are not. Although there are many definitions out there, I prefer to look at efficiency in terms of costs (providing public services at the most reasonable or best costs we can). Effectiveness is the results of providing the service.

Is this now decades-long trend as simple as enhancing efficiency or effectiveness in the provision of government services? State and local government have had several serious periods of revenue shortfalls over the last 20 years, forcing decision makers to either reduce services, find alternatives (like contracting to the private sector) or some combination. The federal government may be able to have expenditures exceed revenues (all the time, it seems), but state and local governments cannot.

"Privatizing" government services has grown in the last two decades. A great amount of federal services are contracted (or "outsourced") to corporations, who in turn subcontract service provisions to others. State and local governments have contracted the management of airports, seaports, transit, corrections, health provision and many others to the private sector. The variety of contracted services is as wide as the 90,000+ units of government in this country.

The discipline of public administration generally evolved from the political science schools to branch out to a number of studies. Though most programs are located in

Originally published as John Carroll (2014). "Private Delivery of Public Services, 20 Years On." *PA Times*, July 21, 2014. Reprinted with permission of the publisher.

the schools of social sciences, our program is housed within the university's business school. One might be hard pressed to discount the similarities in management theories between the disciplines, though their fundamental purposes are quite different (profit versus service).

Our school's namesake and benefactor, H. Wayne Huizenga, built his first megabusiness in part on public contracts. His trash hauling company evolved into Waste Management, Inc., one of the largest of its kind in the world. He also built up other Fortune 500 companies and bought stakes in commercial real estate and sports teams. His ideas of entrepreneurship and building organizations from within to take advantage of opportunities, resonates with elements of the reinventing movement.

The relationship between public and private sectors is not limited to contracting the delivery of services. The public sector has relied on the private sector to build and maintain the products and infrastructure used by government in order to provide public services. We may purchase aircraft carriers from defense contractors, but at the state and local level we also use private manufacturers for the purchase of everything from pencils, to computers, to vehicles, to just about everything government needs or consumes to provide services.

Another trend over the last 20 years has been the eclipse in the compensation for public employees over private employees. Increased salaries, benefits, pensions and other costs, pushed by "the market," the influence of public unions, and the desire of local elected officials to stay that way, finally pushed many public employees past their private counterparts.

Personnel costs comprise the vast majority of public budgets. The no-brainer becomes reducing this overhead by turning to the private sector where employees are now paid less. Reducing personnel costs becomes a multiplier of sorts, because the support personnel and equipment needed are also assumed by the private contractor.

Is this the only way to contract services? No, not at all. Contracts are now tendered to nonprofit groups that are willing to fill in those areas where services are needed but no longer able to be provided by government. Public entities can also contract out to one another for services as well.

The sheriff's office where I served for more than 27 years had a variety of contracts—all of which had to be coordinated with the county commission (the taxing and budget approval authority). Our corrections side (the county jail) contracted its food and health services with private sector companies—the political aspects of which are a discussion for another day. Our vehicle fleet was maintained by private contractors.

The county commission provided separate contracts to the sheriff's office to provide countywide fire rescue services, as well as law enforcement/security/fire rescue for the county's international airports and seaports. The state of Florida contracted with the sheriff's office to provide child protective investigations. The county school board contracted to offset the cost of school resource officers. Fourteen municipalities contracted to turn over their police departments to the sheriff's office, five of which also contracted for fire rescue services.

Osborne and Gaebler can be credited with being among the architects of the recent performance management wave, with a move toward accountability that continues today. Were they the first? Jimmy Carter called for streamlining government in his 1976 presidential campaign. We have heard the calls for government practices to better reflect business methods for some time now (another argument for another day).

A large part of the progressive movement at the turn of the 20th century focused on improving government services. Government looked to the private sector for advice in the contributions of Taylor, Fayol, White, Follett, Gulick and Urwick, Willoughby, and many others from my theory courses. Will the private delivery of public services continue for another 20 years? Very likely, but will we reach a point where we do not recognize the difference between the two? We'll see.

2. Public, Private or Nonprofit Providers

Alicia Schatteman

Everything old is "new" again. For a long time, in times of need, local governments turned to their neighboring communities for assistance such as during a crisis, unexpected decreases in budgets or increased demand for services. This informal cooperation existed because of established relationships and trust. Communities felt a mutual dependence and therefore could call upon mutual aid as needed.

As communities grew in size and complexity, residents requested broader and higher quality services. Competition for property and sales tax put communities in competition with each other, and moved them a little further away from the ideals of mutual dependence. Local governments sought to provide all of the goods and services for their residents within a municipal jurisdiction, which often meant increasing municipal budgets and corresponding increases to property and sales tax. This formula worked in many locales until the Great Recession.

The Great Recession of 2008–2010 taught us all a few lessons. It was the wake-up call many of us needed to reassess our own spending habits and long-term goals. For government, the lesson was clear. The public would not accept expanding budgets and higher property taxes. If families had to tighten their belts, then so did government. Almost daily, newspaper headlines called for government to prioritize, maximum resources, cut spending, eliminate waste.

According to the National League of Cities, 48 percent of cities had reduced the size of the municipal workforce to address fiscal stress on revenues during the recession. With staff reductions, local governments could not continue the same level of services without looking at alternative ways to provide those services at a lower cost. The elephant in the room that is rarely discussed is public employees are the most expensive workers due to public pensions and other benefits. Therefore, if private or nonprofit workers could provide the same services, then the overall cost of that service would be reduced to lower human resource costs. The cost savings of reducing the public workforce could be passed on to residents through stable taxes or budgets. I recently wrote about the tension between government and nonprofit organizations

Originally published as Alicia Schatteman (2014). "The Business of Government Today: Public, Private or Nonprofit Providers?" *PA Times*, July 22, 2014. Reprinted with permission of the publisher.

under contractual agreements to provide public services in *PA Times*.

Although alternative delivery options occurred before the recession, municipalities during and after the recession were looking at all of these options much more seriously.

Alternative Service Delivery Options:

- Contracting out
- Managed competition
- Interlocal agreements (shared services)
- Service consolidation
- Public-private partnerships
- Privatization

The International City/County Management Association (ICMA) has a variety of resources available to local governments to learn more about contracting out. Read more about the use of nonprofits to provide public services through contracts in a paper by Richard C. Feiock and Hee-Soun Jang. ICMA also offers information about shared services (interlocal agreements) which can be found here.

Clearly, there are many considerations before government pursues alternative service delivery options. However there are several tips to keep in mind.

Are you ready to consider alternative service delivery?

- Municipalities must communicate consistent messages to residents and involve all the stakeholders in the process of alternative service delivery options. Communication needs to be ongoing throughout the process so that government is completely transparent.
- Organization culture and the community culture must factor into a decision to pursue alternative service delivery. Certainly, the broader community has a culture as well, which must be considered. Some communities will want reinvestment, others lower taxes, others higher quality services.
- Find the right opportunity to make changes to service delivery. The recession of 2008–2011 certainly made difficult conversations possible and palatable given the devastating impact of the recession on municipal budgets.
- If contracting out is a preferred option, then the municipality will need to invest in good contract managers on staff. In order to have successful contracts, the municipality needs to understand their in-house contract capacity.
- Alternative service options are likely to be more successful if there are a number of alternative providers (public, private or nonprofit).
- Successful alternative service delivery works best when the service is tangible (clear specifications), monitoring costs are not excessive and a competitive market exists for the service.

3. Time for the Plural Sector

Henry Mintzberg

When one sector of society becomes dominant-as the public sector did under communism and the private sector is now doing in the name of capitalism-societies go out of balance and people suffer. A healthy society requires a respected public sector, a responsible private sector, and a robust plural sector. Calling it "plural," in place of inadequate labels like nonprofit or third, will help this sector take its rightful place alongside the other two and also help us to appreciate the unique role it has to play in restoring that balance.

What is frequently called the "third sector" turns out to be surprisingly obscure. No wonder, with vague labels like this one. What does third sector mean to most people? This sector deserves a better name, and it deserves greater recognition of the critical role it will have to play in restoring balance in this troubled world.

What might best be called the "plural sector" (more later on why) has been consistently excluded from the great debates of our time—over left versus right, public sector governments versus private sector markets, nationalization versus privatization (as if these two sectors are the only homes for our important institutions). People argue about the need for government control of health care services to insure equality, compared with leaving control to the marketplace for the sake of efficiency, without recognizing how many of these services are actually supplied by community institutions in the plural sector for the sake of quality. And then we use the term PPP as if partnerships exist only between organizations that are public and private.

The plural sector is not some middle position between left and right, but as different from the other two sectors as they are from each other. Its particular focus is on communities, whereas the other two sectors focus on governments and businesses. It is time, therefore, for the plural sector to take its rightful place alongside the ones called public and private.

The Plurality of the Sector

What, then, constitutes a sector that can be called plural? The answer is any association of people that is neither public nor private-owned neither by the state nor by private investors. Some are owned by their members; others are owned by no one. There are vast numbers of both.

Cooperatives, for example, are owned by

Originally published as Henry Mintzberg (2015). "Time for the Plural Sector." *Stanford Social Innovation Review*, 13(3), Summer 2015. Reprinted with permission of the publisher.

their members—whether customers, suppliers, or workers—each with a single share that cannot be sold to any other member. Amul, a dairy cooperative in India, has three million members (www.amul.com/rn/organisation). Mondragon, the world's largest federation of worker cooperatives, headquartered in the Basque region of Spain, employs 74,000 people, in businesses ranging from supermarkets to machine tools (www.mondragon-corporation.com/eng/). And many of us belong to co-ops as customers, whether in credit unions or sporting goods stores. Indeed, the United States alone is home to 30,000 cooperatives with a total membership of 350 million, more than the country's entire population (community-weaith.org/strategies/panel/coops/index.html). Similar ownership patterns can be found in professional associations, chambers of commerce, and kibbutzim.

Owned by no one are a great many associations of enormous variety: foundations, clubs, religious orders, think tanks, activist NGOs such as Greenpeace, and service NGOs such as the Red Cross. Most U.S. hospitals, called "voluntary," are supported by donors but owned by no one (58 percent, compared with 21 percent by governments and 21 percent by private investors) (kff.org/other/state-indicator/hospitals-by-ownership/). In Canada, close to 100 percent of hospitals are likewise non-owned, even though Canadian hospitals are mostly funded by government. Included in this sector are non-owned organizations that engage in business activities and so form part of what is called the social economy. Red Cross chapters in North America sell swimming lessons, and the Kenyan Red Cross has built commercial hotels to support its beneficial work.

In an article entitled "The Invisible World of Association," a group of us categorized the associations of this sector into four groups: mutual associations, which serve their own members (book clubs); benefit associations, which serve other people (food banks); protection associations, which advocate for their own members (chambers of commerce); and activist associations, which advocate for the needs of others (Amnesty International) (Mintzberg et al., 2005).

Most of these associations are legally registered and formally organized. But especially important are the more spontaneous associations of this sector, in the form of social movements and social initiatives. The former bring people together, often in large numbers, to challenge some aspect of the status quo, as we saw in Cairo's Tahrir Square and the occupation of Wall Street, and continue to see in the American Tea Party movement. Social initiatives, in contrast, are usually undertaken by small groups that champion programs of social change, usually in local communities, although some, like the Grameen Bank, have scaled up to become global.

Environmentalist Paul Hawken's book *Blessed Unrest* includes a 112-page appendix that lists social sector associations under headings such as culture, education, pollution, social justice, and religion. Hawken (2007) refers to all of this as a "movement" of more than one million associations, which he describes as "dispersed" and "inchoate." We need many more such associations, but we also need them to work together in partnership as a force for radical renewal in society.

Why Call It Plural?

This sector has to take some of the blame for its own obscurity, as it has not been able to settle on an acceptable label for itself. Third sector sounds third-rate, an afterthought. Referring to the sector as the home of nonprofits and non-governmental organizations (NGOs) makes little sense, because governments are literally nonprofit and businesses are literally non-governmental. Calling the sector voluntary overemphasizes the role of volunteers, whereas civil society, an old term but of increasing currency these days, is hardly descriptive-in contrast to uncivil society? The social sector is a better label, but logically used only when the other two sectors are called political and economic-which rarely happens.

At a meeting I attended recently of researchers in this sector, in little more than one hour they used almost all of these labels. If the experts can't get their vocabulary straight, how is anybody else supposed to take this sector seriously?

I propose the label plural sector for two reasons. The first is the variety of this sector's associations and their range of ownerships. Forms of ownership in government departments and business enterprises tend to be limited and their structures tend to be more consistently hierarchical. The second reason I favor the label plural is that it can be seen to take its place naturally alongside the labels public and private. Public, private, and civil society just doesn't do it. When I have introduced this label in discussions about the sectors, it has been used quite readily.

Revisiting de Tocqueville

The plural sector has long played an important role in the United States. Alexis de Tocqueville (2003) used the term "association" for the many organized activities he found in the new country. The American people's preference for limiting government encouraged them to organize for themselves, into plural sector associations alongside private sector businesses.

"The political associations that exist in the United States are only a single feature in the midst of the immense assemblage of associations in that country," de Tocqueville wrote in the 1830s. "Americans of all ages, all conditions, and all dispositions constantly form associations…. Whenever at the head of some undertaking you see the government in France, or a man of rank in England, in the United States you will be sure to find an association" (p. 106).

De Tocqueville saw these associations as not only quintessential American, but also a central component of the country's democracy. "If men are to remain civilized or to become so, the art of association together must grow and improve" (p. 10). That it certainly did, in America at least. But more recently, Harvard University professor Robert Putnam (1995 & 2000) has written about Americans "bowling alone," and Institute for Policy Studies scholar Chuck Collins (2012) has commented on the steady "erosion of the community institutions that we all depend on," such as schools, libraries, and parks. (See "Struggling for Sustainability" below.)

If de Tocqueville saw it correctly, then this erosion would appear to lie behind the decline of democratic processes in the United States from decreasing voter turnouts in public elections to private sector lobbying that has coopted so much of the country's political activity. Perhaps, then, the plural sector needs to regain the influence that de Tocqueville described so compellingly almost two centuries ago.

Time to Rebalance Society

Each of us personally, and all of us together, require attention to three basic needs: protection, provided primarily by our governments; consumption, provided primarily by our businesses; and affiliation, found especially in our communities. With regard to the last of these, between our individualized and collective natures, we are social beings who crave human relationships: we need to belong and identify, especially in a world of so much isolated individualism. Accordingly, a healthy society combines respected governments in the public sector, responsible businesses in the private sector, and robust communities in the plural sector. Weaken any one of these and a society falls out of balance.

The communist regimes of Eastern Europe were out of balance because their public sectors dominated the other two. Certain needs for protection may have been served, but at the expense of personal consumption. Many countries today, including the United States and others of the "developed" world, are falling out of balance in the opposite direction. Their private sectors have become dominant, with the result that consumption, alongside the accumulation of wealth, has become excessive, at least for some people, whereas protections have become inadequate for many others. Moreover, under both regimes, communities have been weakened, and so too, as a consequence, have been the local affiliations provided by these communities.

One of the great periods of development-social and political as well as economic-took place in the United States in the four decades that followed World War II. The public sector was certainly strong (consider the welfare programs introduced in those years), businesses and their employees shared the fruits of rapid economic growth, and the plural sector remained robust. All three sectors were in relative balance.

Then came 1989. As the communist regimes of Eastern Europe began to collapse, pundits in the West had a ready explanation: capitalism had triumphed. They were wrong, gravely wrong. Balance had triumphed. As noted, these communist regimes were severely out of balance in favor of their public sectors, and so they collapsed largely under their own dead weight.

But a failure to understand this has been throwing many countries, led by the United States, out of balance ever since, as too much power has shifted to their private sectors. The results are evident in the unrelenting degradation of our environment, the accelerating demise of our democracies, and the ongoing denigration of ourselves, treated as "human resources"—as if we are economic commodities.

In the United States, this imbalance shows up in statistics on rates of incarceration, obesity, the use of antidepressants, the costs of health care (with mediocre results), levels of poverty, high school dropouts, and most surprisingly, social mobility. Income disparities have reached levels not seen since the Great Depression. One poll of U.S. working men reported that 70 percent "either hate going to work or have mentally checked out" (Egan, 2013).

Intent on limiting the power of government, the framers of the U.S. Constitution instituted checks and balances. But these applied only within the public sector. Perhaps, then, it's time to revisit the Constitution to institute greater checks on the private sector for the sake of balance across all three sectors. Radical renewal will require that each sector maintain sufficient influence to be able to check the excesses of the other two. The plural sector, however, has a special role to play in the process of renewing society.

Leading a Radical Renewal

We can hardly expect governments-even ostensibly democratic ones-that have been coopted by their private sectors or overwhelmed by the forces of corporate globalization to take the lead in initiating radical renewal. A sequence of failed conferences on global warming has made this quite clear (James, 2009; Austen, 2011).

Nor can private sector businesses be expected to take the lead. Why should they promote changes to redress an imbalance that favors so many of them, especially the most powerful? And although corporate social responsibility is certainly to be welcomed, anyone who believes that it will compensate for corporate social irresponsibility is not reading today's newspapers.

This leaves the plural sector. Radical renewal will have to begin here, in communities on the ground, with groups of people who exhibit the inclination, independence, and resourcefulness to tackle difficult problems head on. "What now?" asked former UN Secretary General Kofi Annan in 2013 about the repeated failures of the talks on global warming. His answer: "If governments are unwilling to lead when leadership is required, people must. We need a global grassroots movement that tackles climate change and its fallout" (Annan, 2013).

But will a plural sector that has been so marginalized in the battles over public versus private be able to take the lead in restoring balance? It had better, before we are swamped by our problems—if not literally by global warming, then politically by social turmoil.

The plural sector may be obscure, but it is not impotent. Paul Hawken has described, and articles in Stanford Social Innovation Review indicate regularly, the enormous vigor of this sector. A good deal of it can be attributed to the independence and flexibility of many of its associations, whose people are deeply engaged in what they do, especially when the missions are compelling, such as treating the ill or protecting the environment.

These people are not workers forced to maximize "value" for some shareholders they never met, or civil servants who must submit to a plethora of government controls. Many are more like members with a purpose than employees in a job. Consider the health care professionals who volunteer for Doctors Without Borders, the locals who self-organize to deal with an unforeseen disaster in their community, or the protesters in mass movements. "At its best

civil society is the story of ordinary people living extraordinary lives through their relationships with each other" (Edwards, 2004, p. 112; see also Nilsson and Paddock, 2014).

If the private sector is about individual ownership and the public sector is about collective citizenship, then the plural sector is about shared communityship (Mintzberg, 2009). Its associations are able to function as communities of engaged human beings rather than collections of passive human resources. While individual leadership has received so much attention in the private sector, in the well-functioning associations of the plural sector, it is this communityship that matters. Leadership facilitates that.

Aside from functioning as communities, many plural sector associations function in communities, and they often remain rooted there, even after becoming global. As Gui Azevedo and I wrote in another article, "Social initiatives ... seem to be essentially indigenous: they work from the 'inside up,' and out, by people collectively engaged. They are not solving the world's problems so much as their own common ones, later to discover that their own problems are the world's problems" (Mintzberg and Azevedo, 2012, pp. 895–908).

Of course, not all plural sector associations take advantage of their potential. Some structure themselves too formally, thanks to board members or CEOs who force them to adopt unsuitable business practices (including use of the very label "CEO"), whereas others are driven by granting foundations or governments to apply inappropriate controls (Edwards, 2004).

Moreover, even at its best, the plural sector is not some sort of Holy Grail. We hardly need a new dogma: communism and capitalism have provided more than enough of them. It is balance that we require. If, at their worst, public sector departments can be crude and private sector businesses can be crass, then plural sector associations can be closed. The best of the latter may open us up, but the worst of them close themselves down by excluding outside concerns. Bear in mind that the witch-hunts of old were community-based, as are many of today's terrorist cells as well as some of the narrow populist governments of the world.

But compared with what we have been getting of late from so many of our established institutions in the public and private sectors, the associations of the plural sector offer a way forward. And with plural sector success in restoring some degree of balance in society can come more of the reforms we require of our governments and more of the socially responsible behaviors we should expect from our businesses. In other words, constructive social movements and social initiatives, carried out in local communities and networked for global impact, are the greatest hope we have for regaining balance in this troubled world. But something will first have to change in the plural sector.

Time to Get the Plural Sector Act Together

Why is it that with so much energy and activity in the plural sector, the world continues its unrelenting march toward imbalance in favor of private sector forces? This trend can be explained by a variety of factors, for example the sheer size of many corporations and court decisions that have granted them certain rights as "persons" (for example, to make political donations). But one key factor has been largely overlooked: Although many of the associations of the plural sector have their own acts together, collectively this sector does not. Many initiatives are making enormous differences in the lives of people around the world. Yet altogether they don't add up to a consolidated movement for "collective impact," as John Kania and Mark Kramer

(2011) have written in these pages. Hence society continues to fall out of balance.

Years ago, in one of his satirical songs, Tom Lehrer devoted some lines to the Spanish Civil War: "Though [Franco] may have won all the battles, we had all the good songs!" The struggle now going on over the future of this planet will not be won with good songs, however heartwarming they may be.

Is the problem with the plural sector its own plurality? Certainly the dispersal of efforts that Hawken described may be necessary to let thousands of social flowers bloom. "'The landscape of the third sector is untidy but wonderfully exuberant.' It promotes pluralism by enabling multiple interests to be represented, different functions to be performed, and a range of capacities to be developed" (Edwards, 2004). True enough. But unless the sector can get its own act together, many of its flowers will continue to be bulldozed by more powerful forces.

Private sector businesses are no less dispersed; indeed, they compete aggressively with each other. Yet when it comes to their common interests, such as lobbying for tax cuts, this sector is able to get its collective act together. Businesses often speak with one voice, domestically in institutions such as chambers of commerce, and globally through international agencies, such as the World Trade Association and the International Monetary Fund, which have often acted on behalf of economic concerns. In this regard, the plural sector could do well to take a leaf or two from the playbook of the private sector.

This does not mean, however, that plural sector organizations should imitate business practices without careful thought. Each sector can certainly learn from the others-including the private sector from the plural sector, for example about engagement in mission and more open forms of governance. But given the obscurity of the plural sector, it has to focus on its distinctiveness. Let's welcome partnerships across institutions of the three sectors, as long as they are balanced, with full recognition of the contributions that can be made by each of the partners. Examples can be found in the Danish initiatives for renewable energy and in how the Brazilians dealt with their HIV/AIDS crisis (Mintzberg and Azevedo, 2012).

Milton Friedman was quite clear in his emphasis on the distinct role of the private sector-that the business of business is business (Friedman, 1970). This tenet has served businesses well-too well when these interests have led to interference in democratic processes. Right now what plural sector associations need are partnerships with each other, to collaborate for the cause of better balance in this world.

Struggling for Sustainability

Among the forces that have been undermining the plural sector, two merit particular attention: pressures from the other two sectors and the consequences of new technologies.

It is evident that in those countries where they have dominated, communism debilitated the private sector and capitalism has been co-opting the public sector. Less evident is that both have been relentlessly undermining the plural sector. To achieve balance in society, we need to understand why.

Communist governments have never been great fans of community associations (as remains evident in China), for good reason: These are a threat to their omnipotence. De Tocqueville put the point well: "A despot easily forgives his subjects for not loving him, provided they do not love one another" (De Tocqueville, 2003, p. 102). The first real crack in Soviet communism arguably came because of the influence of two

plural sector organizations in Poland: the Catholic Church that survived under communism, and the Solidarity Union that the Church's presence helped give rise to.

But even elected governments have often been hard on community associations. Sometimes for no more than the convenience of their administrators, governments have forced the mergers of community hospitals into regional ones, just as they have promoted amalgamations of small towns into bigger cities. The importance of community figures hardly at all in a prevailing dogma that favors economic scale no matter what the social consequences.

We see much the same pressures, for much the same reason, emanating from the private sector, especially in the global arena. Consider how global manufacturing firms play local communities off against each other to gain tax advantages in locating operations. Likewise, fast food chains are hardly promoters of local cuisines, or global clothing retailers of local dress. There is a homogenizing effect in globalization that is antithetical to the distinctiveness of communities. As a consequence, while private sectors have been expanding their powers globally, plural sectors have been withering locally.

Popular now among many governments is cutting back public services, in the expectation that plural sector associations will provide them instead. This might make sense for certain services, except that alongside cutting their own budgets, these governments have also been inclined to cut their financial support for plural sector associations. The prime beneficiaries of much of this cutting have been the wealthy owners of private sector businesses. Will the foundations that some of these people create alleviate the problem? And if so, will this kind of funding co-opt the independence of these associations? We need true balance in society, not new versions of imbalance.

Also detrimental to the plural sector has

been a progression of major new technologies, from the automobile and the telephone to the computer and the Internet. Many of these technologies have reinforced personal individualism at the expense of social engagement.

Wrap some sheets of metal around many of us and out comes road rage. Have you ever experienced sidewalk rage? Indeed, have you ever been tailgated by someone walking behind you on a sidewalk? (Unless, of course, he or she was texting on a cell phone!) The sidewalk may not be a community, but it exists in one and certainly has a greater sense of social contact than does a road.

Telephones help keep us "in touch," but they can also distance us from people in our local community, because it is easier to call than to visit. And contemporary electronic devices distance us further: They put our fingers in touch, with a keyboard, while the whole of us sits, often for hours, typing alone. No time even for bowling.

The new social media—Facebook, LinkedIn, Twitter, and so on—certainly connect us to the people on the other end. But let's not confuse networks with communities. (If you are not sure of this, try to get your Facebook "friends" to help you rebuild your barn.) These new technologies are extending our social networks in remarkable ways, but at the expense of our local relationships. Many of us are so busy texting and tweeting that we barely have time for meeting and reading (Marche, 2012).

In his *New York Times* column, Thomas Friedman reported asking an Egyptian friend about the role of social movements in that country's protests: "Facebook really helped people to communicate, but not to collaborate," he replied (Friedman, 2012). That is why, although larger social movements may raise consciousness about the need for renewal, it is the smaller social initiatives, developed by groups in communities, that make it happen.

Of course, by facilitating connections among people, these new media help people find others with common cause. Moreover, they make it possible for local communities to connect with each other globally and thus to carry their initiatives into wider movements. Will this connection make up for the debilitating effects that the new technologies have been having on traditional forms of associating? I hope so. As social animals, we will find our affiliations in one form or another. Let's just hope that we find them before it is too late.

References

Annan, Kofi. (2013). "Climate Crisis: Who Will Act?" *New York Times*, November 25, 2013.

Austen, Ian. (2011). "Canada Announces Exit from Kyoto Climate Treaty." *New York Times*, December 12, 2011.

Collins, Chuck. (2012). *99 to 1: How Wealth Inequality Is Wrecking the World and What We Can Do About It*. San Francisco: Berrett-Koehler.

De Tocqueville, Alexis. (2003). *Democracy in America*. London: Penguin Classics (1835/1840).

Edwards, Michael. (2004). *Civil Society*. Cambridge, England: Polity, 2004, p. 112.

Egan, Timothy. (2013). "Checking Out." *New York Times*, June 20, 2013.

Friedman, Milton. (1970). "A Friedman Doctrine: The Social Responsibility of Business Is to Increase Its Profits." *New York Times Magazine*, September 13, 1970.

Friedman, Thomas L. (2012). "Facebook Meets Bricks-and-Mortar Politics." *New York Times*, June 9, 2012.

Hawken, Paul. (2007). *Blessed Unrest: How the Largest Movement in the World Came into Being, and Why No One Saw It Coming*. New York: Viking Penguin.

Kania, John and Kramer, Mark. (2011). "Collective Impact." *Stanford Social Innovation Review*, Winter 2011.

Kanter, James. (2009). "An Air of Frustration for Europe at Climate Talks." *New York Times*, December 20, 2009.

Marche, Stephen. (2012). "Is Facebook Making Us Lonely?" *The Atlantic*, May 2012.

Mintzberg, Henry. (2009). "Rebuilding Companies as Communities." *Harvard Business Review*, 87, no. 7, 2009.

Mintzberg, Henry, and Gui Azevedo. (2012).

"Fostering 'Why Not?' Social Initiatives-Beyond Business and Governments." *Development in Practice*, 22, no. 7, pp. 895–908.

Mintzberg, Henry, et al. (2005). "The Invisible World of Association." *Leader to Leader*, Spring 2005.

Nilsson, Warren and Tana Paddock. (2014). "Social Innovation from the Inside Out." *Stanford Social Innovation Review*, Winter 2014.

Putnam, Robert D. (1995). "Bowling Alone: America's Declining Social Capital." *Journal of Democracy*, 6, no. 1, 1995, pp. 65–78.

Putnam, Robert D. (2000). *Bowling Alone: The Collapse and Revival of American Community*. New York: Simon and Schuster.

4. Public Interest Partnerships

Joaquin Jay Gonzalez III

Largely driven by private sector innovations, the twenty-first century is emerging as a period of unprecedented change. Rapid advances in information, communications, transportation, and internet technologies are changing the ways in which we connect and collaborate with colleagues, clients, and corporations. Social media has surpassed mass media on what news item will go viral. Unprecedented access to education and information are empowering more people with the skills and knowledge to choose their own futures, and to make sure their governments fulfill their promises. All of these factors combine to dramatically alter the context in which public programs, projects, and services are developed and delivered.

Not only have public concerns and needs taken on a new complexity and interconnectedness but the methods to address these issues are changing by necessity. Sources of power and legitimacy to address them are increasingly fractured. We no longer live in a world where the government is regarded as the sole legitimate decision-making actor. In fact, the number of domains in which governments can credibly claim to hold overwhelming pre-eminence in terms of power, authority and influence has shrunk, and continues to shrink.

We have moved from a "government-centered" world to "multiple-centered" world, where power, authority and influence emanate not only from a single source but from a variety of potential actors, sectors, or stakeholders. This shift of power, authority and influence to multiple actors is happening simultaneously upward, downward, outward, and inward. It is upward to global organizations, multinational companies, and international non-governmental organizations; downward to states, counties, and cities; outward to the private sector and the plural sector (a.k.a. civil society); and inward to individuals, families, and community members.

In a world where issues are complex and power to address those issues is diffused, the biggest challenge facing government, business, and community leaders is to find a way to bring together those wielding power and resources, to find common ground, and to combine, share, and align them to efficiently and effectively address public concerns. I have labeled this multi-stakeholder alliance a "public interest partnership" or "PIP" (Gonzalez et al., 2000).

Real-life experiences of how these PIPs are used as a mode of privatization abound among America's communities. It is the core and essence of American democracy. Collaboration in spite of diversity. Individuals and groups from different ethnicities, sexual orientations, family upbringing, political leanings, and socio-economic backgrounds. In this continuing era of privatization of public services emerged yet another delivery approach. Aligning and combining assets, endowments, and resources to form new synergy-one larger than the sum of its parts.

Important Concepts

Stakeholders and Sectors: Who Has the Power and Resources?

Not just government. The power to address issues of public concern is dispersed to many stakeholders. In other words, a wide variety of stakeholders have influence and resources to contribute to solving public issues. Stakeholders are shareholders. No single stakeholder tends to have absolute power. These stakeholders can be usefully grouped in three broad sectors-the public sector, the private sector, and people sector (or the "plural sector" or "civil society").

There are many debates and discussions concerning which individuals and organizations fall into each of the three broad categories, and whether these three categories are appropriate approaches to classifying actors involved in addressing issues of public concern. I do not wish to go into this debate. I acknowledge the complexity of categorization and that some organizations may have fit into overlapping or multiple categories based on actual practice.

Rather, broadly speaking these sectors could be subdivided into the following-the public sector (or government), the private sector (or business), and the people sector (or civil society). The public sector would include the executive, legislature, judiciary, civil service, military and security forces, as well as government owned or controlled entities. They look at citizens, corporations, and communities as taxpayers, voters, and constituents. Communication with them is through town hall meetings, legislative hearings, public announcements, among others.

The private sector encompasses small, medium and large enterprises, multina-tional corporations, marketing and advertising, services and financial institutions. In pursuit of profit and business interests, they view citizens, corporations, and communities as "the market," shareholders, customers, clients, investors, suppliers, contractors, as well as buyers and sellers of products and services. They reach them via advertising, promotions, marketing, etc.

The people sector includes nonprofits, non-governmental organizations (NGOs), community-based and people's organizations (CBOs and POs), religious and ethnic, women's and youth groups, public interest groups, chambers of commerce, unions, professional associations, charities, and foundations. In the name of social justice and economic equality, they advocate for and assist citizens and communities as beneficiaries, the marginalized, the oppressed, the helpless, the poor, and the abused. Outreach campaigns, phone banking, community meetings, are the best way to reach their beneficiaries.

Assets: What Could Each Stakeholder Contribute?

If a PIP is formed, each stakeholder brings to the table a set of assets. These assets, or capital may be usefully categorized as follows:

- *Physical assets* (financial, technical, and material resources),
- *Organizational assets* (personnel, structure, leadership, capacity to manage, plan, implement, monitor, evaluate, and train)
- *Political assets* (power, authority, influence, legitimacy)
- *Intellectual assets* (knowledge or know-how in certain fields of expertise)
- *Socio-cultural assets* (feelings/spirit of trust, friendship and willingness to collaborate, community traditions, ideals or values).

Stakeholders from private, public, and people sectors are endowed with a mix of all five forms of assets although it seems that in actual practice each is only able to contribute certain kinds of resources to a partnership. These mix of contributions and commitments vary, depending on the nature of the problem, the particular context and timing, and the capacities of various participants.

For instance, the government or public sector is typically strong when it comes to political and organizational assets, i.e., policy or program control and coordination, providing institutional stability, and harnessing critical political will and support. Further, the government sector is unique because of its power to create and enforce laws, and exact taxes. But it cannot manage everything on its own. By itself, the government cannot force social energy and civic involvement. That is something that may best done by non-governmental organizations.

Similarly, in many cases the private sector or businesses may have strengths in the areas of organizational and physical assets, i.e., profit making, labour productivity, private sector competitiveness, and entrepreneurial growth. However, the business sector cannot provide political legitimacy or institutional security, which is best done by government. It also cannot guarantee social equity and economic rationality. In fact, many experiences show that the market left solely on its own tends to generate a great deal of economic and income inequalities. Except for their fiscal obligations (i.e., taxes and fees) to the government and corporate social responsibility programs, most businesses seldom participate actively in social and community development concerns. Their forte and focus is profit making. Hence, the need for people and government sectors to check and balance the operations of the free market with regulatory activities and programs that reduce these inequalities.

In the same way, the people sector can often contribute their socio-cultural and intellectual assets, i.e., advancing people participation, promoting self-help, social mobilization, and increasing cultural awareness. These assets go towards addressing inequities and injustices. Yet, civil society tends to be weak when it comes to ensuring stability, security, and institutionalization, and often lacks authority and administrative capacity. Civil society does not have the legal, judicial, and regulatory authority to require the business community to be more accountable and responsible since that is best accomplished by government agencies or judicial authorities. Moreover, the entrepreneurial skills and technical know-how required to continuously raising money, which are critical to sustaining their mission of helping marginalized members of society, are skills that NGOs may have to learn from the businesses.

Typically, actors in any one sector, operating independently, will not have all of the needed resources, all of the public faith and confidence, and all of the knowledge to effectively address issues of public concern effectively.

What Are the Barriers to Forming PIPs?

Despite the inherent logic of forming PIPs to address issues of public concern, there are deep-seated barriers to doing so. Barriers may exist in the broader contextual environment, or closer to home among the stakeholders of the partnership itself.

Most compelling is the inherent lack of trust among the PIP partners. Years of blaming government for its inefficiency, criticizing civil society for its narrow and biased interests and viewing business as interested only in its own bottom line, does not auger well for strong, supportive relationships and alignment. A desire for power and control, and the accompanying reluctance to share power is an additional barrier to partnership.

Finally, the comfort and security of maintaining the status quo is a significant force mitigating against the formation of new partnerships. Changing relationships which have historically been based on adversarial roles to ones which are supportive can be a daunting challenge.

REFERENCE

Gonzalez, Joaquin L., et al. (2000). *Opting for Partnership*. Ottawa, Canada: Institute On Governance.

5. Contemplating Collaboration

David Swindell and *Cheryll Hilvert*

To address today's challenges of decreased budgets and increased workloads, both local government managers and elected officials are embracing the concept of collaboration in new and innovative ways. Collaboration has proven to be an effective tool for jurisdictions to join with others-including other local governments, private sector organizations, and nonprofits-to achieve goals and deliver services that they may not have been able to accomplish on their own.

While there has been a general push by residents, elected officials, consultants, and academics toward the use of collaboration as a key solution to governments' problems, these proponents sometimes fail to recognize that collaborations do not always achieve the goals for which they were established.

While collaboration is appropriately viewed as an option for local governments, the real issue surrounding collaboration is that often the costs and benefits associated with it are not fully realized, nor are strategies effectively evaluated that will motivate the collaborative effort.

The concepts to do so can be complex and confusing, and there have been few tools that give managers the ability to fully "talk through" a collaboration concept and ask such fundamental questions as: Should we engage in a collaboration? If so, what form of collaboration will have the highest likelihood of success?

Defining the Concept

Collaboration is "the linking or sharing of information, resources, activities, and capabilities by organizations to achieve an outcome that could not be achieved by the organizations separately" (Bryson et al., 2009). Collaboration refers to arrangements in which all partners to the arrangement incur costs and share benefits related to their efforts.

These efforts are different from outsourcing or contracting where a separate entity handles certain aspects of service delivery. Because of resident/stakeholder expectations and interactions, local governments may find that those service delivery options in which they create a "partnership" allow an alternative approach to service delivery, yet maintain a level of responsibility between the local government and its constituents.

Originally published as David Swindell and Cheryll Hilvert (2014). "Contemplating Collaboration." *Public Management (PM) Magazine,* 96(7), August 2014. Reprinted with permission of the publisher.

Is Collaboration Right for Us?

Working through a unique collaboration of its own, ICMA's Center for Management Strategies has teamed up with the Alliance for Innovation (AFI) and Arizona State University's (ASU) Center for Urban Innovation (ICMA-AFI-ASU) to determine the factors associated with both successful and unsuccessful collaborations.

Its findings suggest that having a discussion with all stakeholders as to the costs and benefits expected from collaboration—beyond finances alone—as well as a thorough understanding of the environment within which the collaboration will be situated, will do much to contribute to a successful evaluation of a collaboration opportunity.

These conversations can help to identify the "soft costs and benefits" that might be realized in a collaboration. Soft costs include the governance and the monitoring costs. If a collaboration might lead to reduced cost but involve staff cuts, there may be morale and political costs that must be explicitly evaluated as part of a cost-benefit approach.

ICMA's recent survey of more than 1,000 managers highlights some of the most important soft benefits associated with collaborations (O'Leary and Gerard, 2013). Bringing staff from your unit together with those from other units in a collaborative environment can improve the problem-solving process not only for the problem at hand but also for other problems on which the collaborative could work in the future.

Furthermore, these types of conversations can build relationships as well as trust and credibility in overcoming barriers to working on other issues. While cost savings or revenue enhancements might also be benefits, these soft costs must also be explicitly identified as part of the determination of whether a jurisdiction should invest the resources in such a collaborative effort.

Begin the Conversation: Know thy Service

The ICMA-AFI-ASU research project identified a consistent set of factors that tend to be associated with success and others associated with failure in collaborative arrangements. These factors should be part of any conversation about entering a collaboration and fall into two main categories: service-oriented factors and community-oriented factors.

A discussion should begin with a full understanding of exactly what service/project the community is targeting for collaboration. Communities, for example, may want to explore a collaboration on "public safety," but that encompasses a vast array of specific services.

Is the community interested in sharing building, operating, and maintenance responsibilities of a shared forensics crime lab? Patrol officers? Shared purchasing arrangement for capital equipment like patrol cars? In order to begin the discussion, the community needs to be clear about exactly what service is the focus.

Seven characteristics associated with the service/project type can determine whether or not a collaborative arrangement is likely to help achieve desired goals:

1. **Asset specificity.** This represents the degree to which the service relies on investment in specialized infrastructure (e.g., fire trucks, water pipes, treatment plants) or technical expertise (e.g., legal, economic, environmental), which can make collaboration difficult due to a lack of suppliers to compete at the quality level needed by the community. In these situations, collaboration opportunities may be limited, but other alternative service delivery options may still be appropriate or viable. Higher asset specificity also suggests that it is difficult to adapt the investments to produce another service (Warner and Hefetz, 2010).

2. Contract specification and monitoring. There need to be clearly specified expectations among the partners as to which costs, benefits, and management services are to be shared and which entity is responsible for which activity. Services that are harder to specify in a contract or agreement, more difficult to supervise, or require greater performance management expertise are less likely to be successfully produced through collaboration. (Warner and Hefetz, 2010)

3. Labor intensity. Generally, services that are more labor intensive in their delivery and that replicate similar services in other jurisdictions represent the best opportunities for collaboration. An example of this concept is seen in a collaborative effort involving 18 municipalities in Cook County and Lake County, Illinois. These local governments, motivated by the national economic downturn, believed that they might realize some cost saving by relying on the practice of bulk purchasing. The effort has led to savings of approximately $500,000 after the first year for the combined group and involved labor intensive purchasing work that was similarly provided in all of the 18 jurisdictions.

4. Capital intensity. Generally, services that are more capital intensive, yet offer wider benefits than could be realized by a single jurisdiction alone are more amenable to collaborative approaches. In an example of this concept, Westlake, Texas (population 1,065), and Keller, Texas (population 41,923), were facing water shortages in the late 1990s. To grow both financially and physically, these two communities needed to construct water storage tanks. They began a plan to develop their water system and together constructed an elevated joint-use water tank. The combined tank allows each city to maintain its separate water system operations and represented the first time that a joint-use tank was designed and installed in Texas. Each community shared in the $3.1 million cost, saving each city more than $1 million in construction costs. Each also experienced reduced costs for maintenance through an interlocal agreement for maintenance of the tank while maintaining their independent control over their share of the joint tank.

5. Costs. Service/project costs can drive the interest in collaboration by a local government. Costs can also limit the pool of potential partner organizations that may be able to participate in the delivery of more expensive services. When considering available partners, managers must be cognizant of the other participants' financial position, as each must be able to contribute meaningfully to the success of the effort.

6. Management competencies. When discussing costs and benefits of potential collaborative arrangements, communities must be sensitive to the expertise-or lack thereof-for managing the various aspects of a service/project. The greater the managerial expertise on staff related to a service, the more likely a collaborative arrangement can achieve success. A lack of expertise will increase the costs of the collaboration perhaps to the point of exceeding the value of the benefits.

7. Administrative stability. The importance of stability among team members should not be underestimated. High staff turnover creates uncertainties, changes in policy directions, and undermines previously established levels of trust. Turnover is to be expected, and managers should be aware of the trend and likelihood of additional changes in the short- and long-term future, and they should ensure that succession planning is addressed in any collaboration plan.

Discussing and understanding these seven characteristics can influence the likelihood of success in achieving goals when a community delivers a service through collaboration. Fully understanding the service, however, is only one aspect of informing a decision. The other involves explicit awareness of the environment within which the community operates.

New Collaboration Resources

ICMA's Center for Management Strategies has partnered with the Alliance for Innovation and Arizona State University's Center for Urban Innovation to develop a program designed to assist local government managers in navigating the complex work of understanding and analyzing the concept of collaboration.

Underwritten with the support of ICMA Strategic Partner CH2M HILL, this work will provide a set of practical assessment tools that will allow managers to engage their staff, elected officials, and community in the dialogue described in this chapter on whether collaboration is an appropriate approach and what type of collaborative efforts are most likely to be successful.

Also available will be a set of recommended articles and documents designed to enhance knowledge of collaboration; a compilation of case studies on both successful and unsuccessful public uses of collaborative efforts; and, technical assistance to local governments by identified and vetted practice leaders.

Understand the Environment

Communities create strategic plans after an environmental scan identifies factors that can impact a community from both an internal and external perspective. Similarly, understanding these environmental context factors can assist a management team in determining if collaboration is even possible, much less destined for success:

1. **Possible public partners.** Before considering collaboration, a manager should fully understand the number and capacity of potential public partners in the area and identify which can be legitimate partners in a collaborative service delivery effort.

2. **Possible private partners.** In addition to possible public sector partners, managers should be aware of private sector firms that may be viable partners. As with potential public sector partners, private partners may be limited to the extent that the community or region is home to enough competent firms to support a competitive marketplace.

3. **Possible nonprofit partners.** Nonprofit groups are highly capable of partnering in a service delivery collaborative. As with private partners, the size of the local supply of nonprofits will also be driven by the type of service under consideration, as well as the size of the region in which the community is located.

4. **Political environment.** Managers should recognize the support or obstacles that exist among elected officials of the community. Elected officials may be supportive of the concept generally but cautious or even opposed to collaboration on a specific service.

5. **Fiscal/economic health.** The community's fiscal condition may be a motivating factor in wanting to pursue collaboration. Those that are financially challenged may find it more difficult to identify partners with which to collaborate. Communities in a better fiscal position are more likely to be successful in collaborative arrangements. Decisions on whether to collaborate need to take a community's fiscal health into account, as well as the fiscal condition of any partners, be they public, private, or nonprofit.

6. **Employee/labor relations.** Different communities face different kinds of labor and employee relationships that can create pressure on collaborative discussions. There may be resistance to any service alternatives that could impact public sector employment levels. In these situations, the costs of

pursuing collaborative service delivery can increase significantly or decision making be made more difficult. Involving employees in these discussions and seeking their input can be productive.

7. Public interest. Some services are naturally more likely to attract the attention of residents than others. Changes to those services for which residents are particularly connected are more likely to meet resistance. Involving stakeholders in these discussions can help ensure that all points of view are heard and accurate information is shared.

Collaboration Sounds Good, Now What?

If the dialogue described previously identifies supportive information about the service being considered and a receptive environment in which the collaboration could occur, the community will then need to decide which type of arrangement makes the most sense for it. Here are the most common forms of collaborative service delivery:

Public-private partnerships. The form that has received the most attention in the past decade is collaboration that involves a public agency working with a private firm. In truth, this is not as common as one might be led to believe.

While contracting services out to private firms is common, such contracting is not the same arrangement as collaboration. Public-private partnerships, in which a public jurisdiction and a private firm jointly share in the costs and benefits of a service arrangement, are truly collaborations.

These arrangements can be challenging because without the right partner or clearly defined purpose and responsibilities, different motivations can be pursued by the partners (service versus profit) and can impact the viability of the partnership.

Public-nonprofit partnerships. While public-private partnerships receive more attention, local officials should be aware of the potential advantages nonprofit partners might afford for certain kinds of services. One aspect that increases the likelihood of successful collaboration is that, like their public sector counterparts, nonprofits do not work on a profit motive.

On the other hand, while there are a number of potential nonprofits in a community, the number of them capable of being a partner may be more limited, depending on the type of service under consideration. A nonprofit with the expertise to manage a waste incinerator facility, for example, may be difficult to find, but one that has deep talent at operating a community homeless shelter may be an easily identifiable partner with which to address a community need.

Public-public partnerships. Collaboration between units of government is by far the most common form of partnership involving public services. Many may be informal arrangements between abutting local governments, while some are represented by more formalized agreements.

The arrangements involve at least two units of government, but can include more. The earlier example of the 18 municipalities in Lake and Cook counties highlights one type of public-public arrangement known as a "horizontal partnership" between governments at the same level.

There are also examples of vertical partnerships in which two or more units of government at different levels collaborate. Charlotte and Mecklenburg County, North Carolina, for example, have an extensive system of intergovernmental agreements for a wide range of services.

In the area of public safety, the city police department provides basic patrol services for the city and any other parts of the county not patrolled by another municipal police department. At the same time, the county provides jail services for the entire county, including all jail services for Charlotte.

While much has been written that suggests collaboration is the answer to problems and issues facing local governments today, managers must understand what collaboration is and what it is not. While significantly different from privatization or contracting, collaboration can offer excellent alternatives for service delivery if the service is right and the community environment will support the concept.

Understanding the appropriateness of a collaborative effort as well as the environment in which it will occur, and selecting the right form will help ensure that the effort can be a successful and viable solution to the issues and challenges facing local governments today.

Centennial Collaborates for Success

Leaders of Centennial, Colorado, incorporated in 2001, envisioned an "intentional" city-lean, efficient, and with an eye toward outsourcing key services whenever possible. In slightly more than a decade, the city of more than 100,000 has emerged as a model of collaborative service delivery.

Centennial delivers services with its 54 employees in certain areas that make the most sense, including finance, accounting, communications, planning, and engineering management. For other services, the city partners with an array of government, nonprofit, and private organizations to deliver efficient, cost-effective services in keeping with its spirit of right-sized, fiscally responsible government.

Centennial's largest partner is Arapahoe County, which provides a variety of services that include law enforcement, schools, and libraries. For animal services, Centennial partners with the Humane Society of the Pikes' Peak Region, a nonprofit located in nearby Colorado Springs. Other outsourced functions include legal services, contractor licensing, sales and use tax administration, and audit functions.

Partnering for Public Works

Arapahoe County initially provided public works services for Centennial. In early 2008, city leaders took a closer look at needs that revealed gaps in service levels and decided to launch the city's own public works department through a public-private partnership with CH2M HILL, a global consulting and program management firm based in Englewood, Colorado.

CH2M HILL instituted a variety of innovative approaches to service delivery, including updating an old snowplow routing solution, applying updated algorithms, and using consumer-grade GPS units to reduce snowplowing time of city streets by as much as 40 percent.

Within this partnership, even the partner has partners. CH2M HILL collaborates with a number of other private sector companies reaping benefits for Centennial. SAFEbuilt-an ICMA Strategic Partner that offers customized full-service building department programs-introduced process and customer service improvements to the plan review and inspection processes. These include the establishment of two-hour inspection appointment windows, electronic plan review, online permits, and "Rapid Review Thursdays" where customers seeking permits that do not require detailed zoning review-signs, fences, and simple structures-can receive expedited service.

CH2M HILL also established a consolidated customer service center, which serves as a single point of contact for all resident concerns, not just public works. Residents can call the center 24/7 or submit requests online. Information is entered into a work-order tracking system along with the requesters' contact information, so a representative can update them on the progress of work through completion.

It's Working!

"Our public-private partnerships allow us to provide on-demand services at the best value for our taxpayers," says Centennial's Mayor Cathy Noon. "We contract for a base level of service, and any time we have a spike in demand, we can bring in extra resources very quickly."

That flexibility is built into Centennial's various partnership contracts. A value-based system allows the city to adjust service quantities based on changing priorities and demand. If a mild winter requires less snow plowing, for example, the city might decide to use those dollars for additional road striping.

Pre-determined costs of service allow the city to effectively plan its budget over the contract's lifetime, while performance standards enable it to control the timing and amount of service performed, and pass the risk of quality and deadline commitments to the contractor.

In 2012, 79 percent of respondents to a National Citizen Survey™ rated the overall quality of public works services as "excellent" or "good." City leaders also liked the results, voting to extend the public-private partnership with CH2M HILL.

City Manager John Danielson is well acquainted with collaborative service delivery. His 25-year local government management career has included helping create two new cities from their inception, based on the public-private partnership model. He believes the scalability of resources and predictability of costs associated with collaboration can truly benefit local governments.

References

Bryson, J., et al. (2009). "Designing and Managing Cross-sector Collaboration: A Case Study in Reducing Traffic Congestion." *The Business of Government* (Winter/Fall): 78-81.

O'Leary, Rosemary, and Catherine Gerard. (2013). "Collaborative Governance and Leadership: A 2012 Survey of Local Government Collaboration." *2013 ICMA Municipal Year Book*. Washington, D.C.: International City/County Management Association.

Warner, Mildred, and Amir Hefetz. (2010). "Service Characteristics and Contracting: The Importance of Citizen Interest and Competition." *2010 ICMA Municipal Year Book*. Washington, D.C.: International City/County Management Association.

6. Shared Services and Cost-Saving Collaboration

Monte Mercer

Shared services, many of which are public-private partnerships (PPPs), refer to the operational philosophy that involves centralizing functions once performed by individual organizations. In day-to-day operations, problems and opportunities arise that are ideal for collaboration. This abundance of possible shared services and partnership opportunities can be overwhelming though, and it can lead to difficulty identifying which projects to try. The best determining factor for success is for the customer to be the driving force behind any collaborative effort.

The North Central Texas Council of Governments (NCTCOG) serves 240 member governments—or customers—of which 170 are cities. It has had the opportunity to spearhead a large number of shared services and PPP initiatives in recent years, and in this chapter I want to share what we've learned.

In fact, shared services fulfill NCTCOG's mission to strengthen the individual and collective power of local governments and to help them recognize regional opportunities, resolve regional problems, and make joint decisions. These initiatives are primarily designed to solve common needs of NCTCOG's member governments, but they often reach a statewide audience as well.

Steps for a Successful Collaboration

A common recipe for success can be applied to any collaboration effort. By nature, however, shared services are unique and have elements that will apply exclusively to each individual project. For projects to be successful, it is best to tailor an approach that takes individual differences into consideration for each shared services program.

After identifying a problem or opportunity that can be remedied through a shared services approach and also identifying the local government stakeholders, NCTCOG then takes the next step in the process and functions as the coordinating organization. This is followed by determining which entity or entities-also called organizations in this chapter-can serve as a project champion. Project champions need to be recognized leaders within the stakeholder com-

Originally published as Monte Mercer (2011). "Shared Services and Cost Saving Collaboration Deserve Respect." *Public Management (PM) Magazine*, 93(4), May 20. Reprinted with permission of the publisher.

munity because they are crucial for the success of any shared services project, as they lend both credibility and energy to the project.

Create a Winning Approach

When deciding whether a proposed shared services project is feasible to pursue, NCTCOG and the prospective participants use these criteria:

- Does it have the potential to save money?
- Does it have the potential to provide equal or better service levels?
- Can a governance structure or operational process be devised that assures that the participating local governments share in the control of the program?

If these questions can be answered in the affirmative, then we proceed to the next step.

Developing the Request for Proposals

The request for proposals (RFP) process begins with research by the planning organization, the project champions, and any other entity that desires to participate in identifying potential solutions to the chosen problem or opportunity. This leads to an understanding of the project dynamics and sets the stage for initial discussions with prospective private and public sector service providers. Conversations with service providers allow insight into opportunities for standardization and other cost-saving measures while validating the parameters necessary to create a credible RFP.

Identifying opportunities for standardization is one of the most important due-diligence steps, and it should be performed collectively. The 80–20 rule is a good guide for assessing opportunities for standardization. In other words, ferret out the things that each participant does in common 80 percent of the time so that they can be the focal point for maximizing efficiencies and economies of scale.

After this step is accomplished, it is essential to visit with the potential service providers and get their input and understanding of the program being suggested. Doing this allows potential failure points to be exposed.

It is recommended that a significant amount of time be spent with the subject matter experts (SMEs) and the technical experts from potential service providers during this step. Opportunities for cost savings using this approach will generally be significant.

Our experience has been that an element vital to crafting the RFP is understanding how the private or public sector provider will deliver the service. If the procurement is based solely on our understanding of the problem and the solution, we may inadvertently limit the opportunities to provide a more innovative and cost-effective approach to solving the problem.

When the due diligence has been performed, a nonbinding statement of interest is sent to potential users of the service. After these statements are returned, this information will be summarized for the RFP. One critical piece of information for the responders is an indication of the volume of activity or transactions that can be anticipated, as this will be important as pricing discounts are considered.

Participation usually far exceeds the initial statements of interest that are returned. As the RFP is developed, it may take several iterations to reach a version that satisfies all groups; therefore, maintaining some flexibility will allow for creative responses. The RFP should also be scalable to various group sizes. After the RFP draft is completed, it needs to be reviewed by the participants or a representative committee to create the official version.

It is helpful for the committee to be composed of SMEs. For best results, they should be from various-sized entities in order to gain varying perspectives concerning the shared services initiative.

After responses to the RFP have been received, a selection committee should meet to review the submittals. RFPs should be scored on the basis of predetermined selection criteria so scoring is unbiased.

Implementation

It is often a good idea to assemble a pilot group to participate in the initial implementation, again including entities of various sizes for this group. Pilot programs are an excellent way to discover unforeseen problems and remedy them before rolling out the program to a larger audience.

During this implementation phase, encourage communication among the stakeholders to get a reading of components working well and those in need of improvement. These are ready-made networks for exchanging ideas and information and are invaluable during the process. When the pilot has proved successful, a more robust rollout can be initiated.

Planning Organization and Facilitator

The streamlining of administrative activities is one of the biggest opportunities for shared services projects. Here are ways to streamline access to the project:

- The planning organization executes a master agreement with the selected service provider, and it is structured to allow the participating organizations to gain access through interlocal agreements.

- The participants execute an interlocal agreement with the planning organization.
- The participants can then engage the service provider through a service agreement to perform the required services.

The facilitator normally assumes responsibility for many of the administrative duties that would ordinarily be done by an individual organization or a service provider.

Participating Organizations

Participating entities can benefit significantly from shared services. Because individual purchasers are consolidated into an organized, volume-purchase arrangement, the participants are able to realize lower prices while still benefiting from a high-quality provider. This approach also eliminates the need for each entity to go through an individual selection process and to incur the costs involved in issuing and evaluating proposals. This is especially true for small to medium-size organizations.

NCTCOG has been able to leverage the collective bargaining power of several groups to negotiate a lower price for the contract. With the importance of cost reduction during these difficult economic times, it's notable that NCTCOG's shared services programs have been able to generate savings of 25 to 50 percent for participants.

Service Provider

The service provider benefits by being able to reach many organizational clients with just one proposal, thus increasing its market penetration and enhancing its ability to sell other services in the future. The provider also benefits from the standardization of operations realized in the shared services arrangement, which reduces risk for the service provider and allows better pricing to be experienced by the participants.

The clients also can forgo the expense of conducting individual contract negotiations. All of these factors give a service provider ample motivation to reply to an RFP and to partner with the planning organization.

Examples of NCTCOG Shared Services

iCommunities: A Success Story. The iCommunities program created an extensive Internet mapping service that was combined with a set of powerful GIS, database, and Internet technologies. These tools allow local governments to distribute key information to their constituents and other communities within the region.

Residents are able to access specific neighborhood information such as zoning, building and activity statistics, and event notices. Information can be distributed to organizational staff on various program, asset, and work management activities. Traditionally, establishing a tool such as iCommunities would mean that each entity would incur hefty costs for hardware, personnel, and networking. Through this shared services program initiated by NCTCOG, cities can have ready access to this powerful tool for a low cost.

Participants pay a fee to support one network and a group of technicians who service the entire participant list. As individual participants request additional functionality from the iCommunities program, the enhancements become available to all participants. A base-level functionality is automatically applied to all participants.

Additional functionality is offered on a fee basis; specific features can be set up to accommodate unique needs of a specific organization and costs charged according to complexity and extra support needs. The

sharing of knowledge and innovation is one of the most positive by-products of this collaboration.

The Small City Accounting Project: Lessons Learned. Even with the best of intentions, not all PPPs are successful. With each new collaborative effort, however, lessons are learned. NCTCOG's Small City Accounting Project is one such example. Riding on the success of a shared services initiative to acquire enterprise resource planning software to handle accounting, purchasing, and human resources functions for three large-member groups, participants decided that smaller entities could benefit from a similar project.

The project, unfortunately, never really progressed. The reason for this lack of advancement is that, although the larger entities were already interested in the concept and approached NCTCOG to facilitate the purchasing process, the smaller entities were contacted to determine their interest after all the parameters had been developed.

In this case, the project would have found more success had it been customer driven. The best shared services occur when the planning organization is either approached by the entity or seeks ideas from it directly.

Compensation Management Services: Looking to the Future. A current NCTCOG initiative is under way to assist with compensation analysis, design, and best practices implementation. Salary costs usually make up, on average, 70 percent of a local government's general fund budget. Yet tools that readily provide the ability to quickly and accurately analyze, monitor, and control these costs are lacking, as is the ability to assess the impact that changes to salary structures have on benefits and other components of compensation packages.

Various city managers in NCTCOG's 16-county region requested assistance in identifying potential solutions for evaluating these costs in real time. Through the procurement process, a vendor with a multifaceted web-based solution has been identified. The vendor's web tools have the capability to provide projections of personnel costs using scenario-based analytics, and they also contain current salary data so that any participating organization is able to determine the competiveness of its compensation and benefit plan.

Other features make it easy to measure internal compensation equity. A major benefit of this program is that it increases the ability of an organization's human resources staff to carry out many functions that are currently done by consultants. This project was approved by the NCTCOG executive board in January 2011, and we are now in the implementation stage.

Strategy for Success

Consider this course of action for shared services success:

1. First and foremost, under promise and over deliver! It is important to establish achievable results. If you set unattainable milestones or goals, you can undermine your credibility.

2. Begin the procurement process with the end goal in mind. Look toward the future throughout the RFP research, development, and scoring process. With forethought, you can avoid many of the traps and delays that can evolve during the process. Look for opportunities to standardize because standardization is usually one of the largest contributors to reducing risk and achieving cost savings.

3. Use a grassroots approach based on a crawl-walk-run philosophy. It is best to start with a small pilot group and perfect the program before rolling out to a larger audience. Project champions are crucial in building a strong foundation for shared services projects as they have a real interest and commitment to performing the due diligence necessary to support the program and to assuring its success.

For more information on the NCTCOG shared services programs, visit the website at www.nctcog.org/sharedservices.asp. I think our recipe can be used successfully by other local governments that want to navigate the shared services options available today.

7. Strategies for Contract Selection

Cathy Lazarus and Ted Volskay

A decision to privatize a government service requires thorough analysis of the advantages and disadvantages of privatization to determine whether the public is better served by government or the private sector. The process of privatizing a service has three phases:

- Determining if it is appropriate to privatize a service,
- Determining the level of service desired from a contractor and conducting an open, competitive contractor selection process, and
- Negotiating the contract with the selected contractor and monitoring performance over the term of the service agreement.

In all phases, best practices call for transparency, open communication with stakeholders, impartial and unbiased analyses, and the development quantifiable expectations and measures for service delivery.

The decision-making process should ask: What are the problems with the existing service? What will be gained by turning to the private sector? Are there alternatives to privatization?

Privatization can be successful for services with competitive markets, with clear service delivery goals and performance criteria, and where the services involve transactions that are not irrevocable. It requires decision-makers open to the idea of privatization, a government with established privatization policies, a transparent public review process, comprehensive service transition plans, active contract management and a "recovery" plan to take over service if the contractor fails to perform.

When services such as utilities, transportation systems or parks are privatized it should be clear who owns and maintains the public facilities, infrastructure and assets. If "human services" such as child protective services or welfare services are privatized, sensitive client information must be protected and cost savings should not be achieved in ways that are detrimental to vulnerable clients. There must be contractual procedures to assure that the financial statements of the contractor are audited and reviewed on a regular basis and become part of the public record. In all cases, the public must have a way to lodge complaints about the service to the government agency overseeing the private contractor.

Originally published as Cathy Lazarus and Ted Volskay (2011). "Strategies for Best Practice." *League of Women Voters Privatization Study*, Washington, D.C. Reprinted with permission of the publisher.

Introduction

In an era of shrinking resources, federal, state and local governments will continue to view privatization as a potentially viable strategy to sustain services traditionally provided by the public sector. Best practices suggest that the decision to privatize public services should be made after comprehensive review of the advantages, disadvantages and alternatives to privatization, and only after broad based community/stakeholder outreach and comment. The decision to privatize must be based on factual information, principles of good governance, and careful planning for contractor selection and oversight.

This chapter is a review of the essential factors to consider in deciding whether or not to privatize a government service. It outlines key questions to ask policy makers and important policy areas to evaluate before and after making a decision to transfer a public service to the private sector. Links to Pdf attachments to this paper, found after the endnotes, include two tables highlighting the potential advantages and disadvantages of privatization, and a recommended checklist of questions to ask decision-makers throughout a privatization initiative.

Making the Decision to Privatize

Can any public service or public asset be privatized? One of the first questions to ask when considering privatization is whether the public interest is protected and served by the privatization of a service or a public asset such as land, buildings, equipment and information. "Economists and others conclude that certain services can only be provided effectively by government; for example, where continuity of service is essential, where no profits are generated,

and where no competition exists or can exist" (Dannin, 2001).

Conditions for Successful Privatization

Research suggests that, absent extreme circumstances such as default or non-performance by a contractor, there is no definitive way to evaluate whether or not a privatization initiative is a success or a failure. For example, privatization may be viewed as a success by some stakeholders if it reduces service cost; other stakeholders may view the initiative as a failure if it results in a loss of public accountability or a loss of public control. A privatization process may also be considered successful if government self-review leads to improvement without actually transferring services to the private sector. There are, however, private market and government agency characteristics that, when in place, increase the potential for successful privatization. Privatization typically works best for services that have the following characteristics:

- The services are in growing and competitive markets;
- Information associated with the delivery of the service is abundant and public accountability (transparency) is not a limiting issue;
- The service involves transactions that are not irrevocable;
- Externalities that can affect the profitability of a service are limited; and

Service efficiency can be achieved in ways that are not contrary to the public interest. In addition, privatization works best for services that are limited in scope and complexity and the contracting government agency has:

- Officials open to the idea of privatization;

- Clearly defined goals and criteria;
- Established privatization policies;
- Conducted an open public review process;
- Worked closely with affected employees and developed employee transition plans;
- Reliable cost data to accurately compare public service costs to private service costs; and the pricing of public assets to the pricing of private assets;
- A contract monitoring and management system; and
- Performance-based criteria against which the private contractor will be regularly evaluated (Rosen, 2007; United States General Accounting Office, 1997).

Accounting for Public Property, Assets and Information

Privatization often requires private contractors to use public assets (land, buildings, equipment) and information (police records, utility billing information, child welfare files). Whether and how the public agency is compensated for the use of public assets (especially those that generate income) as well as how confidential information is used and protected are major considerations. Also, when service contracts are terminated, thought needs to be given to how the assets will be returned to the public agency. Transactions involving the return of tangible assets are relatively straightforward; however, the return of confidential electronic data and assuring that copies of sensitive electronic files are not retained and used in the future by the contractor are more problematic (Dannin, 2001).

Comparing Government and Private Contractor Cost

Cost savings is a common justification for privatizing government services. Consequently, it is important to accurately compare the total cost of services provided by the government to the projected total costs to the public if a private contractor provides the same service. In comparing the cost of government service to a privatized service, decision-makers must consider not just the cost of the contract but also the cost to transition the service from a public to private provider. The transition costs should include the costs associated with displaced public employees, the cost of contract negotiations and the cost of performance oversight by the government (Dannin, 2001).

Is Privatization the Only Option?

Finally, in making a decision to privatize, decision-makers should be certain that privatization is the best way to provide lower cost services. Sometimes government service delivery can be made more efficient with investment in technology or new delivery methods. Or a "managed competition" process, where the public agency submits a bid to compete with private bidder, can be a good way to determine the most cost effective method of service delivery. As noted in a U.S. Government Accountability Office (GAO) report: "According to Indianapolis officials, competition in the marketplace rather than privatization per se produces the most value for the taxpayer. This view was shared by most state officials we spoke with the primary advantages of managed competition were reduced costs, improved services, improved employee morale and increased innovation" (United States General Accounting Office, 1997).

After the Decision to Privatize

What happens after the decision to privatize is critically important to the success or failure of the initiative. To maximize the probability of success, it is important for decision-makers and stakeholders to remain vigilant throughout the contractor selection process, contract negotiations and approval phase. Once privatization has occurred, it is important for decision-makers and stakeholders to monitor contractor performance throughout the term of the agreement.

There should be open meetings and public hearings about the key terms of all agreements, the selected contractor and the ultimate service contract.

Managing the Contractor Selection Process

Most public agencies have guidelines and procedures regarding the selection of contractors and standard contract language for liability, insurance coverage requirements, payment and other technicalities. Commonly, the public agency will issue a Request for Proposals (RFP), Request for Qualifications (RFQ) or other documents outlining the contractor selection process, the scope of services desired and minimum standards expected of the contractor. It is important to decide contractor selection criteria in advance. Will selection be based on the lowest cost proposal or on proposed service quality, or on a combination of the two? Will potential contractors undergo a thorough screening to verify they have accurately represented themselves, and are reputable and financially stable? Will criminal background checks be conducted on all private contractors? (Whitaker, 2007).

Patronage is a potential problem that involves the assignment of jobs or the offer of favors to public officials (Dannin, 2001). For example, it is alleged that Interior Department personnel responsible for overseeing deep-water drilling in the Gulf of Mexico routinely accepted gifts from private oil companies and conducted negotiations for future employment prior to the Deepwater Horizon oil spill (U.S. Department of the Interior, 2010).

Policies should be in place to minimize the potential for abuse by public officials and contractors. A common method to avoid patronage and assure an open selection process is to have an independent panel screen, interview and rank proposers for the contracting agency. The policies and procedures of the City of Mountain View, California, for example, go further by explicitly stipulating that low-bid pricing is not the primary award criteria in a Request for Proposals (City of Mountain View, 2007). Cost proposals are not opened until after the proposals are reviewed, the interview process is complete and prospective contractors have been ranked by an independent selection committee.

Negotiating the Contract

Government agencies face significant legal risks when a private contractor does not fully honor the contract, declares bankruptcy, or commits fraud or other criminal activity. The governing agency may be liable for the misdeeds of private contractors and is often responsible for making up contractor shortfalls. It is important that protections and remedies for contractor nonperformance or illegal activity be addressed before any contract is signed.

One contractual protection is to require contractors to post a surety bond and/or secure insurance payable to the government agency in the event the contractor is unable to meet the conditions of the contract. This provides an incentive for the contractor to meet the conditions of the contract and also provides financial resources for the agency to intervene quickly and ensure continuity of services if the contractor cannot fulfill the contract (Dannin, 2001).

A second potential remedy is to include in the contract language that establishes the non-performance criteria or conditions that give the government agency the right to immediately terminate the contract and take responsibility from the contractor.

In the case of a renewable, long-term contract, various fees may need to be renegotiated periodically. Specifying key aspects of this procedure, such as the frequency of audits or allowable profit will assure the initial intent of the contractual relationship is not changed over time. Open meetings requirements as well as the accessibility of public records and government documents must not be compromised over the term of the agreement.

Enforcement options and backup plans also should be thought through before the contract is finalized: Who will enforce penalties, and how will they be paid? Are there written legal protections for whistleblowers? When should mediation or arbitration be prescribed? Should these be open meetings?

Employee Considerations

Private contractors often reduce the cost of a service by offering lower wages and fewer benefits than their public counterparts. Private contractors may rely on part time employees who are not offered benefits. "Low waged work is the type of work most prone to frequent turnover, but many public services need long-term workers with historical knowledge of clients, methods and services. Wage levels affect and reflect the quality of worker an employer can attract" (Dannin, 2001). To provide a level of protection, some government agen-

cies require contractors to provide employees with competitive wages and to comply with all federal and state equal employment and anti-discrimination laws.

Conversely, as services are privatized, protections need to be in place for displaced public workers. Sometimes displaced employees are provided other positions, if available, or are offered training for new professions. The public agency may require the contractor to initially hire the existing public employees but at private sector wage and benefit levels.

Managing the Contract and Overseeing Performance

"Oversight must take place on a regular and frequent basis to ensure work is done, quality is maintained, and an early warning system is in place in order to prevent a subcontractor's absconding or engaging in financial improprieties. If oversight is not frequent and regular, problems that could have been prevented may become serious and even irreparable. The oversight process must give the public easy access to lodge complaints, ask questions and get responses. If the public cannot find someone to whom problems can be reported, then no one can be held accountable... (Dannin, 2001). The GAO report found that in all but one agency surveyed, officials reported that monitoring was the weakest link in the privatization process (United States General Accounting Office, 1997).

"There are areas of government services where measures of success can be easily stipulated and efficiently monitored" (O'Looney, 1998). Maintenance services with clearly defined operational procedures and maintenance cycles are perhaps the easiest examples. Are the traffic signals working? Have the trash cans downtown been emptied? What percent of the police vehicles were serviced on schedule? Have the water mains been flushed on schedule?

More difficult to measure are human services where achieving standardized performance measures of success or failure is more challenging. "It is especially difficult to identify and measure desired results for social services. This is because the objectives of many social services, including improved family and child well-being, are often difficult to define simply and clearly" (Winston et al., 2002). In addition, many social service programs involve goals other than pure cost efficiency and require long timeframes to measure success (O'Looney, 1998). An example would be a job training program where it could take years to determine whether clients become successful, long-term members of the workforce.

Despite the difficulties, it is essential to establish metrics in the contract that reflect industry best practices as well as local goals and objectives. It is also imperative that public agencies provide experienced staff to conduct meaningful oversight to assure that goals and objectives are achieved and the public interest is served. Auditors and inspectors may need specialized financial, legal or technical expertise.

Summary

Privatizing a government service is a complex undertaking that requires a major commitment of resources. It involves careful definition of the goals to be achieved, assurance that all efficiencies have been implemented with the existing service model, evaluation of the service "market place" to assure a competitive bidding environment, expert contract negotiation and a thorough understanding of the potential impacts to service customers. Most importantly, the process requires transparency, oversight and ongoing communication with stakeholders to understand their concerns about privatization, because, in the end, the public bears the success or failure of privatization.

REFERENCES

City of Mountain View. (2007). *California, Purchasing Policy No: 2-10.* (Effective Date: July 1, 2000, Revision Date: January 2, 2007).

Dannin, Ellen. (2001). "To Market to Market: Caveat Emptor" in *To Market to Market Reinventing Indianapolis*, ed. Ingrid Ritchie and Sheila Suess Kennedy. Lanham: University Press of America, Inc.

O'Looney, John A. (1998). *Outsourcing State and Local Government Services: Decision-Making Strategies and Management Methods.* Westport, CT: Quorum Books.

Rosen, Mark J. (2007). Privatization in Hawaii. Honolulu: Legislative Reference Bureau, December 2007.

U.S. Department of the Interior. (2010). *Investigative Report Island Operating Company.* Washington, D.C.: Office of Inspector General.

United States General Accounting Office. (1997). *Privatization: Lessons Learned by State and Local Governments.* Washington, D.C.: GAO/ GGD-97-48, March 1997.

Whitaker, Gordon P. (2007). "Service Delivery Alternatives" in *Managing Local Government Services A Practical Guide*, ed. Carl W. Steinberg and Susan Lipman Austin. Washington, D.C.: ICMA Press.

Winston, Pamela, et al. (2002). *Privatization of Welfare Services: A Review of the Literature.* Washington, D.C.: Mathematica Policy Research, Inc.

8. Contracting for Performance

Amanda M. Girth and Jocelyn M. Johnston

With increased fiscal challenges for many cities across America, more local leaders have recently begun investigating alternative means for delivering services, namely contracting or privatization. While contracting is not a new concept, it does alter the service delivery landscape for city officials. More specifically, contracting requires a new set of local management skills and raises issues about the quality of contracted services, new costs associated with contracting, managing vendor competition and ensuring optimal contract performance.

American University, with the support of the National League of Cities, launched the Survey on Local Government Contracting to better understand how public managers view contracting in the nation's cities and towns. Public managers across the country provided critical insights into the "real time" management challenges of local government contracting, helping to highlight the importance of effective governing.

About the Survey

The survey was sent to 2,195 city officials across the U.S., including 487 randomly selected city managers and 1,708 functional specialists who were primarily department directors and their representatives from building inspection services, human services, information technology, parks and recreation and public works. The survey was conducted from July to November 2009.

Results are drawn from 332 respondents for a response rate of 15 percent. With this response rate, it is expected with a 95 percent degree of confidence (i.e., in 95 out of 100 random sample surveys) that if another random sample of municipal officials completed the survey, response results would be within 4.96 percentage points (+/- 4.96 percent) of the results reported here. Survey response rates based on population and region of the country are provided in the following tables.

The results of the survey indicate that while municipal officials generally favor government contracting, many face significant challenges in holding contractors accountable for their performance. This may be attributed to the competitiveness of the market for the contracted service, management capacity of both the government and contractor, and the effective (or ineffective) use of performance incentives.

Originally published as Amanda M. Girth and Jocelyn M. Johnston (2011). "Local Government Contracting." *National League of Cities Research Brief on America's Cities*, February 2011. Reprinted with permission of the publisher.

Attitudes About Contracting

The survey asked managers questions about their general attitudes on municipal contracting. Results indicate that managers generally:

- Support government contracting (93 percent);
- Prefer to provide services in-house if given the option (69 percent); and
- Believe that most public agencies do a good job at contract management (63 percent).

About one in two managers (47 percent) report the greatest drawback of contracting is the difficulty of holding contractors accountable for their performance. he greatest benefits of contracting are distributed across a number of factors, ranging from cost savings (35 percent), greater flexibility in service delivery (32 percent), staffing (14 percent), and higher quality services (13 percent).

Overall, most respondents (69 percent) indicate that their contracts produce high-quality services to citizens. However, there is less consensus among managers about cost savings, as just over half (55 percent) report saving money from contracting services. The vast majority of public managers (69 percent) are generally confident in their level of expertise to manage contracts. However, less than half report having the adequate staff (48 percent) or enough time (40 percent) to effectively manage contracts.

Competition in City Contracts

Just over half of managers surveyed (55 percent) report being satisfied with the market for their contracts. Respondents reveal that they would prefer to work with multiple vendors for their contracts, and 87 percent say that four or more is optimal. Yet one-quarter of the managers surveyed report they often resign themselves to find more have failed.

When asked about their ability to find other vendors, managers reported that:

- It is difficult to find high quality vendors (34 percent);
- The number of contract bidders tends to reduce over time (22 percent), often because contractors buy each other out (14 percent);
- They continue to seek additional vendors for current contracts with the next contract cycle in mind (53 percent); and
- Finding vendors takes away from oversight work (23 percent).

In order to manage vendor competition, managers report using a variety of strategies to increase the number of vendors for government contracts and otherwise strengthen competition for their contracts. Perhaps most interesting is that two in five managers routinely report using mixed delivery (i.e., some portion of the service is contracted out while some portion is produced in-house) all (7 percent) or most of the time (34 percent), and about one in three (34 percent) actively create new vendors (i.e., encouraging outside organizations to set up new subsidiaries for contract work) at least some of the time government contracts and otherwise strengthen competition for their contracts. Perhaps most interesting is that two in five managers routinely report using mixed delivery (i.e., some portion of the service is contracted out while some portion is produced in-house) all (7 percent) or most of the time (34 percent), and about one in three (34 percent) actively create new vendors (i.e., encouraging outside organizations to set up new subsidiaries for contract work) at least some of the time.

Contract Performance

Public mangers also report mentoring and helping contractors with performance. Twenty percent indicate that they spend a significant amount of time helping contractors improve contract performance. More than half of respondents (52 percent) report mentoring contractors to ensure they will continue to bid on their contracts in the future.

When it comes to using performance incentives in dealing with contractors, managers indicate they are more likely to use sanctions to penalize for performance problems (66 percent) than they are to use rewards for satisfactory performance (23 percent).

To gather additional information on the ways in which managers address performance issues, respondents were asked to think of one specific contract that best reflected their experience with unsatisfactory performance. When faced with poor performance, 64 percent of managers surveyed elected to take formal action against the contractor, with the most common responses being financial sanctions or contract termination.

Finally, the ways in which managers reported measuring contract performance varied significantly. Managers report that contractors tend to fall short in performance primarily in the areas of responsiveness, quality and service continuity.

It is clear that performance problems do not generally take long to emerge; 78 percent of managers agree that performance issues appear near the beginning or midway through the contract. Managers their organization was highly dependent on the contractor that was failing to meet performance state that their organization did not have the technical expertise to provide the service in-house and 79 percent did not have the resources to provide service in-house.

These survey results suggest that when municipal leaders are forced to privatize city services, most place a strong emphasis on developing, enhancing and ensuring contractor performance. Whether that's through developing strong relationships, creating vendor competition, or holding contractors accountable, city leaders are generally aware that merely shipping responsibility outside of government ultimately will not improve public service.

9. Contract Management in Contract City

Jonas Prager and John Flint

City and county managers often manage contracts, but managers rarely devote most of their waking hours (and occasionally sleepless nights) to contract management. But the job of the city manager of Weston, Florida, a city with only three municipal employees and about 400 contract employees, is to be the contract manager of Weston for service delivery and finance.

In Weston in 2007 the three employees who are on the city payroll are the city manager, the assistant city manager/chief financial officer (ACM/CFO), and the city clerk. The 400 others are employed by contractors who perform the services that are typical of a community of more than 60,000 residents. This chapter describes the nature of contracting in Weston, the functions of the manager, and some of the challenges and solutions that have characterized local government management in Weston.

The demographics of Weston are important. It is in Broward County, Florida. Miami is 31 miles to the south and Fort Lauderdale 18 miles to the east. A young, ethnically mixed, and affluent group of residents lives within Weston's 26 square miles. In 2005, 47 percent of Weston's inhabitants were white and 41 percent Latino, with African Americans and Asians constituting the remainder. The median age was 34.2 years, with females outnumbering males by 53 percent to 47 percent.

Weston is a community of homeowners; in 2005, 80 percent owned their own residences. Most significant perhaps is the $91,851 median family income, which is 41 percent above the median Florida income and 39 percent above the U.S. 2005 median income. Weston's tax base extends beyond its residents, whose local tax rates are among the lowest in Florida. In fact, tax rates in Weston have been unchanged for 10 years. Weston receives much of its revenue from its 7 million square feet of industrial, office, and commercial space.

The location, affluence, and demographic makeup of the community have much to do with Weston's service obligations to its residents. Many of its crucial services are provided by either the county or the state. Social services for the elderly poor are not an issue because few if any such individuals live in Weston, and the local hospital in Weston is funded privately. Similarly, the local elementary and high schools are not

Originally published as Jonas Prager and John Flint (2007). "Contract Management in Contract City: The Case of Weston, Florida." *Public Management (PM) Magazine*, 89(9), October 2007. Reprinted with permission of the publisher.

a Weston responsibility; administration, education policy, and funding lie in the hands of the school board of Broward County.

Nevertheless, Weston's city government—organized in a council-manager model with an elected mayor and four city commissioners—undertakes a broad variety of duties for its residents. Notable among them are public safety—police and fire response—solid waste collection and disposal, infrastructure maintenance and repair, and recreation and cultural activities. All of these services are provided by contractors.

Weston's decision to contract is not just pragmatic; it is inherent to the philosophy of Weston as expressed in section 3.11 of its charter:

It was the original intent of the city to provide traditional municipal services [i.e., public safety, public works, administrative services, community development, and community services] through public and private contract providers. Accordingly, traditional municipal services shall be rendered through contract providers, not city employees.

The Nature of Contracting in Weston

While technically Weston is not subject to the contracting statutes of Florida, it has voluntarily subscribed to the intent of Florida's laws that require competitiveness in contracting, transparency, and effective contract monitoring (Florida Statutes, Sec. 287.001). Thus, Weston abides by the financial triggers in the state's laws that mandate competitive bidding for contracts that exceed a stated dollar sum. It also seeks via public advertising and other means of solicitation competitive and transparent bids, and it devotes considerable amounts of managerial time to contract monitoring Contracting process.

Weston contracts in three distinct frameworks—commodity procurement, service procurement where existing contracts can be emulated, and uniquely fashioned contracts. In the case of commodity procurement such as park lights, playground equipment, and traffic signs and signals, Weston examines typical acquisitions by neighboring governments and then procures from suppliers on the basis of best terms obtained by its neighbors.

When service contractors have existing contracts with other public entities, Weston can piggyback on those contracts. For policing services, for example, Weston used existing contracts of other Broward County localities with the Broward County sheriff's office (BSO) as the basis for its own contract with the BSO.

When existing contracts are inappropriate or inadequate, Weston devises from scratch contracts designed for its specific needs. This process is, of course, not unparalleled; it is typical of contracting out in both the private and public sectors. Weston is unique because it contracts out the contract process, from evaluating its technical and legal requirements, composing bid documents and conditions, arranging bid solicitation and advertising, to making the final award. Weston typically does not award contracts to the lowest bidder. Instead, the manager negotiates with the most qualified, best-value-for-money proposer for the best possible terms.

Relations with personnel. One of the recurrent features of Weston contracts involves provisions concerning terminating employees. Because city workers are not Weston civil servants but, instead, employees of the contractors, they cannot be directly discharged by Weston government authorities. However, they can be removed from Weston. Every Weston when seen from the viewpoint of the employees, is a decided advantage to the local government. In general, the manager need not devote time and energy to personnel management issues that are endemic to public management elsewhere.

Another relevant feature of Weston service provider contracts is mandated dedicated personnel. Contractors are required to assign a cadre of personnel and equipment for Weston's exclusive use. This provides Weston with the advantage of a permanent staff that can develop local expertise and an allegiance to the community, and this feature still allows labor force flexibility when that is necessary. Thus, in 2005 after Hurricane Wilma left in its wake downed trees and blocked roads, the contractor expanded its local workforce and equipment by bringing in workers from elsewhere.

Contract monitoring. Two methods are regularly employed to monitor providers' compliance with contract terms. First, contract monitoring is itself contracted out. A selected contractor performs a number of services for Weston, among which is "contract administration and supervision of all contracts," while an engineering firm is charged with monitoring construction contracts. But who monitors the monitors, especially since both contract monitoring companies are also service providers?

Enter the manager, whose continuing duty in service provision, in addition to overseeing the entire contracting processes, is to monitor the monitors. Typical monitoring by the manager involves site visits, receiving and responding to resident complaints, and meeting weekly with the city's contract providers.

At each Friday meeting, contractor representatives and the manager, often in the presence of Weston's mayor, review current projects, report on progress and problems, and discuss possible resolutions. Confrontation is rare; mutual confidence allows for cooperative resolution of issues based, for the most part, on long-standing Weston-contractor relationships.

The manager more directly monitors financial disbursements. Although accounting, payable, and receivable activities are performed by a contractor, the manager has final approval and is signatory on all disbursements.

Similarly, financing options relating to new investments (underwriting, terms, placement, and so forth) and to current operations (placement of budgetary surpluses) are explored by a specific contractor. The contractor's recommendations are presented to the ACM/CFO, who bears the ultimate decision-making authority. (An annual independent audit is required under Florida laws.)

Contract renewal. Each Weston service provider contract contains a clause that allows for mutual renewal of the contract. The obvious advantage is to provide incentives to the contractors for adhering to if not surpassing the terms of their obligations. At the same time, Weston does not have to initiate periodic and possible costly searches for replacements whose performance is as yet unknown.

Renewal options, however, may sometimes preclude finding superior providers, suppliers who can provide better service at lower cost. Reletting contracts also provides opportunities for rethinking service goals and objectives. Weston's local leaders believe that, overall, the cost of missed opportunities has been more than offset by the benefits of cooperative relationships with existing contractors. Weston has not renewed contractors whose performance was felt to be or likely to become deficient.

Issues

Weston has not experimented with alternative service provision, specifically with increasing use of civil servants. It is precluded from doing so by its charter unless overridden by a four-fifths vote of the city commission. From a pragmatic point of view, however, we cannot know whether Weston's residents might experience lower costs from a municipal fire department or a city sanitation department using municipal workers and city-owned equipment than from a contracted-out service. Perhaps extremism is not likely to be optimal.

Weston's use of performance goals to assess the effectiveness of its public service providers needs to be revisited. This is a general issue in service provision, where goals are often difficult to specify and even more difficult to measure. Environmental elements also contribute to goal achievement, and it is difficult to distinguish among the contributions of the contractor and other contributing factors. Thus, for example, the BSO is required to "maintain a low crime rate in Broward County." Aside from the question of the precise meaning of "low," whether crime is high or low is only partly dependent upon the performance of the BSO.

Lessons

While Weston may be unique in some ways—residents with above-average income, a local government without civil service and labor union constraints, and an attractive business environment—there are still a number of lessons that local authorities elsewhere might consider after learning about Weston's experiences of more than a decade.

1. Extensive contracting out can work, provided that the local authorities choose wisely. That implies selecting activities that can be easily contracted out, which in turn suggests (1) adequate potential contractors to assure competitive bids, (2) activities whose outcomes can be reliably measured, and (3) devoting adequate resources to

monitoring those results. Once a contractor has been selected, the contractor must be provided with the carrot of performance incentives, including the possibility of contract renewal at the conclusion of the contract, and not just the stick of contract cancellation.

2. Because of the limited resources of most local authorities, consideration should be given to contracting out the contracting process, or at least stages of it. But considerable caution must be exercised in selecting this key contractor.

3. Negotiated bidding, if not prohibited by statute, can lead to better values for the contracting community. But negotiated bidding is also more complex and requires some negotiating and technical expertise that might not be available to the local authorities. Again, contracting out the negotiation aspect of the contracting process might be warranted.

4. Contract clauses should be included to ensure resources (personnel, equipment) be devoted exclusively to the community but with flexibility to increase or decrease them as needed.

5. It would be wise to insert contract clauses that cede to the contracting authority the right to remove undesirable contractor employees without undertaking a lengthy and costly dismissal process.

Is It for Everyone?

Even under the best conditions for contracting, local authorities must always consider the bottom line. Is contracting providing more value for their scarce resources than in-house provision? Weston's success may be due to its unique circumstances. Whether other governments in different circumstances would do as well remains an open question.

10. P3 Structures and Arrangements

Justin Marlowe, William Rivenbark, and A. John Vogt

Public organizations around the world have turned to public-private partnerships (P3s) to engage private sector investment in a wide range of services and infrastructure, such as transportation, utilities, ports, water, schools, and hospitals.

Municipalities considering a public-private partnership should be aware of the full range of possible structures and arrangements. Those structures and arrangements are constantly evolving, and variations arise in response to several considerations. For example, which party owns the asset during the partnership? Which party operates the asset? How are revenues that are generated by the asset shared between the two parties? What portion of the project risks, financial and otherwise, is borne by each partner? What portion is transferred from the public to the private sector, or vice versa? How the parties answer these and other questions defines the structure, dynamics, and, more than likely, the potential for success of the partnership.

P3 structures generally fall on a continuum, with services provided entirely by the public sector at one end and services provided entirely by the private sector with government as the enabler or regulator at the other-with a number of hybrids in between. Here are some of those arrangements.

Passive Private Investment

Government at all levels relies on private capital to finance infrastructure and other needs that cannot be paid for out of current-year revenues. At the local level, the main instruments for private investment are tax-exempt municipal bonds and notes. Municipal bond investors are passive because they are not directly involved in the day-to-day management and governance of the public services in question. They simply loan the jurisdiction money by purchasing the bonds, and then expect a return on their investment through periodic interest payments.

Traditional Public Contracting

Local governments rely on private vendors for a variety of goods and services. In

Originally published as Justin Marlowe, William Rivenbark, and A. John Vogt (2010). "Public-Private Partnership Structures and Arrangements." July 12, 2010, http://icma.org/en/international/resources/insights/Article/101962/PublicPrivate_Partnership_Structures_and_Arrangements. Reprinted with permission of the publisher.

most cases those goods and services are procured through traditional contracting and bidding or through request-for-proposal processes. The government pays for and the private sector provides the services in question, although the private provider plays a limited role in deciding how the service is to be delivered; mainly, it responds to the government's specifications. For infrastructure projects, such an arrangement can include contracts for project design and/or construction of new facilities or other assets. For certain types of economic development services, it might include labor market analysis, website design, and other services in which private partners typically have special expertise.

Operation, Maintenance, and Service Contracts

The municipality hires a private organization to perform some tasks or groups of tasks for a specified period of time. The municipality is responsible for funding any capital investments needed to expand or improve the system, including traditional leasing for such assets as computer technology or fleet maintenance, and it retains complete ownership of the asset. The private partner assumes the risk that the service cannot be provided at the specified level or quality for the specified price.

Joint Ventures

In a joint venture, the municipality and its private sector partners form a new company or public authority. Both assume some portion of the ownership and responsibility for the service in question. P3s for pollution remediation, urban redevelopment, and affordable housing projects are often structured as joint ventures.

Joint ventures follow two basic models, with variations. In the first model, public capital is used to procure the land, buildings, and other assets needed to move the venture forward, and the private partner designs the project, secures tenants, and/or manages the operation in exchange for the right to use the facility and, in some cases, some portion of the revenues received from it. In the second model, the private party finances the construction or expansion of a public facility in exchange for the right to build housing, commercial space, or industrial facilities on the site.

Build-Operate-Transfer

Under a build-operate-transfer arrangement, the private partner takes principal responsibility for funding, designing, building, and then operating a facility. The government retains ownership of the facility and becomes both the customer and the regulator of the service, and formal ownership is then transferred back to the public sector at the end of the agreement.

Most lease-purchase and sale-leaseback arrangements follow this basic model, and a number of variations exist, depending on the private partner's responsibilities.

Concession Agreements

In a concession agreement the public partner grants the private partner full responsibility for all aspects of the design, construction, maintenance, and operations of the facility in exchange for some or all of the revenues generated by it. The public partner's role is limited to regulating the performance, price, and quantity of the service provided. The facility remains government property, but all maintenance and capital infrastructure investments are the sole responsibility of the private partner.

Passive Public Investment

Passive public investment includes equity, debt guarantees, grants, tax expenditures, and other public investments in private enterprise. Most local economic development efforts are of this type. Passive public investment takes many forms—for example, tax credits, tax expenditures, business incubators, and discounted utility rates—and is designed to attract new businesses to the jurisdiction, to prevent existing businesses and industries from leaving, or to encourage existing businesses to expand within the jurisdiction's boundaries. In these types of P3s, the public partner has no role in operations decisions because the operation in question is retail business, manufacturing, or some other decidedly nonpublic service.

Passive public investment has a major effect on local government capital budgeting and finance because it is intended to expand private enterprise, and new private enterprise places new demands on public infrastructure. This is especially challenging because passive public investments are often made incrementally and/or with limited regard for existing capital improvement priorities or programs. For that reason, effective capital improvement programs include a policy or framework of policies that identifies how and when the jurisdiction will make passive public investments. Such policies can help to impose predictability on the economic development process, which can facilitate more effective capital planning and budgeting.

11. Recovery Budgeting and Public-Private Partnerships

Amy Davis

At first glance, the City of Sandy Springs, Georgia—just north of Atlanta—might look similar to other growing cities of 99,000 residents. More than 300 miles of roadway are being improved and maintained, permits are being issued, residents are voicing their views at City Council meetings, and 115 police officers and 97 firefighters are answering calls. But this formerly unincorporated area of Fulton County is also home to residents who wanted change.

They had grown weary of having most of their tax dollars spent on services in other parts of the county and wanted to see their money spent on services at a local level. A dedicated group of volunteers fought for 30 years to get legislative approval to hold a ballot referendum for incorporation. The referendum was held in June 2005 and passed by 94 percent. Just as quickly as the city was born, a five-member governor's commission was set up to guide every aspect of the startup, which would begin on December 1, 2005.

A major task before the governor's commission was deciding how city services would be provided. The commission's decision to explore a public-private partnership for all services was innovative—Sandy Springs was the first city to outsource all municipal services, except public-safety services, to one private-sector entity. The mayor and city council members believe in this unique public-private model and wanted something non-traditional from the beginning. The police and fire departments were excluded from the contract because the liability insurance would not allow the private company to provide these services.

In recent years, public entities have expanded the scope of services performed by outsourced providers, as the benefits of outsourcing have became apparent. Sandy Springs' decision to outsource nearly all city services is an extension of this trend, and since 2005, several other public entities have followed suit and privately outsourced services to this extent. The cities of Johns Creek, Georgia; Central, Louisiana; Bonita Springs, Florida, and Centennial, Colorado, have successfully followed this model.

Contracting Services

The commission chose a global engineering firm that had demonstrated experience

Originally published as Amy Davis (2010). "Thinking Strategically about Recovery Budgeting: A Case Study on Public-Private Partnerships." *Government Finance Review*, 26(5), October 2010. Reprinted with permission of the publisher.

and exceptional performance with local and international government management. The contract included an administrative side to handle duties such as finance, accounting, purchasing, customer service, human resources, communications, and information technology; and a hands-on side to provide public services such as public works, transportation, parks and recreation, and planning and zoning. Most of the public works tasks are done by Georgia-based firms that work as subcontractors for the main vendor.

The vendor, which submitted two RFPs for the project, has been providing services to Sandy Springs since the city's inception. The initial fixed-fee contract for a specific scope of services, which was awarded in September 2005, was for one year. The contract is renewed annually for up to five years and can be adjusted with a change order. Now, after five years, the city has begun the RFP process to ensure that it is using taxpayer money wisely.

Learning Along the Way

As might be expected, there were many obstacles to be faced in starting a new city in 100 days. In most cases, those obstacles have been overcome. City operations started immediately on December 1, 2005, and while the vendor had been selected in September, the partners could not enter into a contract until after the city was officially incorporated and the City Council was seated on December 1. The company invested its own funds to secure office space, recruit and train staff, lease equipment, and put all of the necessary systems, processes, and tools in place—all on, essentially, a handshake. All general government staff remain employees of the vendor, with the exception of the city manager, assistant city manager, court clerk, city clerk, finance director, grants administrator, and public safety employees.

From the first days, Sandy Springs project staff, who consisted mostly of department heads, reported to a transition office that lacked optimal technology-in the first days of operation, staff brought computers, pens, paper, and cell phones from home. These problems were quickly remedied by going to the local office supply store and ordering what was needed. Then, as more staff came onboard, items that were requisitioned came at a continuous clip. In addition, initial call volume from residents to a designated call center, provided by the contractor, was higher than anticipated, and accommodations had to be made. In the first year, the Citizen Response Center answered 69,000 calls. Residents were elated to "hear a voice on the other end," and they called back again and again just to see if someone would answer. (To date, the center has received more than 435,600 calls.)

New project staff began work at a city with no written ordinances in place. Often borrowing models from other municipalities, staff drafted ordinances, standard operating procedures, and departmental guidelines. They learned the expectations of residents and the elected officials, and thought of proactive and innovative solutions to challenges. For instance, when faced with an initial backlog of building permits in the Community Development Department, project staff brought in additional people to help the new department deplete the backlog in record time.

Enhancing Revenue

One of the most important lessons the project leadership staff learned is that revenue streams for the new city should be identified and established as soon as possible, and that adopted ordinances should be tailored to specific municipal needs. Some of the revenue streams Sandy Springs identified were:

1. **Tax Anticipation Note.** Because the city didn't get its first revenue check until April 2006, the vendor helped finance a tax anticipation note for $10 million. This short-term note was issued to finance current operations, to be repaid from anticipated tax receipts. These notes are issued at a discount, have maturities of a year or less, and mature either at a specific future date or when property and other taxes are collected. Tax anticipation notes hold first claim on tax receipts when collected.

2. **Alcoholic Beverage Licenses.** The city inherited 191 alcoholic beverage licenses (restaurant or off-premise and new or transfer) from Fulton County. The city issued temporary licenses for 90 days so establishments could continue operating. Most of the licenses were redocumented within that time, and the city gave the remaining establishments a second 90-day period. All but one of the 191 licensees were redocumented and recertified. This process ensured that the city's records were current and accurate.

3. **Business Licenses.** The City of Sandy Springs took over all operations of business licensing from Fulton County immediately, and new business license fees for 2006 had to be paid by March 31.

4. **Tax Collection.** The finance department devised a collections system for items such as the hotel/motel tax, alcohol excise tax, and auto rental tax. The department created a forms and communications system, accounting system, and deposit system, and it maintained the records. These functions provided the city with an accurate accounting of all capital.

The Priorities

Creating the New City of Sandy Springs (Oliver Porter, AuthorHouse, 2006), says: "The Committee for Sandy Springs mounted a strong campaign to get out the vote and inform voters on the merits of the city. The campaign began with a final poll to determine the top service issues that concerned the voters. By a large margin, the number one issue was zoning. Number two was traffic, by a narrow margin over public safety." Today, the city's elected officials remain true to the voters who elected them by using that poll as the basis of their four priority areas: public safety, transportation, recreation, and parks and code enforcement.

Enhancing Public Safety. The Chattahoochee River 911 Authority, or ChatComm, started in September 2009 as a joint venture with a neighboring city and a new contractor. Not only does this model give residents a more rapid and more reliable response from police, fire, and EMS, it is the largest—and perhaps the only—outsourcing of a 911 center in the United States. The company hired to provide the services must maintain strict standards: answer 90 percent of 911 calls within 10 seconds, and process 90 percent of those calls for dispatch within 60 seconds. So far, the center has done an outstanding job: In a typical week, it answers 465 emergency calls for Sandy Springs, of which 94 percent are dispatched within the response time goal, and 468 non-emergency calls, of which 98 percent are answered within the response time goal.

Keeping Traffic Moving. Continuing traffic improvements on Roswell Road—a major arterial road that runs north and south through the heart of Sandy Springs from the city's southern border at the Atlanta City limits to its northern border at the Chattahoochee River—is a top priority. The Public Works Department continues to improve traffic flow on Roswell Road, and better-timed signals have resulted in a significant savings of time and fuel. According to a recent study the city commissioned, the traveling public saved $1.4 million in time and fuel on the nine-mile stretch of Roswell Road from West Wieuca Road to Dunwoody

Place. The completion of Sandy Springs' Traffic Management Center, a facility linked with fiber optic cable and equipped with real-time video from overhead cameras, played a role in this improvement. Staff was able to see what type of conditions existed on the streets and adjust changes along the whole corridor, as compared to seeing the timing from intersection to intersection via visual inspection.

Time Out. As recreation programs grow, municipalities across the nation are moving toward online registration. Sandy Springs is no exception. For example, the gymnastics program enrollment alone has increased by more than 40 percent, and more than 900 participants are using the newly equipped gymnastics facility this year. The online registration program freed staff to work with the children participating in the recreational programs, provide quality instruction, open more classes, and have more competitive teams on site.

Code Compliance. Community development's Code Enforcement Division made a major commitment to upgrade processes and develop new and innovative approaches to existing programs. Code Enforcement also developed new programs to address customer needs and city issues. The ultimate goal is code compliance to prevent and abate violations on private and commercial property. The division also pioneered the integration of technology into field operations, allowing staff more time to apply their expertise and spend less time in the office. With staff handling thousands of inspections, enforcement actions, and investigations each year, using laptops in the field offers real-time, critical information. Case updates, including permits, licenses, property ownership information, prior code enforcement cases, and photographs, can be seen in vehicles. Inspectors are also able to search city, state, and federal codes, thus providing a superior level of customer service.

Looking to the Future. Sandy Springs is working on a project to improve operational and safety issues on one of the busiest bridges in the city. The city will also widen a major thoroughfare that connects to one of the busiest transportations arteries in the southeast. Finally, the city will address another major concern: water. The residents of Sandy Springs pay the City of Atlanta for every gallon consumed. The mayor and council have passed two conservation ordinances that dealt with creating incentives for the building community to use conservation practices, and also rain and freeze sensor shut offs on irrigation systems.

Summary

A recent online survey indicated that more than 80 percent of the respondents have a high level of satisfaction with the public-private model. The results of the city's 2009 elections back this up: At the end of the first four years, the mayor and four original council members were reelected with overwhelming support or without opposition. (The other two council members chose not to run for second terms.) Residents of Sandy Springs have realized their dream of creating their own city, and they continue to witness changes and improvements as the city lays the groundwork for many great years ahead, according to the mayor. Sandy Springs, which didn't even exist five years ago, was recently named the ninth most affluent city in the United States, and it has an incredible public safety program, public works team, and beautiful parks. The city has much to be proud of and will continue to build on its achievements.

12. Third-Party Agreements

Bob Bland

One of the most pervasive developments since the 1970s across all sectors of the American economy has been the contracting out of services to outside vendors. Outsourcing production to a third party offers the possibility of providing better quality service at a lower cost. But the success of contracting with a third party does not assure either improved quality of service or a lower cost or, even more rarely, successfully achieving both objectives.

Governments have always contracted with private firms and nonprofits for various services. The military depends on private vendors to supply equipment and material. Local governments bid out contracts to vendors for office supplies, vehicles, and technical support. Professional service agreements, such as engineering design or architectural development, are typically the result of negotiating an agreement with qualified firms.

However, since the 1970s governments have greatly expanded their use of third-party providers in producing and delivering public services. Some local governments, such as Weston, Florida, rely on contracts with other governments, private firms, and nonprofits for the provision of all of their services (Prager, 2008). With this expansion has come a wide variety of experimentation in the methods used to select contractors, to compensate them, and greater sharing of financial risk with the vendor. And with this experimentation has also come a new vocabulary and terminology that lacks consistency use or meaning.

When local governments contract with another government, a private firm, or a nonprofit organization, the primary beneficiary is either the government itself (such as a contract for the collection of a city's delinquent property taxes) or citizens (such as a contract with a private firm to collect residential solid waste). For simplicity, these two possibilities are labeled internal beneficiary and external beneficiary.

From a budget perspective, contracting with an outside vendor potentially involves sharing financial risk with that vendor. Financial risk may be unshared to the extent that the local government incurs no loss if the contract is not fulfilled. For example, a contract for the construction of a new city facility will involve virtually no sharing of financial risk. The contractor receives final payment if and when the project is completed. Construction contracts usually include a performance bond-typically up to 10 percent of the value of the contract is

---

Originally published as Bob Bland (2010). "A Typology for Third-Party Agreements." *Public Management (PM) Magazine*, December 1, 2010. Reprinted with permission of the publisher.

withheld until the completed project is inspected and the terms of the contract certified as having been satisfied. Once the project is accepted by the local government, the performance bond is released as the final payment to the contractor.

By contrast, joint ventures, such as a Tax Increment Financing District or a sports arena, involve shared financial risk. In the case of a TIF, if private investment in the redevelopment district does not meet expectations, the local government bears the financial loss. But if the development meets expectations, the benefits from the redevelopment district are shared with investors through lower start-up costs.

These two dimensions to agreements with external parties—beneficiaries (internal versus external) and financial risk (unshared versus shared)—provide a framework for characterizing the types of agreements that have emerged in the past four decades in the public sector.

Under this typology, contracting is more narrowly defined as those third-party agreements in which government itself is the primary beneficiary and the financial risks are not shared with the outside party. For example, most construction contracts fit into this category as do open bid contracts with local vendors for various operating supplies. A state contract with a third-party to operate a state lottery fits in this category. The lottery commission is the primary beneficiary to the extent that a private firm assists the commission in its mission.

On the other hand, outsourcing occurs when the primary beneficiaries are outside the government itself, such as citizens or investors, and financial risk is not shared. For example, outsourcing occurs when a local government retains a third party to operate a toll road, collect solid waste, operate a transit system, provide school bus service to children, respond to burglar alarm calls, or provide insurance for municipal bonds. All of these services provide direct benefits to citizens or entities other than the government itself, and the financial risk is not shared between the government initiating the agreement and the third-party vendor. If a government defaults on its insured debt, the third-party insurer is financially responsible for meeting the obligation per the terms of the insurance policy.

Mildred Warner and Amir Hefetz (2008) introduced the term mixed delivery to describe the growing trend among cities to use a more collaborative approach to the delivery of services. Using the proposed typology, where the financial risks are greater local governments may resort to involving a third party as a way to diversify their risk of financial loss. Mixed delivery occurs when the local government itself is the primary beneficiary from the collaboration but the financial risk (or return) is shared with a third party. (This is a more narrow application of mixed delivery than used by Warner and Hefetz.) An industrial park that attracts private venture capital constitutes a mixed delivery strategy. A university may use a mixed delivery strategy by establishing a research park that attracts start-up industries as collaborators in developing new products.

When the primary beneficiaries are outside the local government and the agreement involves shared financial risk, the collaboration constitutes a partnership. For example, an agreement between a university and a city for the development of a conference center would constitute a partnership under this proposed typology. The primary beneficiaries are conference hosts and their conferees, but the financial risk from the venture is shared by the university and city. An agreement between a city and a professional athletic franchise or symphony orchestra for the construction and maintenance of a facility constitutes a partnership to the extent the financial risks are shared between the two parties and the beneficiaries are patrons or spectators.

Noticeably missing from this typology is privatization, a term that has taken on innumerable meanings. Phillip J. Cooper (2003) provides a useful definition by characterizing "real privatization" as occurring when government is completely removed from the production and delivery of a service. For example, 19 states have an exclusive monopoly on the distribution and sale of some or all types of alcoholic beverages. If a state were to sell its monopoly and completely remove itself from the distribution and sale of one or all types of alcohol, that would constitute privatization.

In a future column, I will offer a typology for the methods for selecting third-party providers. The municipal bond literature provides a useful basis for understanding the range of methods used by local governments in awarding contracts.

REFERENCES

Cooper, Phillip J. (2003). *Governing by Contract: Challenges and Opportunities for Public Managers*. Washington, D.C.: CQ Press.

Prager, Jonas. (2008). "Contract City Redux: Weston, Florida, as the Ultimate New Public Management Model City." *Public Administration Review* 68 (January/February 2008): 167–180.

Warner, Mildred E., and Amir Hefetz (2008). "Managing Markets for Public Service: The Role of Mixed Public-Private Delivery of City Services." *Public Administration Review* 68 (January/February 2008): 155–166.

13. Innovation in Public Management

Katy Singlaub

Innovation—it's what we strive for as public managers to better our organizations and, in turn, better our communities. As a county manager and as a student of innovation worldwide, I've had the opportunity to research, witness, and facilitate the power of innovation in local government. What has become clear is that there are patterns and themes that all of us can replicate; most involve a shift in thinking and not major, new investments we can ill afford.

Public service is noble work. It ennobles us. What could be more worthy than helping people grapple with the questions of how best to design and govern our communities, where the vast majority of the planet's people live, and encouraging prosperity and the achievement of potential and destiny while protecting and preserving the natural and environmental wealth that we and our ancestors have been so fortunate to enjoy?

Although it is ennobling, our work is also challenging, and one of the key challenges for today's public manager is to learn to harness the power of innovation and apply it to solving the simplest as well as the most complex problems of the local government workplace.

I want to share some thoughts on the meaning and place of innovation in local government at this time in our history. This is not intended to be a comprehensive review of all the innovations that local governments have implemented in recent times but, instead, a series of observations about connections, the applicability and transferability of learning about innovation, and a question about how and where local governments will go next.

Innovation as a Foundation

What do we mean by innovation? In general, definitions of innovation point to something that is new or unusual, a breakthrough, something unique. But author Frans Johansson expands this idea in *The Medici Effect*, where he suggests that $4 + 4 + 4 = 35, 372$ is new and creative but also that it is irrelevant. An innovation, then, to quote Johansson, is "the creative idea become realized." That is, it must be implemented, and doing so involves a series of elements that are almost limitlessly available to local government but not always embraced.

Originally published as Katy Singlaub (2008). "Innovation in Public Management: What the Future Will Demand of Us." *Public Management (PM) Magazine*, 90(6), July 2008. Reprinted with permission of the publisher.

Why do we need to accelerate the pace of innovation and change in local government? Thomas Friedman, author of *The World Is Flat*, describes a poster from the factory of his friend Jack Perkowski, chairman and chief executive officer of ASIMCO Technologies, an American auto parts manufacturer in China. It is an African proverb, translated into Mandarin, and posted on the factory floor:

Every morning in Africa, a gazelle wakes up.
It knows it must run faster than the fastest lion or it will be killed.
Every morning a lion wakes up.
It knows it must outrun the slowest gazelle or it will starve to death.

It doesn't matter whether you are a lion or a gazelle.

When the sun comes up, you better start running!

We are all in a race for survival, even in government.

Although local governments do not face the same kind of competition for profit and cost reduction among their industry that private sector firms do, business leaders and citizens are increasingly unwilling to sit by and watch local governments' cost of service escalate far more rapidly than the rate of inflation because of governments' reliance on a traditional model of labor-intensive service delivery.

Corporate leaders in our cities and counties ask why we are not introducing the same innovations they must introduce or face the failure of their enterprise. All of us have an investment in stimulating an environment for radical innovation—not only because it is demanded by our citizen-customers but also because it is imperative to the survival of our quality of life.

I don't mean to imply that local governments in the United States are not already innovating and implementing relevant, imaginative new strategies for fulfilling their missions. This impressive foundation provides an excellent base from which to launch the next level. Let's look at the chain of forces that Thomas Friedman cites and how these forces are demonstrated in local government innovation.

Friedman's Forces

1. **Fall of the Berlin Wall.** The end of the Cold War shifted the world from a two-system economic environment, with free-market capitalism on one side and centralized authoritarian communism on the other, to a single predominant economic system supporting democratic, free-market forces. Local governments have similarly moved from a strongly centralized funding of service delivery to a decidedly more entrepreneurial system, with many communities, like Carrollton, Texas, moving toward competitive service delivery.

2. **Netscape and the explosive success of Web browsers.** The Internet and smart Web browsers enabled users, independent of time and geography, to access each other's knowledge about anything and everything. The early Web browser technology was founded on a basis of trust and integrity, with an assumption that the early users, all researchers, would quickly help to improve it.

Their interest in recruiting people to use it at little or no cost assumed that people would use it wisely and, by using it, would quickly expand the database of knowledge available for browsing, thereby increasing the value of the browser technology. And they were right. Local government professional e-networks and discussion groups now provide instant access for colleagues to answer one another's queries and share lessons learned.

3. **Development of workflow software.** Computer software has connected such systems as different e-mail or word-processing systems with each other. Local governments throughout the United States now use

workflow software to connect completely independent, stand-alone technology systems in public and private not-for-profit agencies. The software is used, for example, to improve the efficiency and outcomes of service delivery to mentally ill homeless individuals who often do not carry identification and cannot recall where they are.

4. **Open sourcing of software.** Open sourcing has fostered self-organizing collaborative communities founded on continuously improving intellectual property owned by no one. Because open-source software is openly and freely shared, it is constantly improved by its users and is available, free, to anyone. In return, users who develop an enhancement make that improvement available to everyone for free. Local governments like Palo Alto, California, now use "wikis" as an open information source for all users who want to post interesting information to improve the knowledge base.

5. **Outsourcing.** Organizations now frequently hire outsiders to perform limited functions such as research, call centers, and publishing. In this practice, increasingly common in local government, agencies contract out functions as diverse as custodial services, solid waste management, transportation, human resources management, fire departments, police and detention services, libraries, and medical care for indigents, as some examples. As long as quality standards and efficient performance can be maintained at a lower cost, local governments will continue to widely use outsourcing to deliver services.

6. **Offshoring.** Organizations now have the ability to take their entire operations and move them offshore. Local governments in the United States have not readily adopted offshoring for obvious reasons— many citizens, employee labor unions, and elected officials do not tolerate public services being done remotely by people who are not U.S. citizens or legal residents. I expect, however, that enterprising local governments will soon find ways to offshore entire functions and processes of government, invisibly and without objection, and may do so because of rising costs and declining revenues.

7. **Supply chaining.** The master of supply chaining, of course, is Wal-Mart, where the transaction in which you buy a product is monitored by the bar code on the purchased good, which electronically and automatically sends a signal to deliver another one, which is then picked, packed, shipped, and distributed onto the shelf within hours or days.

In local government, one of the areas that has been successfully and vertically integrated in a limited kind of supply chain is building permitting, which ultimately delivers a product (the inspection report). When the chain becomes fully implemented, each step in that automated, successful inspection report may one day electronically trigger a request for the next person in the supply chain of building your house, such as the grader, framer, plumber, electrician, finish carpenter or landscaper, to get to work. Ultimately, it would automatically notify the building inspector to come and perform each inspection, up to the final inspection.

8. **Insourcing.** In this case, organizations can bring entirely independent functions in-house in order to create more powerful integrated supply chains. One example that Friedman uses is UPS, which not only picks up your Toshiba laptop computer in response to that work order for a repair that you already sent to the manufacturer, but also completes the repair and handles the delivery of the laptop back to you, the customer, after UPS's Toshiba-certified computer repair technicians—according to their contract with Toshiba—actually repair your computer to Toshiba's standards.

By reducing the number of separate transactions to complete the work, UPS makes money for itself and for Toshiba, and increases value to customers. Many local governments, dissatisfied with the quality and cost of local community access television providers, have already insourced their own television production units. They can thus control message, content, quality, and time of viewing, and they can link to Web and other media, saturating the local bandwidth with their own unique programming.

9. **In-forming**. That dominant search engine Google not only connects you with information about friends, colleagues, and business associates, it gives you information about them that they may not even be aware is knowable. Meanwhile, Google is keeping data about what and who you are looking for and will link you up with advertisers and service providers based on your unique personal preferences.

The younger generation knows this well, and they will expect local government to find them, hence the entry of some local governments into Facebook and MySpace, as well as the enormous popularity of local government use of customer relationship management (CRM) software to connect citizens with the specific information and services that they are interested in. This is done quickly and automatically, and no intervention or contact from a government employee is required. Recent legislation to push text messages during emergencies also uses this force.

10. **The steroids**. Friedman's "steroids" refer to all the technology that amplifies all the other forces to make them digital, mobile, personal, and virtual. This force is widely used by constituents to shape local governments; you can bet that during the next public meeting of your city council or state legislature, a lobbyist or concerned citizen will be sending the mayor or the assemblywoman an e-mail or text message with a caustic question to pose to staff during the presentation!

The Medici Effect

In a keynote presentation on September 23, 2008, that is based on his bestselling book, *The Medici Effect: Breakthrough Insights at the Intersection of Ideas, Concepts, and Cultures*, author and entrepreneur Frans Johansson took ICMA conference attendees on a journey to "the Intersection": a place where ideas from different fields and cultures meet and collide, ultimately igniting an explosion of innovation.

Johansson's presentation explored his proposition that breakthrough ideas are best found at this intersection of different cultures, occupations, ways of thinking, and points of view, and that it is there that open-minded people can see patterns and find analogies, look at things from different angles, and challenge the first principles that often become intellectual straitjackets.

Johansson revealed how people can use the "Medici effect"—a reference to the proliferation of new ideas enabled by the Medici banking family in Renaissance Italy—to find intersections in their own lives and turn the ideas they find there into groundbreaking innovations that will benefit themselves, their organizations, and their communities.

Ten Key Principles

Based on Friedman's forces, I propose that there are 10 key principles for successful innovation in local government.

1. Build on vision and values. There is surprisingly little correlation between technical expertise and successful innovation. The correlation, it seems, is with passion. Innovation is successful more often when it is guided by core values and a vision for better outcomes and results for those served.

2. Create and sustain a culture of innovation. A culture of innovation demands

many things, and among them is diversity. Exposure to differing perspectives, cultures, and thought patterns exponentially increases the opportunity to see something in an entirely new way. Do we routinely encourage our managers and supervisors to hire nontraditional candidates for jobs? They are likely to bring new ideas that may help us find solutions we wouldn't have thought of otherwise.

3. Use a significant crisis or opportunity to innovate. Crisis stimulates our thinking and compresses our available time for study; in other words, it favors action. Local governments report using such techniques as examining reverse assumptions to find an innovation during a crisis. Reverse assumptions require that we consider what might make the problem worse, and then we work backwards.

Fire professionals know that if we examine the aftermath of a catastrophic wildfire for those factors that can make the catastrophe worse, we might discover that patterns of high winds, heat, slopes, and certain vegetation can predict with great accuracy when and where fires will occur. We then can plant different vegetation on those slopes and assign more firefighters and brush crews on shifts and in locations meeting those criteria.

4. Create collaborations. Bringing diverse interests together expands the likelihood that ideas will bear fruit. Like opensource technology, collaborations improve the ideas and share power. When Washoe County contracted with SAP for its enterprise resource planning solution, we brought together and housed off-site a team of staff from purchasing, human resources, finance, and even the district attorney's office—not just technology professionals—and implemented our system in one year, on budget.

5. Identify and nurture a champion. Like the angel investors who provide seed capital for entrepreneurial ventures, the champion—an elected official, a manager, a key department head, or a citizen—gives moral support and hope to the innovator, enhances the credibility of the innovation, and can remove or neutralize the organizational barriers.

A local city councilwoman led a successful effort to fund and build a new state-of-the-art regional animal services center by helping forge a partnership between Washoe County and the humane society, which is co-located in the facility and handles the adoptions. This new partnership dramatically reduced the rates of euthanasia of animals in the county.

6. Seek innovation at the intersection of seemingly unrelated fields or concepts. Frans Johansson describes the explosive growth in the number of opportunities for unique combinations, and therefore innovation, at the intersection of seemingly diverse and unrelated concepts and fields. To innovate this way, we must break down associative barriers—those filters that cause us to habitually relate familiar things in familiar ways. If we were able to integrate functions of the police department with our libraries, for example, what might we create? If our engineers were linked with senior services, what innovations could they discover? The Alliance for Innovation is just such a creation at the intersection. A partnership was formed among Arizona State University (research), the International City/County Management Association (practitioners), and the Innovation Groups (pioneering organizations) to transform local government through an alliance that is stronger, more nimble, and more innovative than any of us could be alone.

7. Demonstrate courage. As Alvin Toffler wrote in his important book, *Power Shift*, it's not enough to be right; we have to be effective. We can't rest on knowing our solution is right; we have to lead by example and be willing to sacrifice, demonstrate flexibility, and have courage to stay the course.

How many of us have lost ballot issues, only to bring them back and win, perhaps many years later?

8. Persevere if the innovation is important. The difference between a creative individual and a successful innovator is often the discipline to keep going and keep trying. Keep at it, and consider using a pilot program to demonstrate the effectiveness of your innovation. When the overhaul of the child welfare system in the state of Nevada was proposed, Washoe County created a pilot program that ultimately led to vastly improved child outcomes and won the support of our state legislature.

9. Cultivate the credibility of the leader. The credible leader can guide the organization toward innovation, attract innovators to the team, and inspire confidence from the elected governing body. Credibility involves envisioning the future and using that vision to inspire others, but it also involves building a track record of following through with implementation of new and exciting ideas.

10. Share the gift. This is the most important principle of successful innovation in local government. Like the viral dissemination of information through browsers and open-source technology, innovations in local government will need to replicate quickly because that lion is running faster than people are. Innovations will become better and more relevant, and they will have more impact to the extent that we can accelerate their adoption.

We must help to ensure that the tools, the training, the equipment, and the human infrastructure of systems and processes are provided for all to operate effectively after innovations are in place and up and running. It is the manager's task to integrate and empower employees, citizens, businesspeople, and elected leaders in the process of continuously identifying and improving innovations. As we do this, we re-create the origins of local government: small groups of people that came together to improve residents' conditions and their very lives by doing it better together than they could have done it alone.

14. Managed Competition: Ten Years of Progress

Tom Guilfoy

No one knows the exact date when managed competition started at the City of Carrollton. There were a lot of decisions made and actions taken during late 2001 and early 2002 that collectively made a big difference in the way our City has operated ever since. We have decided to celebrate March 20, 2012, as the tenth anniversary of the beginning of Carrollton's Managed Competition philosophy and program. Why March 20? This date marks the Vernal Equinox or the beginning of Spring. This season brings increasing daylight, warming temperatures and the rebirth of flora and fauna.

In many ways, managed competition was a rebirth for the City of Carrollton. It helped establish us as an innovator in local government operating methods and practices. Our approach to providing competitive services has received national recognition and has been imitated by other cities and counties around the country. We want to recognize this major milestone by reflecting on our progress to date, sharing some lessons learned and talking about the challenges that lie ahead.

How Our Journey Started...

Discussion of the 2002-2003 City budget began in April 2002 with a presentation to Council of the five-year financial forecast. While the City continued to see growth in the assessed valuation of property and new construction added to the property tax rolls, sales tax revenues saw a significant decline from previous fiscal years.

Leonard A. Martin, City Manager: We started the Managed Competition transformation of our organization as the recession of 2001 was in its infancy. Today, ten years later, the world is in yet another recession experiencing a slow and unstable recovery. The latest national job reports reveal a trend in the private sector of adding back jobs lost during the worst economic downturn since 1929. However, the numbers also revealed that government is still reducing employees, while taxpayer demands for accountable performance from their government is not going to go away.

Over the last decade, I have been extremely proud of how our organization made difficult decisions to become competitive before economic calamity forced it

---

Originally published as Tom Guilfoy (2012). "Managed Competition: Ten Years of Progress." March 20, 2012, Carrollton, Texas. Reprinted with permission of the author.

upon us. We made painful decisions for the right reason: to better serve our customers, the taxpayers who live and do business in Carrollton.

You are looked up to and admired by local governments throughout the United States. The processes you have created to provide services cheaper, better, faster and friendlier are being adopted by other organizations that are mired in traditional government cultures whose taxpayers are in revolt over the waste and inefficiencies they see.

Congratulations on such admirable achievements. I look forward to our continued innovation to provide our customers even better valued services—the highest quality at the lowest possible cost. Thank you for your commitment to becoming the standard by which all other cities are measured.

In June 2002, the Mayor and City Council met for their annual strategic planning retreat. These eight community leaders established a new long-range goal for City staff:

Transform the city organization to a service business

- Achieve high citizen satisfaction with services and organizational values
- Ensure services are provided in a cost-effective manner
- Establish a managed competition attitude and program
- Create a well trained and professional workforce focusing on performance and productivity
- Focus on providing essential services and core businesses

Key Action: Establish a Managed Competition Plan

With the vision and leadership of City Manager Leonard Martin, the City began to change its culture, operate with a greater sense of focus and urgency and behave more like a competitive service business.

Back in 2002, traditional governments believed that there were only two ways of dealing with a budget shortfall:

1. Cut services, service levels or programs and/or
2. Raise fees and taxes

Carrollton thought there was a better way, and created a third option:

3. Transform the culture to a Competitive Service Business-reduce costs, streamline processes, adopt best practices, leverage technology, share resources and increase employee productivity.

The managed competition philosophy, program and toolkit helped leaders who embraced it follow this third option. Through the use of structured operational and competitive assessments, reengineering and right-sizing processes, and employee involvement and empowerment, many City business units were transformed into competitive service businesses. These units were able to increase service quality and customer responsiveness, eliminate waste and inefficiencies and provide essential services more efficiently and effectively with fewer resources.

Over the past ten years, the following Carrollton business units have achieved a mark of distinction and have been declared "substantially competitive" by City Manager Leonard Martin.

Managed Competition "Honor Roll"

- Traffic Operations (2004)
- Parks Maintenance Operations (2004 and 2010)
- Water/Wastewater Operations (2005 and 2011)
- Utility Billing & Collections (2006)
- Facility Maintenance Services (2007)
- Workforce Services (2008)
- Payroll Accounting (2009)
- Building Inspection & Planning (2010)

- Streets & Storm Drainage Operations (2011)
- Accounts Payable (2012)
- Library Services (2012)

The Bottom Line...

While it is difficult to calculate the total cost savings and cost avoidance due to managed competition, we conservatively estimate that our managed competition program has saved the City at least $30 million over the past ten years. That equates to about 40 percent of the City's General Fund budget or $38,000 per full-time equivalent City employee.

So, What's Next?

The Next Frontier ... More Innovation & Cooperation

Mike Eastland, executive director of the North Central Texas Council of Governments, said that in the future, cities may see more opportunities to merge services. Carrollton, Farmers Branch, Addison and Coppell are working together on a shared Public Safety radio system and regional dispatch center. The cities have also discussed opportunities to collaborate and share certain "back office" functions.

Larry Williams, Carrollton City Council Member 2000-2009: Will this be easy to do? No. Just like getting competitive is not easy. We know there is resistance in some cities to sharing services and facilities with others. These challenges can be overcome for the long-term benefit of our citizens and community. Just like we've seen with managed competition, the rewards are worth the struggle.

Council Point of View

"Managed Competition (MC) to me, is like a breath of fresh air for a government entity to embrace—to operate government like a business is not only a fresh idea, but one that is long overdue in coming.

As a taxpayer, I appreciate City staff, starting with the top, who had the concept that City government needs to be efficient. I am glad to see MC principles consistently applied from department to department.

I had hoped the MC process would identify operational weaknesses, and I think it did—I appreciated that fact the City staff did not try to hide the inefficiencies, but was transparent in providing an accurate assessment. Allowing the first department reviewed to be outsourced, when all of the facts were known, sent a clear message to all City functions that the City Manager's Office, backed by the Council, was serious in this attempt to be able to prove efficient operations.

When one of the departments went through the MC process, and were deemed to be operating efficiently, I believe the staff of that department experienced a feeling of pride in their work—a feeling of pride that could not be gained in any other way—I did not expect that to be as strong as I believe it was."

15. Unloading Assets

Christopher Swope

Richard M. Daley might say with a wink and a nod that he's got a bridge he'd like to sell you. Except that Daley has already sold it. It's called the Chicago Skyway, and a Spanish-Australian consortium gave him $1.83 billion for it. The mayor might also like to offer you his four downtown parking garages, but as it happens, he's just recently sold those too. Morgan Stanley, the Wall Street investment bank, paid Chicago $563 million for them.

For those who feel they've missed out on Windy City souvenirs, not to worry. Mayor Daley is putting more pieces of his city's infrastructure up for sale. Next: Midway Airport, the busy hub for Southwest Airlines. Daley wants a deal for the city-owned airport, and he wants it this year. (Buyer beware: Bring lots of cash. We're talking billions.) After that, the mayor wants to unload several recycling centers. He may also put a for-sale sign on a bunch of city-owned marinas.

Chicago is in the midst of what's looking more and more like a liquidation sale. There may not be an "Everything Must Go" banner hanging at City Hall, but the new attitude there is that certain public assets SHOULD go if the price is right. "The city will never give up schools, police programs and parks—things we do well," says Daley's dealmaker, Chief Financial Officer Dana Levenson. "But what's the incentive to hold on to the things we don't do well when there's a market now that will pay the city lots of money for them?"

Chicago's way of thinking about infrastructure is still unusual in the United States. But ever since Daley sold the Skyway—or more accurately, leased it for 99 years—more state and local leaders have begun asking whether they, too, might unload a few hard assets. So far, toll roads are getting the most attention. In Indiana, Governor Mitch Daniels sold a 75-year lease on the Indiana Toll Road for $3.85 billion. Soon after, Virginia facilitated a 99-year lease of the 9-mile Pocahontas Parkway for $603 million. Pennsylvania's Governor Ed Rendell is putting the Pennsylvania Turnpike out to bid, and governors in Illinois, New York and Delaware all have expressed interest in seeing what their states' turnpikes might fetch on the world's financial markets.

More than just toll roads are in play, however. In New Jersey, Governor Jon Corzine asked the investment bank UBS to scour state government for items to consider privatizing. The study put the New Jersey Lottery

Originally published as Christopher Swope (2007). "Unloading Assets." *Governing*, 20(4), January 2007. Reprinted with permission of the publisher.

and development rights around transit stations at the top of the list, right alongside the New Jersey Turnpike, Garden State Parkway and Atlantic City Expressway. Treasurer Bradley Abelow is now winnowing the list down to items the state will take bids on. "I was worried that people would view it as a fire sale," he says. "In fact, it's quite the opposite. We're starting with the presumption that we don't know what the answer is, just the questions to ask."

These kinds of deals would have been unthinkable not long ago. But in the past year or two, pension funds and other investors have decided that American infrastructure makes a good long-term investment. At first, this emerging market was dominated by companies from Australia and Europe, where private concessions for toll roads and airports are nothing new. (Macquarie Infrastructure Group, an arm of an Australian bank, and the Spanish highway manager Cintra successfully teamed up on both the Skyway and Indiana Toll Road deals.) But now U.S. firms such as Goldman Sachs and the Carlyle Group are raising their own multibillion-dollar investment funds. In total, as much as $100 billion is waiting to be invested in public assets that produce their own revenue streams from tolls or fees.

As Dana Levenson sees it, that's a seller's market. Chicago, which has been called the "Silicon Valley of infrastructure privatization," has used proceeds from its two concession agreements so far to pay down huge sums of debt and raise its credit rating. Levenson believes that governments have an obligation to at least consider selling off some of their infrastructure, even if they ultimately opt to hang on to it. "With as much money as is amassing in these funds, I can't imagine anything less intelligent than dismissing it out of hand," he says.

There are plenty of critics, however, who see Chicago-style sell-offs as a sellout. In Indiana, where public-opinion polls showed 2-to-1 opposition to leasing the toll road, the idea of paying tolls to foreign firms made many residents uneasy. The same was true in Harris County, Texas, which studied selling its network of local toll roads last year. The county council decided not to do it—despite eye-popping estimates that put the market value as high as $20 billion. "We're not leaving that money on the table, we're taking it over time," says Edwin Harrison, the county finance director. "It has to be quite obvious," Harrison adds. "If anyone comes in and gives you a billion dollars, they certainly expect to make twice or three times that. They're not doing this because they want to do a public service."

A Question of Capital

When Macquarie's D.J. Gribbin makes the case for privatizing infrastructure, he likes to invoke Hernando de Soto. Quoting a Peruvian economist to an audience of state and local officials may seem an odd choice, especially since de Soto's area of expertise is third-world poverty. But Gribbin thinks de Soto's book, *The Mystery of Capital*, helps explain why public infrastructure belongs in private hands.

De Soto writes that trillions of dollars of "dead capital" is locked up in the shanty-towns of developing nations. This is so because inadequate systems of property law prevent people from using their primary asset—their homes—to create more wealth. In the United States, Gribbin also sees dead capital spread across the land. It's not locked up in tin roofs and mortar but rather in toll roads and other assets that government doesn't manage aggressively. "Though the state has title to the asset, it's trapped in a non-market context," Gribbin says. "As soon as you move that asset into a market context, now all of a sudden you've opened up the world to value that asset."

The Indiana Toll Road is a good example

of what Gribbin is talking about. Before Governor Daniels took office, toll rates had stayed put for 20 years. For five of the past seven years, the road experienced negative cash flow. To get a handle on what the status quo was worth to Indiana, the state's accountant projected out revenues and expenses over 75 years, assuming that the road would continue to be managed basically as it has been in the past. The accountant came up with a net present value of $1.9 billion.

By contrast, Macquarie/Cintra cut Indiana a check for $3.85 billion. In addition, the companies agreed to immediately pay for an electronic toll-collection system, widen 7 miles of congested road and not only build a new state police post but also contribute to the salaries of new state troopers. What's more, the private operators will pay for all operations and expenses, as well as any further capital improvements necessary to keep traffic moving at levels spelled out in the concession agreement.

By Gribbin's calculus, Indiana is bringing $2 billion of dead capital to life—more if you consider all the road improvements. Where does that "unlocked value" come from? First and foremost: higher tolls. After a few years, Macquarie/Cintra will be allowed to set toll rates at whatever the market will bear. As John Schmidt, a Chicago lawyer who advised Indiana on the deal, puts it, "The reality is public entities are not capable of raising tolls in an economically rational way. By shifting toll-setting power, within limits regarded as politically acceptable, you can create additional value."

Other sources contribute to that $2 billion windfall. Macquarie/Cintra thinks it can run the toll road more efficiently than Indiana did—electronic toll collection is a big first step. In addition, the concessionaire is able to depreciate the toll road on its federal taxes—a break that Indiana can't leverage since states don't pay taxes. And long-term investors seem willing to pay a premium for the sort of stable revenue stream that a proven toll road such as Indiana's can produce. Macquarie/Cintra expects to earn a return in the range of 12 percent. That beats the bond market any day, with less risk than investing in equities.

Governor Daniels and his staff couldn't be happier with the deal. Before, Indiana was looking at a $3 billion backlog in highway projects around the state and no money to pay for any of them. Now, Indiana claims to be the only state with a fully funded 10-year transportation plan. The state treasurer's Web site shows interest on the up-front lease payment piling up at a rate of $6 per second. "Nobody knows what will happen in 75 years," says Daniels' finance director, Ryan Kitchell. "There might be flying cars that don't use the Toll Road, and we'll look really smart. Nobody knows. What we do know is we have $4 billion in the bank earning interest today. And we'll put it into the ground building and maintaining roads that should throw off jobs and economic benefits that last the whole time."

The Road Not Taken

Daniels' critics aren't convinced. Forget the dead-capital argument, they say. This is a desperate and shortsighted play for cash. Had Indiana instead committed itself to aggressive public management of the Toll Road, it would be the taxpayers, rather than private investors, who would be enjoying those comfy long-term returns. "The fact is that the road was never intended to be a money-maker," B. Patrick Bauer, the incoming Democratic House speaker, wrote in an op-ed last year. "However, now that the governor has installed a plan that eventually will increase those tolls, why not keep control of the Toll Road in our hands?"

Similar thinking is what ultimately turned Harris County against leasing its own toll roads. "Government does not inherently have to run the thing poorly," Harrison says, noting that he believes the county does a solid job of managing its toll roads. "So why should I have my people—Americans, Texans, the people who live here in Harris County—pay tolls to somebody in Spain or Australia?"

If much of the opposition to privatization is philosophical, there are also pragmatic reasons to worry about these infrastructure deals. Most have to do with the risks inherent in leases that last for as long as 75 or 99 years. For example, how does one predict what an asset such as a toll road will be worth in 2081? Even privatization proponents admit that valuations are mostly guesswork. In other words, $3.85 billion sounds like an awful lot of money for Indiana to get for its Toll Road, but nobody can say with authority that the state shouldn't have gotten more—or less.

Another long-term risk is that expectations will change over time. In Indiana, as in Chicago, lawyers have done their best to predict what sorts of operational issues may come up over the decades. Look no further than the thickly detailed leases, specifying everything down to who's responsible for cleaning up road kill (Macquarie/Cintra is). The risk is that unseen issues may come up, or that terms agreed to in 2006 may seem like a bad deal in 2056.

Or sooner. North of the U.S. border in Toronto, it took only five years for a $3.1 billion toll road sale to go sour over the issue of toll increases. When the concessionaire (Macquarie/Cintra again) began raising tolls—as was its right under a 99-year lease—drivers and elected officials balked. Ontario took the concessionaire to court to stop the toll hike. The government lost, and the tolls were allowed to go up.

Toronto's lesson for U.S. officials has nothing to do with whether the government was right or wrong in its actions. Rather, the lesson is that the billion-dollar glow surrounding these deals lasts for only a little while. Once that light fades, what's left is a public-private marriage that goes on for almost a century. For better or worse, Mayor Daley and Governor Daniels have agreed to transportation and infrastructure policies that won't just outlast their administrations. Those policies will outlast the lifetimes of their own grandchildren.

High Flier

None of this fazes Dana Levenson. A former banker, Levenson came to work for Chicago at the end of 2004, just before the Skyway deal closed. Soon after, Levenson got to work on selling Chicago's parking garages. Now he's working on the Midway Airport deal. When a reporter suggests that Chicago has shown the way for other states and local governments considering infrastructure sales, Levenson replies only half-jokingly: "Yeah, they should send us a gift. We'll take the money."

In Levenson's mind, there is no doubt that the private sector runs certain operations better than government can. Take parking. Chicago's four downtown garages, beneath Grant Park and Millennium Park, were priced below-market yet still had lots of empty spaces. Levenson describes how he and other city officials would get regular e-mail reports about parking revenues. "We'd see the numbers go up and the numbers go down. The question is: Do we care? I care, because I'd like to see more people park there because that means more revenue to the city."

The way Levenson reasons, city government will never give the person monitoring the garages a performance bonus if he gets the garages to 99 percent capacity and won't fire him if it continues at 70 or 80 percent. "If the asset can be run better," Levenson concludes, "why not see what the market would bear?"

In the case of the parking garages, the

market bore $563 million. In a sign that the infrastructure market is growing more competitive, 13 companies bid on the concession—compared with five on the Skyway deal. Chicago went with an offer from Morgan Stanley, which partnered with a parking manager that will run day-to-day operations at the garages. Chicago plans to use proceeds to pay off outstanding debt on the facility and create a trust fund that will generate enough interest to replace the park department's lost revenues. That will still leave $122 million to invest in capital improvements in neighborhood parks around the city.

Negotiating a deal for Midway Airport, Levenson admits, is much trickier than selling parking garages. For one thing, there are safety and homeland security concerns to contend with. But the bigger challenge is red tape. U.S. airports can be privatized only under a limited federal pilot program,

so any deal Chicago strikes will require approval from the Federal Aviation Administration. Federal law also requires that most of the airlines at Midway sign off on the agreement. Historically, U.S. airlines have opposed airport privatization for fear that the landing fees they pay would inevitably increase. (Levenson declined to comment on how negotiations with Southwest and the seven other airlines that serve Midway are going.)

What's clear is that other states and cities will be watching closely. If Chicago reaps billions, expect more deals to follow—and pressure to build on Congress to open airports across the country to private management. "If Daley pulls off the Midway deal," says Robert Poole, a transportation expert at the Reason Foundation, "it will be as big an earthquake to airport privatization in this country as the Skyway deal was to toll roads."

16. Got Nightlife?

Jim Peters and *Alicia Scholer*

For almost two decades, the transition from suburban development to investment of public and private resources in city and county infrastructure has demonstrated the power of the New Urbanism and smart growth movements. Housing has grown denser, public transportation has been enhanced and streamlined, and improvements to public space design and landscaping have increased the aesthetic appeal of communities.

Yet when people with rapidly changing social demands and lifestyles are added to the space created for them, local government managers are forced to reevaluate these traditional pillars of development. A focus on planning for people and their need to socialize is an emerging challenge for managers as dining and entertainment venues as well as later hours are integrated into residential areas.

The Rise of Nightlife in Mixed-Use Communities

Many communities have experienced a transition from an industry-based economy to one that is primarily services based. Abandoned factories and warehouses have been replaced with lofts and such nightlife venues as bars, clubs, lounges, and restaurants.

To tap into the revitalization catalyzed by the development of hospitality venues, boutique businesses and start-up companies often relocate to districts with these social amenities. Convention centers draw association business, filling up hotels and nearby restaurants. Downtown sport stadiums and arenas have reclaimed abandoned districts. Communities that offer these "live, work, and play" experiences can host tens of thousands of people in a single evening.

In this 50-minute seminar, *PM* author Jim Peters offers insights on trends and effective strategies on managing hospitality zones and nighttime economies.

Anticipating people's need for social interaction at different times of the day, and particularly at night, is critical for the success of a mixed-use community. Properly planned and managed, hospitality zones where people gather to share food, drink, music, and dancing can be a prosperous investment, centralizing both attractions and services.

Unplanned hospitality zones can be costly, lead to conflicts, and produce an excessive burden on police and demands for appointed

---

Originally published as Jim Peters and Alicia Scholer (2010). "Got Nightlife? Manage Sociability as an Economic Engine". *Public Management (PM) Magazine*, 92(10), November 2010. Reprinted with permission of the publisher.

and elected officials to manage safety and quality-of-life impacts. Considerations include transportation, parking, utilities (water, energy, sewerage), and trash management to ensure that a high standard of living is met for both visitors and residents. An expansive network of stakeholders is required to create a comprehensive system for district development and management.

This chapter will introduce demographic trends, establish a framework for action, define terminology, and highlight the six core elements of a hospitality zone-entertainment, public safety, multiuse sidewalks, venue safety, late-night transportation, and quality of life.

Downtown San Jose: Nightlife 2.0

San Jose, California, reoriented its entertainment zone policing model to improve safety budgets that had been surpassing $1 million and introduce more visitor-friendly policing tactics. Businesses share in policing costs that are used for roving foot and bike patrols. Results have included reductions in policing costs, assaults, and gang presence as well as greater civility among patrons.

Background

During the past 20 years, San Jose's downtown core has emerged into a vibrant destination with a high concentration of dining and entertainment establishments catering to the 21- to 25-year-old demographic. Entertainment zone police officers worked overtime hours to monitor the district, respond to incidents, and generally ensure the safety of large crowds of late-night patrons—up to 12,000 people—as they made their way home.

In 1997, the city council approved the city's first entertainment zone policing model to address public safety downtown during the evening and late-night hours. In 2005, a downtown working group was formed to address issues related to nightlife. In 2006, the police department instituted initiatives to deter cruising, address youth curfew, actively enforce public nuisance laws, and regulate entertainment permits more closely.

Although it is consistently ranked as one of the safest large cities in the nation, San Jose is still seeking to overcome lingering perceptions surrounding safety downtown and to minimize police costs further.

Initiatives Undertaken

Downtown coordinator. In 2008, the city allocated a position in the city manager's office to serve as liaison between city government departments, downtown businesses, and residents. The downtown coordinator position is responsible for analyzing current policies and ordinances and recommending areas for change and improvement. The objective of this position is to strengthen the city's capacity to address key operational issues and opportunities in the downtown that involve several city departments that are responsible for nightclubs, zoning overlay, and successful high-rise housing.

City manager's downtown advisory committee. Recognizing that accomplishing the city's goals would require successful partnerships, the city manager established a downtown advisory committee to guide this process. The committee is charged with facilitating implementation of action items recommended in a report generated by a hospitality zone assessment.

Further, the committee, with staff support from the downtown coordinator, reviews and evaluates new and existing policies. The composition of the committee encompasses all stakeholders in the downtown community and those who participated in the assessment outreach process.

New entertainment zone policing model (EZPM). In 2009, the city began to reevaluate the way police patrolled downtown. The city's downtown coordinator led a small working group consisting of the police department, city attorney's office, downtown businesses, and an outside consultant to facilitate interviews, observations, and community meetings on what would help downtown businesses succeed.

EZPM is focused on attitude, training, and collaboration. The police department's downtown services unit uses bikes and plainclothes officers to work with businesses in the early part of the night. The city requires all nightlife business employees to attend Alcoholic Beverage Control LEAD (Licensee Education on Alcohol and Drugs) server training, and security staff members are required to attend 16 hours of security training. Police officers who work downtown are also required to attend specialized training.

Understanding the nature of people to cluster into groups, often seeking space conducive to their life stage or lifestyle, leads to insights on better zoning for the intensity of activity in an area. In addition to the critical aspects of physical planning of a community's core, it is necessary to plan for social interaction. Whether dealing with such public spaces as parks and plazas or commercial venues providing dining and entertainment, policymakers and planners need to consider different social generations' need for interaction.

Media of the last decade, including television shows like *Seinfeld*, *Friends*, and *Sex and the City*, inspired a new culture of urban living among friends, which redefined socializing in stark contrast to the family-oriented environments depicted in the earlier television shows like *Father Knows Best*, *Leave It to Beaver*, and *Ozzie and Harriet*.

Demographics

Birthrate data can often provide clues to the past and present and also serve as a barometer of the future patterns in a community's evolution. Age is often a factor in the frequency that people go out to meet and socialize. Two of the critical ages are 18 and 50. The age of 18 is a transition into adulthood; 18-year-olds often go away to college or enter the workforce. The age of 50 is a time when children are grown and sometimes move away; it is also usually a peak earning period of an adult's life.

U.S. birthrate data shows patterns of the U.S. population turning 18 and 50 since the 1970s, when the rise in the number of young adults led to the expansion of the disco nightlife scene. Meanwhile, the past decade shows a merging of the two age groups' growth rates.

This simultaneous growth in the two population groups corresponds with the competing demands of these two groups for the vitality and amenities of the urban community. Conflicts can arise from the two different times of day during which they patronize dining and entertainment districts—the 50+ market tends to enjoy hospitality before 10 p.m., while the 18+ market only begins to arrive at 10 p.m. or later.

Social Generations

Lifestyles and social interaction can often be correlated with age and life stage. While this represents a broad generalization, understanding the essential needs of people and the demographics of your local government, district, or the markets you are trying to build can determine the best mix of dining, entertainment, and events.

Integrating potential social interaction into revitalization and development planning can result in a stronger and more vibrant social economy, with less impact on city and county resources for management. The major question then is: How well does your community meet the needs of each generation?

Assessing Your Community's Sociability. Conducting an economic assessment of dining and entertainment businesses is the first step in strategic planning by local government for issuing permits and licenses and allocating resources for an active nightlife.

Hospitality Zone Development. The terms mixed-use district and multiuse district traditionally describe the blend of residential, commercial, and retail development within a particular location. A hospitality zone, meanwhile, is an area of mixed or multiple uses that is distinguished by a high concentration of dining and entertainment businesses such as restaurants, pubs, taverns, cafes, and nightclubs. A hospitality zone often has an active street life and may serve as a center for community fairs, festivals, and events.

Recognizing that hospitality zones evolve and change over time is also key to proper planning of the social economy. Emerging zones where creative culinary entrepreneurs seek low rents in deserted warehouse districts can be nurtured with infrastructure improvements, expedited permitting and licensing, and zoning updates for the new development.

Integrating dining and entertainment venues into mixed-use districts can be coordinated strategically. Questions to ask include:

- What are current and potential areas for growth and development in your community?
- Where is there overconcentration?
- What systems exist for maintaining a balance of businesses to meet day, evening, and late-night economies?

SINGLES: Individuals in their late teens and early twenties who are exploring relationships.

MINGLES: Older singles, couples, and social groups of any age with a common interest.

FAMILIES: Introduction of children into couple relationships requires adjustment to going out.

JINGLES: Business travelers on expense accounts, vacationers, and empty nesters.

At the same time, a declining district with an overconcentration of businesses engaging in risky practices and promotions requires a tightening of permits, higher standards for new businesses, and more dedicated resources for increasing compliance.

Sociable communities provide spaces to socialize that appeal to all four social groups' interests and also address the stages of development and six core elements of a safe and vibrant hospitality zone.

1. Entertainment. Progressive communities nurture dining and entertainment opportunities for diverse ages, lifestyles, and cultures with incentives for business development and talent retention.

What barriers to dining and entertainment exist and how can they be minimized? What support systems—for example, subsidized housing and health care for musicians—are in place, need to be enhanced, or need to be developed? What education and training are available for talent development—for musicians, chefs, bartenders, servers, management?

2. Public safety. A continuum of collaborative partnerships-ranging from business associations, to neighborhood organizations, to licensing, permitting, enforcement, and regulatory agencies-is required to manage hospitality zones.

What resources exist or need improvement in the licensing and permitting process? How can safety and compliance agencies in your city and county work together to streamline initiatives?

3. Multiuse sidewalks. Vitality and

vibrancy extend outside of buildings to the streets and sidewalks, and they encompass such experiences as sidewalk café dining, kiosks, food vendors, street entertainers, and public markets.

What is your vision to enhance vitality and minimize chaos on your hospitality zone's streets and sidewalks? What systems, tools, resources, and people will you need to initiate desired changes?

4. Venue safety. There is increased pressure for licensed beverage businesses to prevent sales and service to underage and intoxicated persons as well as assure the safety of patrons both inside the venues and as they exit.

What impediments exist for venues to access qualified labor and educational training? How can your community assist businesses in the creation of a safety plan and connect business owners to mentors?

5. Late-night transportation. Providing safe and efficient access to and exit from hospitality zones can enhance the visitor experience, reduce alcohol-related accidents, and expedite clearing the zone at bar-closing time.

What challenges does your community face in providing safe rides to and from the hospitality zone? How can impaired driving and disorderly conduct be addressed through multiple transit options?

6. Quality of life. Mixed-use districts place residents and commercial businesses in close proximity, often resulting in conflicts about noise, trash, vandalism, fights, and public urination.

What resources and partners need to be engaged to update codes and to define community standards that address sound management and undesired behaviors?

Contrary to common belief, the key component for each element's success is not infrastructure or system changes. It is people. In the end, it is people who will enjoy a hospitality zone's vibrancy, and it is the communication and cooperation among various stakeholders who will facilitate implementation of necessary changes and ensure sustainability.

Steps to Managing the Nighttime Economy

Conduct an Economic Assessment: To strategically allocate resources to an active nightlife and determine how many permits and licenses to issue, take an inventory of existing social amenities, occupancy totals and revenue generated within the hospitality zone.

Identify Gaps and Resources: Assess how well your community currently meets the social needs of each generation by identifying strengths, gaps and resources in the following areas-entertainment, multiuse sidewalks, quality of life, late-night transportation, venue safety and public safety.

Dedicate Staff: Select a neutral individual as a nightlife coordinator who will oversee planning and management of your hospitality zone. They will serve as a liaison among key stakeholders to communicate key information, resolve conflicts and facilitate implementation of next steps.

Planning for People

The "people factor" creates dynamically different impacts in a bookstore and a restaurant, even though each might take up the same square footage. While the bookstore may have 10 to 15 customers and three to four employees present at any one time, the restaurant may host 100 customers with 10 to 20 employees.

Contemporary planning usually specifies in great detail the physical space and the structures, but it only implies the addition of people. Highlighting the 3,000 housing units to be built can be translated to approximately 7,000 people located in this concentrated residential area. Showcasing 100,000 square feet of retail space can include reference to 20 new dining and entertainment venues, with total seating capacity (occupancy) of 15,000 people, many in the area in the evening and after 10 p.m.

For these reasons, planning for a concentrated hospitality zone requires involvement of many diverse and often adversarial stakeholders, including business owners; residents; police; fire personnel; and staff who regulate alcohol sales, public works, planning, health, and more. The late-night and weekend hours mean that adaptation of such local government services as trash removal, transportation, traffic and parking control, and safety compliance inspections is required.

This may require staff dedicated to manage the nighttime economy. Seattle, Washington; San Jose, California; and Edmonton, Alberta, Canada, are among those cities with a downtown or nightlife coordinator serving as a liaison among the key stakeholders, identifying gaps in service, resolving conflicts, and setting proactive schedules for planning. (See the accompanying case study about San Jose, California.)

Finally, with changing demographics, it is important for local government managers to consider time and generational continuums as well as use of office, retail, and residential space. The inherent value of smart growth planning is that less time is spent commuting. In turn, with efficient public transportation and less distance traveled, this time savings can be translated to more community time, which is often spent socializing with coworkers, families, and friends, and thus more demand for nightlife.

Adapting traditional zoning, licensing, and permitting systems to the smaller, more flexible, and consumer-oriented businesses is one way local government managers can enhance this industry sector. A new form of concierge governance designed with streamlined systems presenting a "how can we help you succeed" attitude can facilitate progress.

Final Thoughts

Every community has buildings, streets, sidewalks, lights, and parks. What distinguishes one community from another are the people and the opportunity to share food, drink, music, and dance in safe and convenient venues. It is the social connectivity and relationships that make life worth living and that define a vibrant community.

Sociable cities attract conventions, tourists, residents, and a creative class of talented professionals who provide an economic base that helps emerging industries that are clean and sustainable. Planning for people in a 24/7 economy requires adaptation and efficient management of resources through common vision, communication, and collaboration.

17. Business Improvement Districts

Lawrence Houstoun

There are more than 1,000 business improvement districts (BIDs) in North America, and their numbers continue to increase. Although roughly one in 10 never completes the pre-ordinance organization phase, once up and running their private sector sponsors almost never abandon them. BIDs have been formed in localities with as few residents as 10,000. They are popular with their authorizing governments as well as the private sector people who manage them and share their costs. While most are in the United States, the first BIDs were formed in Toronto, Canada, and their numbers are increasing rapidly in Britain and South Africa.

Most BIDs start with business leadership, although some are launched at the initiative of local governments. Maplewood, New Jersey's, planning board launched two in that suburb. Trenton, New Jersey's, economic development office started the downtown BID there. The borough administrator of Netcong, New Jersey, encouraged BID formation and serves as its part-time manager. The mayor of Jacksonville, Florida, challenged business leaders to form one. Most BIDs have at least one local representative, manager, or councilmember on their boards of directors. Most are nonprofit corporations.

Eighty or 90 percent of them have modest budgets and low shared costs, enabling them to produce effective marketing that attracts customers and investors. A district with 200-odd properties may have an annual assessment budget of $200,000, supporting a BID manager and services essential to improved business profitability and property values. Charges are usually based on each property's share of the total valuation of all affected properties in the service area; less-valuable properties may incur a bill equal to 50 cents a day, substantially below property taxes or common area maintenance charges.

BIDs are popular with local governments and sponsoring private sector people for these reasons:

- They are self-financing. The sponsors agree on a cost-sharing formula at the outset and are comfortable knowing that they can rely on the planned benefits because the assessment is a multiyear resource. In contrast, when the revenue stream is dependent on year-by-year voluntary contributions, contracts for services and agreements with a district manager are tenuous.
- BIDs help build local revenues.

Originally published as Lawrence Houstoun (2009). "Business Improvement Districts: Partnering Local Governments and Business." *Public Management (PM) Magazine*, 91(7), August 2009. Reprinted with permission of the publisher.

Improved properties have greater value to the local governments and add to the basis for local sales and other taxes.

- A well-run BID is entrepreneurial and will attract grants and other outside money to the locality. In addition to funding for closed-circuit television, BIDs have attracted funds for commercial facade improvements, pedestrian lighting, and directional signage.
- BIDs are well tested and adaptable to diverse needs and opportunities. Many formed in recent years are intended to improve the district's competitive position and are geared to exploiting economic opportunities. BIDs are as common in small towns and suburbs as they are in larger city neighborhoods.
- Commercial centers with poor shopping, little foot traffic, and poor reputations are typically the most visible evidence of the community's economic health and worth. A bad downtown image negatively affects even residential property values. BIDs successfully overcome these deficiencies.

What Do BIDs Do?

There is no formula for BID services. They work best when the service mix is attuned to local needs and local leadership. Large BIDs differ from small ones, partly because they function in more urban contexts and because they have higher revenues to support their work. They are all, however, defined in the same state laws and have the same general economic purposes.

The few large ones, some with annual revenues above $15 million and often with legal capacity to float bonds for capital projects, work in areas of concentrations of high property values. Large BIDs have been performing to their sponsors' satisfaction for decades in New York City; Washington, D.C.; Philadelphia, Pennsylvania; Baltimore, Maryland; Seattle, Washington; Denver, Colorado; and elsewhere.

Often launched in areas where crime and grime were economic problems—loss of shopping, premium pay rates required to compensate for unsatisfactory employee conditions, high insurance costs, loss of strong businesses, poor reputation among investors and potential residents—these BIDs were formed to overcome serious economic problems.

Most large BIDs formed and maintain foot patrols—uniformed, supplementary security forces that work with police and are in radio contact with local precincts when needed. These well-trained men and women can and do answer visitor questions, and they get a lot of them because they are so visible on the sidewalks. They have and use first-aid training, help motorists connect with repairs, and help police in emergencies.

They are unarmed and without police powers. Contrary to some early skeptics, they are popular with rank and file police, sometimes working from the same headquarters. Some BIDs—Denver, Colorado; Arlington County, Virginia; and Hollywood, California; among them—employ off-duty police because a lesser form of supplemental security is not sufficient to the needs. The hourly rate, of course, is substantially higher for off-duty police than for BID patrollers, often called ambassadors.

BIDs are also used in industrial areas. Most of the assessment revenues in these locations support mobile security patrols in vans, mainly operating during the night and on holidays. One in New York City was so successful that the board of directors stopped the patrols, retaining the BID authorization in the event new threats emerged. Some industrial-area BIDs also support landscaping, brighter lights, and improved parking.

BIDs, large and small, create marketing programs, most often designed to attract consumers and sometimes commercial tenants, investors, and visitors. Even small ones produce attractive electronic newsletters by which they keep their various constituencies—owners, operators, residents, and local officials—informed of their own work and the variety of activities sponsored by other organizations that also have a stake in the commercial centers.

Commercial BIDs adopt logos, branding slogans, color-consistent directional signage, and commercial locator maps. Many sponsor special events and farmers' markets, adding an entertainment draw to the shopping and more reasons to come downtown. Several have sponsored summer-long outdoor sculpture exhibits and others, including Ardmore, Pennsylvania, organize "First Friday" strolling visits to art galleries and other enterprises that collect artwork for the monthly event.

Among the most important BID investments have been financial incentives to property owners and realtors that produce a defined business that the district board considers important to strengthening the commercial center's appeal. Typical rewards consist of a $5,000 bonus and lots of favorable publicity and also inducements to work hard to land a strong merchant, not settling for the first one that comes along. Other incentives consist of matching funds for exterior upgrades or to alter interiors to fit the needs of a shop the business community wants to attract.

Small BIDs today are increasingly turning to closed-circuit television systems, planned with local police, to support evening shopping and dining. Board meetings often include regular police participation, and some have a board seat reserved for the force. Where needed, districts maintain security committees composed of board members and others most concerned about this condition.

Different Applications; Same Principles

BID principles are highly adaptable to local economic needs. Use of BID revenues should be applied to a need or opportunity that is, generally speaking, district wide. Here are some examples:

- Some large BIDs have organized supplementary bus systems to move shoppers and employees.
- One mid-size BID, plagued with unattractive vacant lots, landscaped them, keeps them tidy, and includes a sign indicating the property is for sale and listing the agent.
- One small town put together a modest incentive package that saved a movie house, an important anchor especially for evening shoppers and diners.
- Finding that only 20-odd businesses were open on Sundays (a condition that discouraged strong new businesses from moving there), one suburban BID campaigned with ads, music on the street, promotions, and marketing, and in less than a year it raised the total to more than80.
- A small BID in the West, using a grant, purchased an empty building, fixed it up, rented portions, and used part for itself, producing another income stream.
- One BID, dissatisfied with the number of restaurants with outdoor dining, purchased bright pink chairs and gave them to any sidewalk bistro that requested them.
- A small BID in a large city secured an agreement that enabled the district to set rates and manage the parking lot, producing more revenue than had been the case under city management.
- A small city district invented a win-

ter holiday with a patriotic theme and created a cluster of gift and flower shops in a commercial building that had been empty since renovated.

- One BID organized a district-wide rodent control program.
- One small suburb with a long-established district created a second one within the original service area to help finance a supermarket that has greatly improved walk-in trade for the other shops.
- Another BID, organized in a commercial area with 30 percent of the shops vacant, helped transform the area by promoting it as a restaurant center. When that lost momentum, it helped expand the furniture niche.
- Some BIDs help new business prospects get acquainted with the community and negotiate the permit process. Some are official and others are unofficial advisers to planning bodies on issues affecting downtowns.

While the tools applied may differ somewhat from those of the typical shopping or office center or industrial park, the fundamentals are similar. People want to work or shop or visit or live in a place that is convenient, safe, clean, and fun. To make these favorable conditions apparent requires effective marketing, and to support that requires a multi-year compulsory charge on benefiting properties. BIDs add value to real estate, and the cost-sharing mechanism means that the individual charges are small in the context of overall business costs.

The mix of services needed to make such places more profitable differs, if only in degree, from the service mix that local governments can generally undertake. Urban commercial centers, for example, often require more intensive cleaning, various investments to reduce possible fear, and activities that please the various user groups.

Because the district organization produces private sector benefits, it is reasonable that the foundation revenues come from all those beneficiaries.

BIDs also produce various efficiencies. Legally required pavement cleaning by owners and tenants rarely produces consistent and satisfactory results. Where BIDs take on this responsibility, the results are everywhere satisfactory. Removal of sidewalk litter also reduces the amount the local government must remove from the cart ways.

Bids Face the Recession

Because they are directly involved in the local economy, BIDs are adapting their priorities to help business operators and property owners engage in cooperative steps to survive the prospective (and current) loss of business, foot traffic, and local purchasing power.

A dozen BIDs, mainly large ones, recently produced a joint paper on priority actions that BIDs can take themselves and can urge on their host communities. This bullet list reflects their report and also includes material found in newsletter reports by small districts.

The BID leaders note their relatively favorable positions in an unfavorable time:

- BIDs are principally concentrated in centrally located areas, close to population centers, often with transit service. BID leaders believe that they are already and will remain more favorably positioned than out-of-town shopping centers as gasoline prices again rise.
- BIDs have well-established marketing programs, and the amenity improvements they have produced are recognized as key ingredients in economic growth.
- Because all beneficiaries share the

compulsory charge, they believe they are in far better positions than organizations highly dependent on voluntary contributions. BID revenue declines are not likely to affect them until 2010 or 2011.

- The organization in the United Kingdom in touch with all BIDs there reports that, since the recession, there has been increased interest in adopting BIDs as an important economic tool.

BIDs are adjusting to the recession in various ways:

- The most common response consists of convening economic stakeholders to pool their best suggestions and to emphasize money savers (energy-saving tips, marketing improvements). Expert speakers are sometimes featured at these "sunrise semesters." The Ardmore, Pennsylvania, BID compiled its own list of anti-recession actions after a local private sector planning session.
- Some are changing their marketing strategies.
- A few are proposing uses for stimulus funds. One American and one British BID are compiling papers on stimulus measures that BIDs can advance.
- Without ignoring shopping, more attention is being given to real estate, including residential opportunities, in commercial BID newsletters and BID policy priorities. The Pittsburgh, Pennsylvania, BID promotes a nearby residential neighborhood in each newsletter edition.
- More newsletter emphasis is being given to new business arrivals and the number of jobs added by new or existing businesses.
- Some newsletters are broadening their previous attention to local businesses, especially restaurants. Pittsburgh's

BID newsletter describes bargains— $100 jeans available for $10 at a shop that might otherwise be overlooked.

- BIDs are giving greater emphasis to promoting positive messages and I voicing local optimism. One BID featured an anti-rumor campaign in its newsletter.
- Some are strengthening their research capacity to keep track of changes in conditions and the markets and to sell new initiatives— counting counts.
- Some are reexamining goals, tools, and priorities. They are pruning activities that are producing less economic value. Can sidewalk cleaning costs, for example, be reduced without economic loss? Can that money be better spent on financial incentives for new businesses, job expansions?
- Some are exploring such financing tools as tax increment financing. They are negotiating advance payments from active developers where adverse construction impacts are expected.

Where Are the BIDs Going?

While the recession is reshaping BIDs, the best course for most is to reexamine priorities rigorously, to invest more in business and job attraction, and to work harder at the initial goals: improve business and property values and the commercial environment.

To be competitive, successful districts need to be, first of all, convenient. They need stronger destinations, more reasons for people to be there, clear directions, and simple parking arrangements. Those that have been passive purveyors of clean sidewalks will need to upgrade their attention to people—business employees, visitors, shoppers, and residents—now more than ever.

18. Help Businesses, Shop Local

Ken Pulskamp

When the economy began to seriously decline in 2008 and businesses both small and large started to feel the hit to their bottom lines, Santa Clarita, California, already had several programs in place that helped both businesses and the city weather the storm. The city along with a young, close-knit community of business leaders and residents believed there was only one way they would get through an economic downturn without leaving anyone behind, and that was through the old adage: We are all in this together!

Years prior, Santa Clarita began laying the groundwork for successful business retention. While surrounding communities had lost businesses of all sizes and their residents began attending going-out-of-business sales at many retailers, Santa Clarita's elected officials found themselves at one grand opening after another, with two of northern Los Angeles County's largest retail construction projects opening right in their own backyard during the third and fourth quarters of 2008. Was Santa Clarita just lucky?

Starting with Square One

For localities that want businesses to stay in place, especially when the economy is struggling, local leaders must make it more cost effective for businesses to open their doors in the first place. Starting at square one, Santa Clarita made a commitment to its business community to keep taxes on businesses as low as possible, yet still deliver high-quality services, including streamlined and expedited permit processing.

As a result, the city has consistently ranked among the top 10 least-expensive California cities in which to do business by the *Cost of Doing Business Survey* (published by the Kosmont Companies and the Rose Institute of State and Local Government at Claremont McKenna College). The survey objectively compares 402 cities nation-wide according to the array of taxes and fees cities impose on businesses, including sales, utility, income, property, and business taxes. The survey gives companies an opportunity to narrow their short list of cities by comparing the hard numbers and helping them make a comprehensive and strategic decision to remain, expand, or relocate.

Further recognition for Santa Clarita's longtime business-friendly practices came in late 2008 when the city was named as the most business-friendly of the 88 cities in Los Angeles County by the Los Angeles

Originally published as Ken Pulskamp (2009). "Local Government Mantra: Help Businesses, Shop Local." *Public Management (PM) Magazine* 91(7), August 2009. Reprinted with permission of the publisher.

Economic Development Commission (LAEDC).

With the California state deficit now at its highest point in history, many communities are struggling to afford the increasing costs of gas, health care, and pension plans. As a result, local governments are turning to hikes in fees to businesses and higher permitting costs to aid in the balancing of their budgets. This could be perceived as an easy answer, but Santa Clarita's leaders decided to forgo increases to local businesses that might otherwise cause them to cease altogether!

The council reaffirmed its commitment to not issue business licenses or assess a business permit fee and to continue providing businesses with its traditional low-cost-to-do-business approach, free of any unnecessary costs or bureaucracy. This strategy led the city to better provide the city and businesses with an ability to attract, expand, and retain.

This spring, the Santa Clarita City Council approved a $5.1 million 21-Point Business Plan for Progress. This first-ever economic stimulus program is aimed at helping further enhance local business partnerships, encourage quality job creation in the area, bolster retail spending, and attract external dollars to the community.

In May, the council increased the city's local preference purchasing policy to 10 percent (from 5 percent) to create more opportunities for local businesses to do business with the city, who has also partnered with many local business organizations on a new Think Santa Clarita Valley campaign to promote the local economy.

In June, the council approved three items that are part of this program: a grant program for encouraging new building facades in the city's redevelopment area of Newhall; a grant program for encouraging energy efficiency on local businesses; and a grant program to encourage new jobs and investment in city-based businesses. Updates are available at http://www. santa-clarita.com/recovery/local.asp.

As a result of these strategies, Santa Clarita assesses fewer taxes than any other city in the county of Los Angeles. The city does not assess a utility user tax, allowing businesses to save up to 7 percent or more on their utility bills. Santa Clarita also does not require a gross receipts tax, allowing businesses to save tens of thousands of dollars on their bottom lines. In these ways, the city is doing everything it can to keep businesses doing what they do best: business!

Impacting the Bottom Line

While the city has control over keeping local government taxes low for business, the taxes assessed by the state remain beyond the city's control. Realizing this fact, Santa Clarita applied for and successfully secured a state of California enterprise zone designation for city-based businesses in July 2007.

This important state designation allows businesses located in the city to reduce their state income taxes up to 50 percent. Because the amount of taxes that city businesses are obligated to pay is reduced, businesses can invest that money for the benefit of employees or to acquire equipment, helping make the business even more successful. As the word spread through the Santa Clarita business community about the new tax incentive program, calls started flooding city hall.

City-based businesses that have taken advantage of the program have seen an estimated savings of $8 million collectively in the first year alone. The savings to date have been so great that several local businesses went on record to tout their savings in television commercials and radio spots.

"Thanks to the enterprise zone, I have money in my pocket that I wouldn't have had otherwise," commented local Valencia Acura dealership owner, Don Fleming. The stage was set for the business community and the city to become partners in ways some had never imagined.

Taking It to the Streets

As the economy turned sour and more businesses began looking for help from government, Santa Clarita stepped in and began hosting stakeholder meetings for business leaders. The mayor's economic development summit helped create a "meeting of the minds" of leaders from the chamber of commerce, the industrial association, as well as industry professionals. A well-attended luncheon for commercial brokers was held in the fall to target rising vacancies and share resources for attracting new tenants to the city.

As part of the city's strategy, the luncheon was held in an empty office building. By providing local business leaders with a voice, these stakeholder meetings offered both insight and opportunities for additional ways that the city and the business community could proactively come together in the current economic climate.

During discussions with local business leaders, city management acknowledged the expressed concerns for business safety. The city in response partnered with its sheriff's department and formed a first-of-its-kind program for the Los Angeles County Sheriff's Department with the inception of the Santa Clarita City/Sheriff's Business Alliance. The city now funds a full-time, dedicated sheriff's sergeant to work exclusively with Santa Clarita's business community.

The sergeant responds promptly to needs and educates businesses on how to prevent crime at their sites. The staff member also informs them of crime trends and various crimes occurring near or around their locations. The response from the business community to this new program has been positively overwhelming, with letters of thanks and calls of appreciation regularly about the difference this program has made in safety in the business community.

Despite a 3 percent increase in population annually, Santa Clarita has been ranked by the California Department of Justice as the third-safest city in California and has reported decreasing business crime year after year.

Retail Roundup

Santa Clarita's success at retaining local retailers is unique. While communities of equal size and demographics across the nation were losing one big-box national retailer after another in 2008, Santa Clarita's 180,000 residents were enjoying growth and expansion. Santa Clarita ranked among the top 25 retail markets in California and was named the 11th-fastest-growing retail market in California, according to the 2007 California Retail Survey.

Santa Clarita's regional mall, Westfield Valencia Town Center, is undergoing a major expansion and renovation, adding 234,500 square feet of retail space. Despite the national slowdown, Santa Clarita residents enjoyed the grand opening of several national chains and unique franchises during this time.

The city's previous conservative approach in master planning for the community, complemented by the under saturation of the retail market in the area, created the perfect opportunity for a retail expansion to occur during a time when most communities saw a mass exodus of retail opportunities.

Stores opened their doors to residents who were eager to embrace the new retailers and who lined up for grand-opening sales and ceremonies. The message about the importance of shopping locally, a long-time community initiative for Santa Clarita, rang true in the hearts of residents, while the sales tax leakage to neighboring communities slowed.

The city's online directory of businesses at www.ShopCityofSantaClarita.com showed an increase in traffic from both residential and business users (averaging some 2,000 visitors each month), and the message began to spread: The only way residents of Santa Clarita would get through this downturn without losing their favorite businesses was by shopping locally!

Coming Full Circle

There is no doubt that the economic slowdown has impacted communities of all sizes. In our case, the city, along with the business community, banded together on several key programs to create an environment where businesses can succeed even when times are tough. This has been a mantra in Santa Clarita during the past several years: The decisions made during good times are more important than the decisions made during bad times.

Consistent, conservative budget practices and innovative cost-saving solutions for businesses when the economy was booming are allowing Santa Clarita to weather the economic downturn with successful business retention and expansion. The council, the residents, and the business community all came together to prove that no business would be left behind and that we are truly in the tough budget time together.

19. Love at First Site

Jennifer Grzeskowiak

Every city, neighborhood and street has its own story. Unfortunately, some of those tales are of suburbs that drew away residents, large manufacturers that abandoned the area, increases in crime and decreases in investment. To keep those stories from ending tragically, communities are enlisting the help of private partners and residents to collaborate on physical improvements and events that help forge identities, attract businesses and bring vitality back to the neighborhoods.

San Francisco, Indianapolis and Milwaukee each have identified districts that could use some special attention and are working with residents and businesses to redevelop the neighborhoods. The projects have started small, but they have made a significant difference in the selected districts. "If you look at any major city, you don't get much bang for your buck if you focus on too big of an area," says Keith Stanley, Milwaukee South of Highland (SOHI) district manager. "But when you focus on a specific area or street and create a plan, it works better."

Attracting Business

New York–based Local Initiatives Support Corporation (LISC) is one organization that is facilitating relationships between communities in need and businesses looking for opportunities. LISC selects districts that show promise for revitalization, often in lower-income neighborhoods. Then, nonprofit groups develop action plans for the districts and are responsible for implementing them. To help accomplish their plans, the districts receive $70,000 in Community Development Block Grant funds annually for three years, as well as $70,000 in technical assistance from LISC. The districts must raise at least $10,000 each year on their own. Using funding pooled from cities and other donors, ranging from individuals to corporations, LISC typically pays for a staff member for each nonprofit group and technical assistance, and distributes donated services, such as architectural or business consulting.

One of the key goals for the districts is attracting new businesses. "As people moved away from the city, so did the retail businesses, which is typical of many cities," says Maury Plambeck, director of the Indianapolis Department of Metropolitan Development. "Over the years, there was a big push to get people back to residential parts of the neighborhoods with good, affordable housing. One of the ways to attract residents

Originally published as Jennifer Grzeskowiak (2008). "Love at First Site." *American City & County*, 123(11), November 2008. Reprinted with permission of the publisher.

is to have the same services as in the new developments." A strong retail presence not only keeps residents in the area, but also provides jobs and attracts visitors from other neighborhoods.

Attracting retailers, however, is not easy. "The hardest thing to revitalize in this district is the visibility of the area itself," says Nick Wolff, program manager for Visitacion Valley Business Opportunities and Outreach to Merchants (VV BOOM) in San Francisco. "It's often overlooked in San Francisco. We do a lot of marketing and paint the picture that we know exists here."

Visitacion Valley is one of nine districts in the San Francisco Neighborhood Marketplace Initiative (SFNMI), which receives funding from the Mayor's Office of Economic Development. The program began in 2002 when a city council member from Excelsior approached LISC about starting a commercial corridor program there. Since then, LISC has added districts by issuing requests for proposals to merchant and neighborhood associations and selecting areas with a track record of improving their financial districts.

To attract businesses to the area, the first step is determining who lives there, Wolff says. VV BOOM made brochures that compiled the neighborhood demographics. "The median income per household in Visitacion Valley is very high," Wolff says. "It's a misperception of the people who live here and how much money they have. The spending power is very under-recognized."

Understanding the importance of market data, Indianapolis set up a Web site with the information prospective retailers need. The tool is a project of Focusing Commercial Urban Strategies (FOCUS Indy), a partnership between LISC, the Central Indiana Chamber of Commerce, the Indianapolis Coalition for Neighborhood Development, and Indianapolis.

The city and LISC split the cost to set up IndySiteFinder.com, which is hosted by the city's server and has a database of market information, such as available properties based on size or units; economic and demographic data; and maps. Prospective retailers can search a location and pull up data for a three-mile radius, including how many people live in the area, their net incomes, and how many dry cleaners or coffee shops already occupy space. Property owners also can list available sites and include aerial photographs. "A lot of that information is out there, but it's not easy to find for free in one place," says Will Pritchard, program officer for LISC Indianapolis.

FOCUS Indy also prepares marketing materials, brochures and site profiles, and works with architects and designers to draw images of potential uses for the buildings. "The districts do what a commercial broker would if they were marketing the site," Pritchard adds. Some of the districts under FOCUS Indy's Neighborhood Business District Program also have designated people to call prospective retailers and sell them on the benefits of locating in the area.

In Milwaukee, the SOHI Economic and Restructuring Committee meets once a month to discuss businesses they want to attract to the area. "We try to work with residents, business owners and property owners to make those decisions," Stanley says. "We want to keep them in the loop and let them guide decisions." The committee also maintains a database of approximately 600 businesses and sends them weekly updates about what is happening in the district. SOHI even has set up a YouTube channel to post videos about available properties, including interviews with property owners who have rehabilitated the buildings.

SOHI is one of six districts in the Main Street Milwaukee program, which launched in 2005. As of April, 68 businesses had opened or expanded in the districts, 57 buildings had been updated and $4.4 million in private investment was allocated in the form of funding or services.

Once businesses move into the districts, Indianapolis, Milwaukee and San Francisco have support programs, ranging from business coaching to assistance in finding grants for improvements. In Milwaukee, architects have adopted some of the districts and offer design services. The neighborhood district managers in the cities also work closely with the city to help with permitting, code violations and other planning issues.

Once businesses move in, street festivals, benefit auctions, and art- and food-based events help the districts increase their visibility. More than just fluffy functions, they help the areas express their identities, bring volunteers together, give the community a place to gather and draw visitors that might not otherwise come to the area.

In October, the *San Francisco Chronicle* ran an article addressing how fairs in the city's Neighborhood Marketplace Initiative districts have attracted attention to the areas. One of the most successful of those fairs has been the Portola Festival, which is in its sixth year and features arts and crafts, dining, children's activities, and a stage with live music and other performances. This year's event took place on three blocks and attracted more than 5,000 visitors.

VV BOOM also just held its third annual Leland Avenue Street Fair, with 4,000 people attending the family oriented event. More than 70 residents volunteered to help. "It's a good time for people that maybe overlook this corridor to come down and leave with a positive impression of it," Wolff says. "They look at the businesses on Leland Avenue and maybe notice a produce market, taqueria or coffee shop that they didn't know existed. It also corrects misperceptions about cleanliness and safety."

Dressing Up

Revitalization, however, cannot occur without physical improvements. FOCUS Indy offers a Facade Improvement Program, which distributes grants of up to $20,000 to businesses in the city, with preference given to buildings in the designated Neighborhood Business Districts. "It's a great public-private partnership," Pritchard says. A representative from the city is on the committee that makes decisions. "We try to cluster the awards," Pritchard adds. "If the city is working on properties on a block and we get an application from a nearby business, they're more likely to get a grant." The committee also steers grants away from properties that are not cooperative with the city or that are not current on their taxes.

In Milwaukee, the Mosaic on Burleigh district is using physical improvements to strengthen its identity. Working with a business consultant provided by Main Street Milwaukee, it chose the mosaic theme to represent the diversity of businesses in the district and is complementing it with streetscape improvements, including seating areas along the street with obelisks decorated with mosaic tiles. "Main Street Milwaukee is so important to taking an urban environment and creating something whole and beautiful and useful out of it," says Jean Meyers, main street manager for The Mosaic on Burleigh district.

In May, at its annual Burleigh Blooms event, the community planted foliage obtained with a Home Depot grant and cleaned Burleigh Street. Volunteers later enjoyed an Art Window Crawl, during which they traversed the street to view the photographic displays that University of Wisconsin Milwaukee art students created to fill boarded-up windows in the district.

In San Francisco's Visitacion Valley, a major streetscape renovation on Leland Avenue is in the pipeline that would involve planting trees, installing sidewalks, digging up concrete and expanding corners on curbs. Since the Schlage Lock Co. closed its Visitacion Valley factory in 1999, the city has been working with a variety of community groups to create a master plan for the 20-acre site, which will include retail and housing. San Francisco–based Universal Paragon has purchased the site and plans to transform it into retail and up to 1,200 housing units, with an eye toward sustainability. In addition, an 8,700-square-foot library is slated to open in 2010.

Revitalization does not take place overnight, particularly when the process of disinvestment in the neighborhoods took decades to occur. The lengthy nature is due, in part, to the time it takes to form connections among the stakeholders. In Indianapolis, for instance, FOCUS is working on building new relationships with the mayoral staff after a new mayor was elected last year, Pritchard says.

While the partnerships take time, they are also the key to the revivals. "Public-private partnerships are the most effective way to accomplish a lot of our goals—overall community and economic development, along with safety, design and cleanliness," Wolff says. "These things are achievable when partnerships are formed."

20. The Station at Potomac Yard

Helen S. McIlvaine

The Station at Potomac Yard is a creative and cooperative approach to meeting multiple community needs in the City of Alexandria, Virginia. Located within a former regional rail yard, which is to be redeveloped into a walkable "urban village," the project's innovative mixed-use design maximizes the use of land by combining a fire station, 64 units of affordable and workforce rental housing, and retail space, above two levels of underground parking. The project was made possible through a unique public, private, and nonprofit collaboration.

The efforts of these groups—the City of Alexandria; Potomac Yard Development (PYD), a joint venture of national homebuilders; and the Alexandria Housing Development Corporation (AHDC), a local nonprofit housing entity—allowed multiple public and private resources to be accessed to complete the project, despite the implosion of national credit markets and increasing constraints on city fiscal spending during the development period. More than 92 percent of the Station at Potomac Yard's $34 million total development cost came from non-city funding sources. While Alexandria's investment of actual dollars was limited, the city's superior bond rating, strong financial position, and willingness to provide back-stop guarantees were critical to securing other financing and investment.

Getting Started

The Station project was conceived in early 2006 when city staff, reviewing PYD's plans for the first neighborhood to be developed, realized that the dense, urban design being proposed might hinder optimal emergency response time. The plans had already been extensively and positively vetted with the community, so all parties were interested in keeping the development schedule on track while mitigating the response time issue. PYD executives suggested that PYD would be willing to donate land and $6.6 million toward the cost of constructing a fire station within the 160+ acre Potomac Yard redevelopment site.

The city, which had not built a new fire station in more than 30 years, eagerly accepted the offer. Keeping in mind that Alexandria had lost more than half of its affordable rental housing since 2000 (a decline from 18,000 apartments to fewer than 9,000), the city also opted to use the air rights above the fire station to build a residential

Originally published as Helen S. McIlvaine (2011). "The Station at Potomac Yard: Public, Private, and Nonprofit Collaboration." *Government Finance Review*, 27(3), June 2011. Reprinted with permission of the publisher.

facility that would meet the urgent need for new affordable housing. PYD responded by offering to donate a substantial portion of its voluntary affordable housing contribution (estimated at approximately $10.5 million for the overall site) early to help fund the affordable housing project, if approved.

In summer 2006, the project team (including city fire, housing, code, and planning staff, and developer and nonprofit representatives) held weekly informational meetings with a mayor-appointed citizen task force and the community. These meetings led to two important outcomes. First, the community communicated its desire to include some workforce housing in the development, with rents that would be affordable for residents with incomes of up to 80 percent of the metropolitan area median income. These units would potentially serve city employees, including first responders and teachers. Second, it was confirmed that this new municipal structure would be designed and constructed according to green building standards, in accordance with Alexandria's commitment to becoming an eco-city.

In September 2006, the task force issued its report endorsing the project; at its October retreat, the city council preliminarily approved $1 million to fund LEED elements. In February 2007, the planning commission and city council unanimously approved the development proposal, which included 64 apartments, with 44 "affordable" units and 20 "workforce" units. In March 2007, AHDC submitted a successful application for $10 million in low-income housing tax credits. With this award of additional equity, the station project was able to move ahead. In fact, Internal Revenue Service rules governing the low-income housing tax credit program required that the project be delivered and the affordable units occupied by the end of 2009, so construction got underway in January 2008 and the project was completed in August 2009, allowing AHDC to meet its critical December 2009 milestone.

The Role of City Finance Staff

The complexity of the project—i.e., the number of entities involved, multiple sources of funding, varied reporting requirements of investors and lenders, a rigid construction schedule necessitated by the tax credits, and challenges encountered due to dynamic market conditions during the development's construction and stabilization periods (2008–2010)—necessitated regular participation, collaboration, and leadership from the city's financial, management, and budget executives and their support to keep the project moving forward on time and on budget. Their contributions included:

- Initial determination of project feasibility
- Assessment of city financial support required and potential funding sources
- Management of public and political support for budget items related to the project
- Guidance and support in establishing Alexandria Station LLC, a special-purpose entity comprising the city and AHDC, to develop and construct the project
- Technical assistance to set up finance and accounting systems to track all project expenses, funds, and payments according to uses, funding sources, and participants
- Strategic advice to troubleshoot and pragmatically navigate difficult market conditions
- Bookkeeping and accounting for all aspects of the project: making payments to contractors, vendors and consultants; tracking and allocating

PYD contributions and deposits from all funding sources; helping all parties with record keeping and audits; and responding to information requests from lenders, banks, and investors
- Technical support to AHDC and its accounting team
- Regular participation in monthly Alexandria Station LLC steering committee meetings to anticipate and resolve issues affecting project construction, financing, and operations
- Ongoing assistance to the condominium unit owners association that governs station operations (the city is a member of the association, as it owns the fire station)

The city's top financial executives were available primarily in a regular consulting capacity, as needed, and finance and accounting administrative staff provided daily support for operations from 2007 to 2009. On one occasion, too, the city consulted its third-party financial advisor for independent counsel regarding soliciting a letter of credit to benefit AHDC.

By associating with AHDC on this project and providing technical assistance, the city also helped AHDC build its capacity and develop greater self-sufficiency to successfully undertake future projects. Although AHDC did not have full-time staff until the station was nearly complete, AHDC board members with affordable housing development, legal, and finance experience provided regular leadership to Alexandria Station LLC's development efforts.

Financing the Project

The most important financial concept demonstrated by the Station at Potomac Yard is the tremendous potential for accessing resources through collaborations among public, private, and nonprofit entities. So many local and state governments face fiscal constraints similar to those experienced by Alexandria, and this model will allow them to deliver capital projects with community benefit. Municipalities that have the capacity and willingness to adopt more entrepreneurial business practices will be able to enter into effective partnerships and attract, marshal, and maximize third-party resources.

Creating a special-purpose entity corporation allowed Alexandria to act more nimbly in financing, building, and managing the overall development for the station (necessary to meet the deadline imposed by the tax-credit funding). And the technical assistance, participation, and oversight provided by city finance professionals throughout the development process ensured that the requirements and fiduciary interests of the public trust were fully safeguarded.

In addition to loans and grants, the city was able to provide a short-term bridge loan of $1.4 million to help AHDC pay the general contractor when the planned closing on tax credits was delayed for several weeks in the fall of 2008. The city's willingness to provide flexible interest-rate terms, to make residual receipts loans, and to subordinate its financing at different stages of the project all helped AHDC secure non-city financing.

While the city's investment of dollars in the project was proportionally smaller than some other sources (exclusive of land, around 8 percent of the total development cost), the city's active participation in the station and its willingness to provide backstop guarantees, as needed, enabled AHDC, a startup nonprofit organization with no balance sheet or development track record, to secure a tax credit investor and to arrange for favorable construction to permanent financing with the Virginia Housing Development Authority (VHDA).

On AHDC's behalf, the city backed two

letters of credit and provided a completion guaranty to the tax credit investor. PYD's donation of land made the project both possible and affordable over the long term. The developer's willingness to stake early dollars for predevelopment and feasibility studies (typically the most difficult project phases to finance because of risk) and to fund the initial period of construction helped AHDC get tax credits. Developer dollars also helped fund "non-eligible" (for tax credits) costs associated with the underground parking, the community room, and the workforce housing. By using consultants and vendors that had a relationship with PYD, the station was able to take advantage of efficiencies and knowledge that resulted in savings for the project.

Because of the strict deadline for completion, financing and constructing the project had to be fast tracked as soon as the development concept was approved and tax credits awarded. Alexandria Station LLC, the special-purpose entity established to own, develop, finance, and construct the project, allowed the city, as the managing member of the corporation, to act nimbly.

Costs and Benefits

Between 2006 and 2010, Alexandria provided significant staffing resources to this important capital project, in addition to finance staff. The city provided technical support to AHDC in order to enhance the capacity of this start-up nonprofit development organization. City departments and agencies involved included representatives from code administration, fire, general services, housing, planning, transportation and environmental services; the Office of Historic Alexandria; the city attorney's office; communications; and recreation, parks and cultural activities.

The investment of city funds in actual non-personnel hard and soft costs associated with the development of the Station at Potomac Yard was approximately $3 million. Of that amount, $1.9 million was secured by a loan to AHDC that is expected to be repaid from project cash flow from the residential component over the next 15 to 20 years.

In addition to PYD's donation of land and its contributions to the fire station ($6.6 million) and to the housing facility ($7.5 million), other funding for the $34 million project included $8.6 million in low-income housing tax credit equity, $8.35 million in loans from the Virginia Housing Development Authority, city loans and grants, AHDC's deferred developer fee, and some ancillary project-generated revenue.

The station project provided much needed, very tangible benefits to the City of Alexandria—a new, state-of-the-art fire station and affordable and workforce rental housing. The new station houses multiple vehicles, stores modern firefighting and equipment for dealing with hazardous materials, and provides a suitable living environment for a male and female workforce. Both the fire station and the housing facility are green: The fire station is LEED-certified and the residential units meet Earthcraft program standards for energy efficiency and savings. The project has provided many opportunities for community engagement and education regarding affordable housing and its demographics; the very visible and iconic station building has helped change the public's perception of affordable housing.

Conclusions

While mixed-use projects and public-private partnerships are not new, the station represents a unique combination of uses. Despite initial concerns about combining a fire station with residential apartments, the engineering and design measures taken to mitigate sound and vibration within the structure appear to have been very successful. Building residents and members of the fire station both report that the station community is thriving. Visitors from other cities, states, and countries have toured the station with the hope of replicating the concept. City staff is providing technical assistance and information to several similar projects being explored in Arlington, Virginia; Washington, D.C.; New Brunswick, New Jersey: Durham, New Hampshire; Wilmington, Delaware; the City of Frisco, Texas; and Shanghai, China.

The Station at Potomac Yard design concept, which combines a municipal use with affordable housing, could be easily adapted and replicated in urban, suburban, and rural communities as part of smart growth or efficient land use planning. With monetary resources limited, governments are challenged to find and adapt new ways of providing meaningful support: mutually beneficial public, private, and/or nonprofit collaborations offer excellent opportunities for local governments to maximize new resources available through strategic partnerships.

The Station at Potomac Yard has won the following awards:

- Virginia Municipal League 2010 Achievement Award
- Brick in Architecture Award, 2010
- Housing and Non Profit Developers 2010
- Achievement Award for Innovation, June 2010
- 2009 Virginia Housing Award-Best Mixed Use or Mixed Income Housing Development, November 2009
- Fire Chief Magazine, 2009 Bronze Award for Fire Station Design
- Finalist, Affordable Housing Finance 2009 Reader's Choice Award, Master Planned/Mixed Use Category
- American Planning Association Award, 2008
- Outstanding Project, National Capital Area
- U.S. Conference of Mayors Award for Excellence in Public Private Partnerships, January 2008
- Finalist, National League of Cities Award for Municipal Excellence, August 2008
- Finalist, Urban Land Institute Ronald J. Terwilliger Center Workforce Housing Models of Excellence Award, October 2008

21. Somber Spots and Bright Spots

Craig Chavez

In 2001, Ann Arbor had 1,000 employees. Today, it has fewer than 750 employees. Because of Michigan's statewide policies limiting property taxes, each fiscal year it became necessary to reduce expenditures to match limited increases in revenue. Now, after 11 percent expense reductions in the current year, slumping revenues will mean another 11 percent cut across the board, including the likely closure of some recreation facilities, and significant layoffs, beginning July 1, 2010.

The state of Michigan has further complicated Ann Arbor's financial scenario. Because the state's budget is in limbo, Michigan has reduced its revenue sharing between the state and its local governments. Roger Fraser, Ann Arbor's city administrator, said, "This is problematic because our budget was calculated with the state's contribution of revenue sharing. Its 10 percent reduction, announced in October, further compounded a bleak revenue outlook."

Although the current situation is bad, Ann Arbor's job restructuring and involvement in the creation of an economic development group called Ann Arbor SPARK have helped mitigate the negative effects of the current recession.

Labor Restructuring

Several years ago, declining revenues, coupled with an influx of early retirements and a Byzantine organizational structure, created the perfect opportunity to reshape Ann Arbor's organization for the better. Following a major reorganization in 2002–2003, and with the help of a consultant, Ann Arbor's management and human resources staffs involved line supervisors, employees, and their unions in the restructuring of various job functions.

Employees got together in facilitated work groups and used their hands-on knowledge to examine the work processes and make suggestions for process and staffing improvements. From these examinations, service area managers and human resources staff were able to work with the unions and create what they call "career progressions," which are new job classifications with clear, five-level pay and skill progressions. These job classifications and their required skills were formed with input provided by the employee work groups.

Before the restructuring, job descriptions and work structures were so separate and rigid that they hindered Ann Arbor's ability

Originally published as Craig Chavez (2010). "Somber Spots and Bright Spots." *Public Management (PM) Magazine*, 92(4), May 2010. Reprinted with permission of the publisher.

to function efficiently. Fraser said, "There were, for example, 32 different clerical job classifications, and, due to the work structure, any clerical job opening required a cumbersome posting process because the job classifications prevented people from being moved around as needed."

After the restructuring, all of the clerical positions were reformed into one job classification with a five-level skill and pay progression. Ann Arbor has seen similar benefits from restructuring other departments like field operations that include water, sewer, public works maintenance, and park services. With this added flexibility, Ann Arbor can now move employees around from an unneeded area, like parks maintenance, and have them work on snow removal during the winter.

Both the city and its employees benefited from the restructuring and the new career progressions. The employees received opportunities for increased pay and a new career path, and the city achieved needed flexibility. Richard Martonchik, Ann Arbor's human resources service partner and a member of the restructuring project, said of the labor flexibility: "It is useful during any economic downturn, especially during this recession. The restructuring allowed Ann Arbor to keep providing services even with the reductions in funding and staff."

SPARK

Created in 2005, Ann Arbor SPARK is a collaborative effort among the city of Ann Arbor, Washtenaw County, other local communities, Eastern Michigan University, the University of Michigan, Washtenaw Community College, and the private sector. The economic development group has three functions: traditional economic development, new business development and assisting start-ups, and managing employee talent.

Employee placement is done by partnering with local businesses that cannot find talented employees. SPARK also has ongoing programs of support for folks seeking jobs. With this effort, SPARK maintains direct contacts with thousands of talented job seekers. Through this and other imaginative tools, SPARK provides any given company the means to attract the best and brightest to that company. SPARK also holds more than 200 networking events a year, and these events assist small and start-up companies with every facet of business development.

SPARK puts a big focus on new business development. Through research, SPARK found that new businesses lacked the needed resources to thrive. The resource dearth included funding and business knowledge, so SPARK focused on increasing business education and funding. Entrepreneurs can attend SPARK networking events and learn from attorneys and other professionals about the basics of business.

The training includes such topics as business and patent law, information technology, developing business plans, and building and using professional networks. The training also includes how to get business funding. Funding has been a crucial part of new business development. By working with local banks, the city of Ann Arbor, Washtenaw County, and the Michigan Economic Development Corporation (MEDC), SPARK has generated micro-loans from $5,000 to $50,000 that can be used for a variety of business needs. These loans are essential to start-ups who lack working capital in the best of times and especially during the down economy because the state of Michigan has seen a sharp increase in people trying to start their own businesses.

Although the demand for funding is high, start-ups were not able to borrow from banks. The SPARK microloans and training programs fill this gap and provide new and fledgling businesses with needed funding and knowledge. In addition to the microloan program, SPARK has committed nearly $9 million in venture capital funding to start-ups through the state-wide Michigan Pre-Seed Capital Fund. Michael Finney, SPARK's president and CEO, said, "We're successful because we're focusing on supporting businesses in every stage of development and growth and supplying them with the tools that they need to succeed."

SPARK, a private, not-for-profit company serves as the sole economic development agency for the region, consisting of 28 local governments and two major universities. This arrangement streamlines economic development, creates efficiencies, and eliminates economic turf wars between neighboring local governments. Instead of each local government funding its own economic development efforts, the governments now contribute to SPARK, and SPARK works to develop the economy in a broader and more efficient manner. This process pools resources and is especially useful in a tight funding environment.

During this fiscal year, Ann Arbor contributed $75,000 to SPARK, and Washtenaw County gave $250,000. Based on benchmarking, similar sized cities and counties typically spend $2 to $3 million to staff their own economic development organization. By pooling resources, local governments in the county enjoy significant cost savings while benefitting from a $7 million economic development organization with 15 full-time employees. "By fostering a regional approach to economic development and working with partners in the Ann Arbor and the greater Detroit area, we've been able to achieve a high level of results in a collaborative environment," said Finney.

A Silver Lining

Ann Arbor's experience provides guidance to other local governments dealing with the recession. Although it was painful to reduce the number of city staff by 25 percent, and reduce recreation, police, fire and other services, Ann Arbor's labor restructuring softened the impact. In fact, Martonchik said, "The restructuring allowed us to maintain services even with reductions in staff, and up to this point the residents have hardly noticed changes in service levels."

SPARK also helped Ann Arbor navigate through the economic uncertainty. Pfizer was a major employer in the city, but when the company left, it took 5 percent of Ann Arbor's property tax revenues and 3,100 jobs with it. Yet, there was some relief, according to Fraser, because, "SPARK created 2,900 jobs after Pfizer left."

With the labor restructuring and involvement in SPARK, Ann Arbor used creativity and innovation to respond to budget shortfalls and a changing economy. This meant there was a silver lining to Ann Arbor's efforts. Despite various and increasing economic challenges, the city was able to develop better, more efficient ways of operating and minimize service impacts to its residents.

22. The Park That Paid Off

Greg Beato

For a quarter-century, the Presidio of San Francisco has been a contested terrain. At the center of that battlefield is the Presidio Trust, a government agency that represents an alternative model for funding and managing a public asset. Here's how the trust turned a large military facility into a large urban park.

In 1776, Spanish explorers established a fortified outpost on the northern edge of what would become San Francisco. Over the next 200-plus years, this outpost, dubbed the Presidio, was a military base-first under Spain, then under Mexico, then under the United States. In all that time, the forces based at the Presidio never fired a shot in anger. Then, in 1989, the Pentagon announced that it was planning to close the Presidio as a military post. According to legislation enacted by the U.S. Congress in 1972, the Presidio would eventually pass into the jurisdiction of the National Park Service (NPS).

It was at this point that the Presidio turned into a battlefield. The combatants have included members of Congress, federal agencies, advocacy groups, environmentalists, and billionaires with art collections that they want to share with the world. At issue: How to maintain a 1,491-acre park-a large tract of open space and developed land that features historic architecture and iconic views of the Golden Gate Bridge-in a way that honors its past, serves present users, and remains financially viable in a political climate where Congress often trims NPS budgets with an unsparing hand.

For nearly two decades, an entity known as the Presidio Trust has played a central role in the Presidio saga. Created by Congress in 1996, the trust is a corporation wholly owned by the federal government that manages most of the parkland at the Presidio. Congress gave the trust a mandate to "increase revenues to the Federal Government to the maximum extent possible," and many onlookers worried that this provision would doom the Presidio to a bleak future as a heavily privatized business park-a place where corporate logos would bloom like wildflowers. "There were elements to what Congress did that made the trust threatening to the National Park Service," says Craig Middleton, who signed on as the trust's first employee in 1997 and became its executive director in 2001. "The trust reported to the President of the United States, not the Secretary of the Interior. It had lots of flexibility relative to hiring and firing, contracting, all the things that [other] government [agencies] complain about."

Originally published as Greg Beato (2015). "The Park That Paid Off." *Stanford Social Innovation Review*, 13(3), Summer 2015. Reprinted with permission of the publisher.

In fact, the NPS had taken part in developing the trust model for the Presidio. Yet NPS leaders viewed the Presidio Trust cautiously once it came into existence. "We were really suspect," says Middleton, who announced in February that he would be leaving the organization after serving there for 18 years. "People were saying, 'What does this mean for the parks? Does this mean that Yosemite is next—that they're going to privatize that?'"

So far, no multinational has managed to purchase naming rights to any part of the Presidio. To be sure, the trust has replaced some old buildings with new ones, and a film production company and a sporting-goods retailer now occupy space where soldiers once spent their days. But that's only part of the story. The trust has rehabilitated hundreds of structures, built or rebuilt trails and scenic overlooks, and cleaned up landfills and toxic-waste areas.

Perhaps most remarkably, the Presidio hasn't received or required federal funding since 2012. When Congress created the trust, it imposed a strict deadline: If the Presidio wasn't financially self-sufficient within 15 years, the General Services Administration would take possession of the land and dispose of it by means that could include selling it to private developers. That didn't happen. And today the trust brings in revenues that exceed its operating costs by about $30 million a year.

The battle over the future of the Presidio has not ceased. But the Presidio Trust, in part by organizing its work around cross sector partnerships, has demonstrated the feasibility of one model for funding and managing a large public park.

Marking a Transition

Along with being a strategic location for Army operations, the Presidio was a favorite post among high-ranking officers who looked forward to winding down their careers by battling the sand traps of its 18-hole golf course. Local politicians loved the post, too, because it poured millions of dollars into the San Francisco economy without requiring many services in return. It had its own police force, its own fire department, and its own utility systems. The Presidio also had a long history as de facto parkland for San Francisco's civilian population. "The Army would put on a parade or an artillery demonstration, and thousands of people would come out and sit on the sand dunes and have picnics," says Whitney Hall, a retired U.S. Army colonel who served as the Presidio's commandant from 1978 to 1981.

In 1972, Congressman Phillip Burton drafted legislation that would eventually create the Golden Gate National Recreation Area (GGNRA), a non-contiguous area that covers about 28 miles of coastal lands north and south of the Golden Gate. Although the future of the Presidio as a military post seemed fairly secure at the time, it was situated amid what would become GGNRA land. So Burton included a provision that would have far-reaching consequences: When the Presidio was "determined by the Department of Defense to be excess to its needs," it would transfer to the jurisdiction of the Secretary of the Interior and become part of the GGNRA.

Ultimately, it was a simple economic truth that determined the Presidio's fate. "The cost to support each uniformed person at the Presidio was the highest of any Army post," Hall explains. As early as 1979, the Army began to explore the possibility of divesting itself of the Presidio. A decade later, in 1989, the end of the Cold War prompted a large-scale restructuring of U.S. military facilities, and the Presidio turned up on a list of imminent base closures.

Parks advocates in the San Francisco Bay Area rejoiced at the possibility of adding the Presidio to the GGNRA. But they also faced an immediate practical consideration: How much would it cost to operate as a park? By NPS standards, the Presidio is tiny. Yellowstone National Park could contain 1,488 parks as big as the Presidio within its borders. But over more than two centuries, the Presidio had developed a robust infrastructure that included 870 buildings—barracks, single-family residences, hospitals, a bowling alley, a golf course, and more. Maintaining all of those structures, hundreds of which were subject to the National Historic Preservation Act (NHPA) and to California preservation laws, would be quite expensive. "No one knew exactly what the numbers were, but it was believed that the Army had been spending $70 million a year to run the place," says Middleton. The NPS didn't have that kind of money. Even the "crown jewels" in its system, such as Yellowstone and Yosemite, were not nearly so costly to maintain. (In 1995, the appropriation for Yellowstone was $18.3 million.)

Building a Trust

The Army did not plan to leave the Presidio until 1994, so the NPS had five years to figure out how to pay for its new park. The agency turned to a local nonprofit, the Golden Gate National Parks Conservancy (GGNPC), which had formed in 1981 to raise funds to benefit the GGNRA. The GGNPC advised the NPS to create a standalone advisory group—the Presidio Council—to help determine the park's purpose, its features, and, most important, its funding model. The council recruited the consulting firm McKinsey & Co. to work on the project. "They donated hundreds of hours of volunteer time to look at management models around the country that were dealing with sites that involved a combination of public, private, and nonprofit talent and funds," says Greg Moore, president and CEO of the GGNPC. "Their research

was the foundation of the Presidio Trust idea."

At the heart of the trust idea lay a critical insight: The problem of funding the Presidio contained its own potential solution. All of those buildings were costly to maintain, but all of those buildings could generate rental income, too. "The Park Service people who were involved on the ground realized that their legislative authorities were insufficient for this," says Moore.

Historically, the NPS has operated on an appropriations basis. Each year, the agency as a whole submits a budget to Congress, and Congress allocates the funding that it deems appropriate. In turn, individual parks must submit most of the user fees that they collect to the U.S. Treasury. Over the past two decades, Congress has modified that structure, and parks are now able to retain some user fees for their own purposes. But in the early 1990s, every dollar that a park collected went to the Treasury. As a result, the NPS had little or no institutional capacity for enabling parks to maximize their revenues.

What McKinsey and the Presidio Council recognized, however, is that the Presidio would require an organization that possessed both special administrative powers—such as the ability to retain its own revenues—and a more entrepreneurial mindset. It would need managers who had experience in borrowing capital, crafting partnerships, negotiating leases and other contracts, managing facilities, and cultivating private donors. And that would mean tapping private-sector expertise.

The NPS accepted this solution, at least in part. In October 1993, it published "Creating a Park for the 21st Century," a document that presented its "grand vision" for the Presidio. The agency envisioned the new Presidio as "a national park unlike any other," a place where nonprofit tenants would join forces to pursue work on "sustainable design, global climate change, environmental cleanup, resource protection, biological diversity, and other significant environmental concerns." In partnership with the NPS, a "federally chartered partnership institution" with "new legislative authorities" would manage the Presidio. The site would be divided into two sections. Area A, which the NPS would oversee, would consist of 323 mostly undeveloped coastal acres. Area B, which the new institution would govern, would encompass the remaining 1,168 acres.

The NPS plan assumed that the new entity would be able to generate considerable revenue on its own. Even so, the plan called for annual appropriations of up to $25 million. At the time, the federal debt stood at $4 trillion, and Congress had no appetite for additional spending. Convinced that the Presidio would "drain money from every other park in the Nation," Rep. John Duncan, a Republican from Tennessee, introduced legislation to sell the Presidio. So did Senator Pete Domenici, a Republican from New Mexico. Domenici even put a price tag on it: He said that sale of the land could yield as much as $550 million.

But other members of Congress—including Nancy Pelosi, a Democrat from California whose district includes the Presidio—continued to push for the creation of a new federal agency to manage the Presidio. Eventually, that side won the debate. In 1996, Congress voted to establish the Presidio Trust. It also agreed to provide the trust with annual appropriations that would start at $25 million. But each year thereafter, those appropriations would decrease. And in 15 years, they would stop entirely.

Conserving Authority

In some respects, the structure of the Presidio Trust mirrors the conservancy model that has grown in popularity over the past few decades. Across the United States, private citizens have formed nonprofit organizations—the Central Park Conservancy in New York City, for example, or the GGNPC—that help fund and maintain parks and other public spaces. In this model, a city or other government entity typically owns the parkland in question, but the conservancy ends up playing an integral role in daily park operations. The GGNPC, which has raised more than $300 million for the GGNRA, also oversees restoration projects in GGNRA parklands, manages six native plant nurseries, operates eight gift shops, organizes a wide range of volunteer and outreach programs, and leads tours. The rise of conservancies, not surprisingly, has generated concerns about the danger of privatization and the possibility that the public will lose control of public assets.

The Presidio Trust was designed to provide the kind of entrepreneurial orientation and private-sector expertise that conservancies often bring to park management. Yet it differs from a conservancy in significant ways. For one thing, it's wholly owned by the federal government and thus wholly accountable to the government. Empowered by an act of Congress, the trust can potentially be dissolved by an act of Congress. Equally important, having a statutory foundation gives the trust a crucial measure of authority. If its legitimacy had derived only from an informal agreement or even from a memorandum of understanding, it might not have lasted in its original form.

Indeed, in the early days of the partnership between the trust and the NPS, the two organizations clashed repeatedly. "There is a section in the Presidio Trust Act that gives the NPS a formal role with respect to interpretive functions for visitors," says Toby Rosenblatt, who served as the first chair of the Presidio Trust Board of Directors. "Other than that, in terms of uses and budgets and every other operating aspect of the Presidio, it had no jurisdiction, and the Trust Act made that really clear." Still, the NPS often tried to assert its institutional preferences. "They [NPS leaders] were never great believers in the trust having its independent operations and budget," Rosenblatt says. "So they kept saying, 'You've got to do things the way we do them.' And the trust's board and staff, with the help of attorneys, said, 'No, that's not what the Trust Act says.'" Congressional authority gave the upstart agency the ability to move quickly and boldly—even when a much larger and more established agency pushed back.

Saying Yes

In 1999, two years after it launched, the trust needed to summon all of the authority that it could muster. That's when it announced that it was moving forward on a proposal by the filmmaker George Lucas to build a new corporate headquarters for his company, Lucasfilm, on the site where the Letterman Army Medical Center (LAMC) and the Letterman Army Institute of Research (LAIR) then stood. Those structures, built in the late 1960s, were not particularly beloved. ("It was a big ugly high-rise and a wretched-looking research center," says Moore.) But the plan to demolish them and replace them with new construction of comparable square footage—about 900,000 square feet—drew howls of protest from non-profit watchdog groups, including the Sierra Club, the National Trust for Historic Preservation, and dozens of other organizations.

Amy Meyer, a longtime Bay Area parks advocate who served on the Presidio Trust board from 1997 to 2003, recalls the reaction that the Lucasfilm decision prompted. "People were saying, 'What is this anomaly, this "trust"? It's supposed to be taking care of a national park, and now we're going to have Star Wars on it?'" For many trust skeptics, the deal appeared to signal that the Presidio was on the verge of becoming, as the San Francisco Bay Guardian put it, "an intensively developed office complex."

The NPS, in its 1993 plan, had suggested that "replacement construction" of LAMC would be necessary. Yet the NPS also took issue with the trust's plan for the site, characterizing the "overall size, scale, materials, detailing, and siting" of the Lucasfilm project as "incompatible with Presidio's status as a National Historic Landmark District." Although the NPS had envisioned the Letterman Complex as a site of fairly extensive development, it had proposed to fill the space with tenants "devoted to scientific research and education focusing on issues of human health." The licensing department of a billion-dollar movie production company wasn't what the agency had in mind.

The terms of the Presidio Trust Act did not support the grandness of the original NPS vision. The act specifically charged the trust with finding "tenants that enhance the financial viability of the Presidio." And in this case, that meant finding a tenant that could finance the Letterman Complex renovation on its own. The act enabled the organization to borrow up to $50 million from the U.S. Treasury, and Congress was providing annual appropriations of about $25 million. But this one project would cost at least $200 million. In the judgment of the trust's board, the Lucasfilm proposal was the best available option. Lucas's company would cover the costs of renovation in return for a long-term lease, and when it moved into its new building, it would start paying about $5.8 million annually in rent. As a result, the trust would gain some of the capital that it needed to continue renovating other parts of the Presidio.

Tactically, though, it was a risky proposition. Choosing to make Lucasfilm a marquee tenant gave the trust's critics a high-profile target around which to organize their protest efforts. "It was a very a controversial deal," Middleton notes. But saying yes to Lucas brought substantial benefits that went beyond the direct revenue that resulted from the deal. "Those first few years, we were practically having to beg [non-residential tenants] to come out here," says Middleton. "It was too far away. Nothing had been repaired yet. If you were lucky, the lights went on when you turned the switch. Lucas gave others the confidence that somebody had really placed a big bet on the Presidio-so they could, too."

Engaging All Sectors

The trust, in other words, regarded Lucasfilm as an anchor tenant that would help draw other potential tenants to the park. That kind of synergistic approach has been typical of how the trust operates. Indeed, the Presidio Trust Act put a strong emphasis on collaboration. It specifically encouraged the trust to "maintain a liaison with the Golden Gate National Park Association," for example. (That was the original name of what's now the GGNPC.)

In addition, the act laid out clear guidelines for selecting a board of directors that would bring a variety of perspectives to the endeavor. Although the Bay Guardian claimed that the trust's founding board was "made up largely of big business leaders and real estate developers," the board was in fact fairly diverse. It did include Don Fisher, founder of the Gap; Toby Rosenblatt, a San Francisco developer; and May Murphy, a real estate lawyer. But the remaining members were Meyer, a parks advocate; William K. Reilly, a former administrator of the Environmental Protection Agency; Edward Blakely, dean of the School of Urban and Regional Planning at the University of Southern California; and John Garamendi, a high-ranking official at the U.S. Department of Interior (who is now a U.S. congressman).

The range of viewpoints that the original board embodied set the course for a culture of collaboration. "The fundamental magic of the Presidio comes from the trust's ability to take a cross-sector approach, to combine public funding and public expertise, nonprofit funding and expertise, and private-sector funding and expertise to achieve a public vision and a public mission," says Moore. As an example, Moore cites the effort to restore Crissy Field, the onetime airport of the Presidio. Moore's group raised funds for the project, attracting $36 million from local foundations and other donors, and the NPS managed the restoration. "Together, we created this landmark site, beautiful and popular, and that made the buildings around it more leasable," Moore says. "In every case, it's been one improvement helping to leverage the other."

The structure of the trust also provided a framework for philanthropic investment. Most important, it reassured donors that the Presidio had a future as a public place. "For philanthropists, there was a practical realization that the restoration of historic buildings for leasing was a business proposition," says Moore. "It was important to get done, because without self-sufficiency, there wouldn't be a Presidio national park." By focusing on building restoration, meanwhile, the trust created an opening for philanthropists to make an impact in other areas. "Crissy Field, the trails and overlooks, the restoration of Mountain Lake and the Presidio Forest, youth programs—that's where private foundations and individual donors realized that they could contribute to the public dimensions of the Presidio," says Moore. To date, private donors have invested about $150 million in the Presidio.

Leasing the Future

In the early days of the Presidio trust, both advocates and critics of a new federal agency assumed that most of its revenue-generating efforts would involve commercial leasing. Both the NPS and the trust, after all, assumed that successful redevelopment of the Letterman Complex was crucial to the Presidio's long-term success. Many critics, meanwhile, worried that the place would become a vast office park where corporate fat cats would ultimately push out every other species.

To a large extent, however, it is residential leasing that has shaped the economic fortunes of the Presidio. "Jim Meadows, the trust's first executive director, made the important recognition that the most valuable and marketable asset in the Presidio was the residences," says Rosenblatt. "The early money that came from appropriations was all devoted to rehabilitating and upgrading the residential property and getting it leased." The trust applied much of the $50 million that it was able to borrow from the U.S. Treasury toward this end as well.

Investing most of its capital in residential real estate allowed the trust to generate significant returns very quickly. By 2001, the trust had 872 rentable housing units. In the wake of the dot-com bust and the recession that followed, its efforts to rent commercial space faltered. But its residential revenues continued to increase rapidly: They rose from $7.3 million in fiscal year 1999 to $21.3 million in fiscal year 2001.

The trust's decision to use most of its available capital to develop residential housing also had a significant long-term impact. "There were two ways we could have approached residential leasing," says Middleton. "We could fund it ourselves and then charge market rate [rents] on short-term leases. Or we could do a deal where we gave someone a 50- or 60-year lease and then let them pay for the cost of fixing up their housing." The trust had adopted the latter approach in the case of the Lucasfilm project because it didn't have enough money to do otherwise. With its residential property, however, the trust was able to take the other approach—a move that proved to be extremely fortunate. "Rental prices in San Francisco have skyrocketed," notes Middleton. By 2013, the trust was bringing in $44.2 million annually from residential leasing (compared with $19.6 million from non-residential leasing).

Renewing the Space

The trust has used its ample revenue to rehabilitate both the natural and the built environment over which it has responsibility. Today the Presidio is a cleaner, more beautiful, and more vital public place than it was when the trust took it over. The trust has dredged and purified the once-toxic Mountain Lake, removed hundreds of non-native koi, carp, turtles, and other creatures that people had dumped into the lake over the years, and made the surrounding area safe again for native species like the chorus frog and the Western pond turtle. So many coyotes now inhabit the park that they have their own Yelp page. (They get mostly good reviews.)

To rejuvenate the Presidio's 300-acre forest, the trust has removed aging trees and planted nearly 4,000 cypress and pine trees where those trees had stood. In May 2014, it completed a 20-year environmental remediation project to clean up waste that the Army had left behind. "There were 15 large landfills, hundreds of leaking underground petroleum tanks, toxic chemicals and materials, lead-based paint," says Jan Blum, a longtime Presidio volunteer who helped with the cleanup process. "Over that 20-year period, more than 350,000 tons of contaminated soil were removed or, in some cases, capped to make it safe for everyone. It was a very big deal."

Working in concert with the NPS and the GGNPC, the trust has constructed eight scenic overlooks in the park and added or improved 22 miles of trails and 15 miles of bikeways. It has also rehabilitated the vast majority of its 433 historic buildings. In September 2014, the trust completed a $30 million makeover of its historic Officers' Club. The club, a 37,000-square-foot structure that stands on the site where Spanish soldiers first set up a permanent residence in the late 1700s, features portions of adobe walls from that era, along with meeting rooms, a restaurant, and other modern amenities. In addition, there is a museum exhibition space where uniforms, weapons, and other artifacts from the Presidio's period as a military post are on display. Other recent building efforts include the Inn at the Presidio, a 22-room boutique hotel, and the Military Intelligence Service Historic Learning Center, a project of the National Japanese American Historical Society.

Fielding Criticism

The scope of what the trust has accomplished is impressive. Yet the fight over the best use of Presidio land continues. People cherish the Presidio in different ways and from different perspectives. So it's not hard to find critics of the trust. Blum, for example, says the trust has done a great job with building restoration but that it could do more to showcase the Presidio's ecological attributes. "The Presidio is home to 16 different rare or endangered species," she says. "It has over a dozen different ecological habitats. This park is really a biological treasure, but most of the public doesn't know it."

Others fault the trust for taking insufficient care of the Presidio legacy. "Restoring the Officers' Club, restoring the Inn at the Presidio—we're very happy with what the trust has done in both those places," says Gary Widman, president of the Presidio Historical Association (PHA), a nonprofit advocacy group. "When it comes to new construction, that's where they run away from their responsibilities under the Presidio Trust Act, part of which says that they

have a responsibility to protect the Presidio from development."

Two development proposals were especially controversial. In 2007, former trust board member Don Fisher put forth a plan to construct a new museum in the park. "He had an extraordinary modern art collection, and he wanted to build some place to show it off," says Middleton. Fisher wanted to build in the most historic area of the Presidio, the Main Post, and he wanted to build big: His proposed structure would have had 100,000 square feet of space. Like the Lucasfilm project, this project has the potential to serve as a much-needed magnet for further development. "This was when the Main Post had almost nothing in it. All these buildings were empty, and nobody wanted to touch them because they were going to be so expensive to rehabilitate," Middleton explains. But the scope and style of Fisher's museum design sparked criticism. "It was a gorgeous building, but it didn't fit with the rest of the site," Middleton says. "People had a bad reaction to it, and we couldn't overcome that." In 2009, Fisher withdrew his bid and moved his collection to the San Francisco Museum of Modern Art.

During the same period, the trust also unveiled a plan to construct a lodging facility on the Main Post that would consist of 110 rooms in 14 buildings with 90,000 square feet of total space. The project drew complaints from the NPS, the National Trust for Historic Preservation, and the PHA. "Building a 14-building hotel in the middle of the single most historic piece of real estate on the Presidio is not protecting it from development," says Widman. In 2012, the PHA and the Sierra Club filed a federal lawsuit in an attempt to block the project, claiming that it violates the Presidio Trust Act, the National Historic Preservation Act, and the National Environmental Policy Act. In 2013, a judge ruled in favor of the trust, but the PHA has appealed the case, which is now before the U.S. Court of Appeals for the Ninth Circuit.

Another point of criticism is that the trust could do more to present and interpret the history of the Presidio. At present, Hall suggests, the Presidio functions well as a recreational space for the people of San Francisco, but it does too little to attract national and international visitors by highlighting features that make it a national historic landmark. "The history display in the back of the Officers' Club [was] the result of years and years and years of being hounded and pecked at by neighborhood groups and others, who said, 'Where's the history? What is this place?'" Hall says.

Fulfilling Its Promise

None of the issues raised by critics is likely to fade anytime soon. In fact, as the trust continues to solidify its financial position, criticism of its actions will probably intensify. For much of its early history, the trust was able minimize expectations because it had to focus on the basics—repairing infrastructure, renovating buildings, cleaning up landfills. To a large degree, therefore, it deferred attending to the question that the NPS posed in 1994: What kind of park should the Presidio be? The trust has, in many ways, been more conservative in its stewardship than the NPS had intended it to be. The NPS, after all, had envisioned the Presidio as a new kind of service institution. It had wanted to create enough short-term lodging options to host as many as 720 people a night. (The trust has fallen far short of that goal.) Most of all, the NPS had aimed to create something that would be different from Yosemite or Gettysburg or any other park in the NPS system.

Now the Presidio Trust is in a position to explore such ideas. Leaders at the trust note that they're entering uncharted territory. "With the Trust Act, Congress provided us with a very clear North Star," says Joshua Steinberger, chief strategy and communications officer at the trust. "It offered a clear picture of what success or failure looked like. But there was less direction about what happens after 15 years."

In 2013, the trust provided funding to launch the Presidio Institute, a nonprofit organization that seeks to promote leadership and service through a cross-sector fellowship program. That organization also uses office space at Fort Scott, a former Army training center. Developed in partnership with the White House, McKinsey & Co., and other entities, the institute echoes the original NPS vision of the Presidio as a global center for exploring social and environmental issues from a cross-sector perspective.

The trust is also pursuing a large infrastructure project called the New Presidio Parklands. For decades, a highway that connects downtown San Francisco to the Golden Gate Bridge has separated Crissy Field from the Main Post at the Presidio. Now the California Department of Transportation is constructing a series of at-grade tunnels that will replace the highway; above those tunnels, the Presidio Trust will be able to create a 13-acre landscape. As this project moves forward, familiar questions arise: How much new construction should there be? What are the best uses for the new parkland?

"The trust is in a transition from real estate development and financial sustainability into park-making," observes Blum. "They say they want to 'activate' the Main Post. They want to 'activate' the Parklands. And they want to create a place that is welcoming to visitors from everywhere. But we already get 1.6 million visitors a year. How many people do we want to attract, and how will that affect the visitor experience? What is the ultimate goal?"

While Blum suggests that the Presidio might become too busy, others argue that the trust has fallen short in efforts to draw people to the park through programming. Currently, the trust spends about $6 million a year on presentations at the Officers' Club, a weekend food truck event on the Main Post, and other fare of that kind. Over the next five years, the trust plans to increase that figure to $7 million. "That's almost no increase at all," complains Don Green, a retired economist who has been a member of various advocacy organizations with an interest in the Presidio. "The program budget should at least double, from $6 million to $12 million, because that's what the trust is supposed to be doing—providing services to the public."

Saying No

The NPS, which will celebrate its 100th anniversary next year, now faces an estimated $11 billion in deferred maintenance costs. All across the country, U.S. national parks are filled with leaky water systems and crumbling buildings. But because Congress controls their purse strings, they can do only so much to fix those problems. The Presidio, by contrast, stands as a beacon of self-determination. The Presidio Trust—often criticized for leaving the Presidio vulnerable to commercialism and undue private-sector influence—has grown into a powerful mechanism for ensuring the park's autonomy. Not only does the trust enjoy a strong financial position, but it's able to choose (or not to choose) new projects as it sees fit.

Just ask George Lucas. In 2012, he and his team submitted a bid to build a new museum on a prime location within the Presidio. The site, which boasts postcard-worthy views of the Golden Gate Bridge and Alcatraz Island, now is home to a nondescript structure that once served as the Presidio's commissary. (Its current lessee is a discount sporting-goods retailer.) For more than a decade, the trust has planned to develop "a cultural institution of distinction" at this location. Lucas proposed to build a museum on the site that would house his $1 billion collection of narrative art—a collection that includes works by illustrators like Norman Rockwell, along with works of animation and cinematic set design.

In many respects, it was an extraordinarily attractive proposal. Lucas was planning to pay the entire cost ($300 million) of building the museum. He was also going to create a $400 million endowment that would cover all operating costs in perpetuity. And he was ready to pay millions of dollars per year in rent to the Presidio Trust. Lucas's high profile and the museum's tourist-friendly content, moreover, would attract hundreds of thousands of visitors every year. There would be learning opportunities for children, research libraries for scholars, and meeting facilities for visiting artists. For all of these reasons, the project had won the support of California Governor Jerry Brown, Senator Dianne Feinstein, House Minority Leader Nancy Pelosi, San Francisco mayor Ed Lee, the director of the Smithsonian American Art Museum, and other luminaries.

When the Lucas team unfurled its sketches for the Beaux Arts style building that it envisioned for the site, however, the designs prompted a wave of criticism. The proposed museum looked stolid and sepulchral, particularly in the context of the open space that it would inhabit. "People were calling it the museoleum," says Meyer. It was also too tall and would potentially block views from the Main Post. Others noted the project's lack of a thematic or historic connection to the Presidio.

In February 2014, the Presidio Trust board unanimously rejected the project, along with the two other proposals that it was considering for the site. According to the current chair of the board, Nancy Heilman Bechtel, none of the projects "quite hit the mark." Many park advocates applauded the decision. "I give them a lot of credit for standing up to this push to bring a vanity project into one of the most beautiful sites in America," says Blum. "That took a lot of courage." But courage alone would not have been enough. The trust, thanks to its access to other sources of revenue, had reached a point where it could afford to say no-even to a $300 million museum.

Providing a Model

Despite the success of the Presidio Trust, even many of its strongest allies are reluctant to vouch for the portability of its model. "If there are places like the Presidio that face the same challenges, maybe smaller in scale, I think the trust model is worth considering," says Moore. "But when you look at Yellowstone or the Grand Canyon, or the majority of our national parks sites, they're too different in their composition for an approach like this." Rosenblatt sounds a similar note: "The NPS and some of the major Friends of the Park groups always worried that the Presidio Trust struc-

ture would be a precedent for other national parks. And we've always said, 'You shouldn't make that leap,' because very few other national parks or monuments have so many leasable resources."

In Middleton's estimation, however, the trust does illustrate at least one important and broadly applicable principle. "The trouble with these big [government] systems is that they create policies that have to apply to everything equally. So whether it's a little historic park or a much bigger park, they've got the same template," he says. "The lesson here is to be flexible enough and autonomous enough to design for the place, instead of trying to impose the same solution throughout the system."

Middleton also believes the trust stands as a powerful example of what government can do well. "It's a demonstration of how the public sector can be really effective," he says. "In our culture, the myth is that the only people who can innovate are in the private sector, and the people who stop you from innovating are in the public sector. In the Presidio, we're the regulators and the safeguarders, but we're also the implementers. And I love that."

23. Mission: Green

Ed Brock

Landfill space is cheap and plentiful in Texas. But, with Austin officials concerned with environmental conservation and sustainability, they set a goal in 2005 to eliminate all (or at least most) waste going to the city's landfill by 2040, says Matt Watson, policy director for Mayor Will Wynn. "We're not running out of space, but, landfills are not popular pieces of public infrastructure," he says.

Because sustainability—planning for the most efficient use of community resources—is a complicated process, however, many cities and counties are enlisting consultants to plan waste reduction programs, preserve water resources and help measure carbon emissions. Austin already had a recycling program and incentives to encourage residents to produce less waste, however, Watson says it needed somebody with expertise to analyze how it could most efficiently achieve the zero-waste goal. "We determined that if we were really going to be serious about it, we ought to bring in some national-level expertise," he says.

"[Sustainability consulting is] a new field. As we speak, the metrics of it are being written," says former Pittsburgh Mayor Tom Murphy, now a senior resident fellow for the Washington-based Urban Land Institute (ULI), a nonprofit organization that researches land use and development issues. "From what I'm seeing, every major engineering firm will have a sustainability division [in the near future.]"

Taking Out the Trash

Solid waste planning can reduce a landfill's physical as well as carbon footprint-the amount of greenhouse gas emissions produced by sources in the community. In late 2007, Austin hired Loomis, Calif.–based Gary Liss & Associates to help the city reduce the amount of waste going to its landfill by 20 percent in 2012 and 100 percent by 2040. "They've been meeting with stakeholder groups, our solid waste advisory commission, our Solid Waste Department, and council offices," Watson says. "They're coming up with some pretty detailed proposals about how we can achieve the next set of measurable increments of improvement."

To reach the zero-waste goal, the city, in conjunction with the consulting firm, is introducing single-stream recycling—where recyclables are placed in one bin to eliminate sorting—that will encourage res-

Originally published as Ed Brock (2008). "Mission: Green." *American City & County*, 123(4), April 2008. Reprinted with permission of the publisher.

idents to recycle more. Austin also has limited the use of non-compostable plastic bags and requires producers of electronic devices to recycle their old products. "We've taken all the normal, progressive steps a city takes to try and have advanced waste management, but until now, we haven't really gone beyond that to achieve a zero-waste goal," Watson says.

Watson says the city needed consultants because they have experience city employees do not have. "Since their entire business is focused on this, they've already run through a lot of the scenarios that we might think up, and [they can] help us anticipate which ones would work better here and which kind of strategies might not work so well," he says.

While many best practices are freely available, Watson says they are not "one-size-fits-all." Consultants can help communities pick the most cost-effective means for achieving their individual goals.

Protecting the Source

Maintaining the water supply is increasingly important to communities across the country, especially in areas that have been experiencing severe drought, such as the Southeast. Florida has the second-highest water consumption rate in the nation, according to the Office of Sustainability at the University of Florida in Gainesville, Fla. There, the average person uses 150 gallons a day, more than twice the national average.

Tampa Bay Water, which serves 2.5 million people in three counties and three cities, depends heavily on groundwater, but growing demand has been placing stress on the aquifer. In the last several years, the utility has considered alternate water sources, says Water Quality Assurance Officer Christine Owen.

The utility turned to several consultants to help determine what water sources to use, when to use them and how to best manage them. "On our groundwater sources, we would like to operate in a way that's consistent with sustaining that resource for generations," Owen says. "That is looking at systems—ecological, natural water systems—and seeing how much of the system can [be used and] can [the system] rebound from that use. Not pushing a system too far, but getting what you can out of it."

The utility works with New York–based Hazen & Sawyer to create computer models that predict the reliability of water sources based on supply and demand. The models, which predict future use, allow the utility to balance the amounts of water it extracts and puts into the reservoir, which holds only a six-month supply. "Our surface waters are pretty ephemeral, [and] the availability from stream flow is [seasonally] dependent," Owen says.

Overland Park, Kan.–based Black & Veatch also helps the utility manage demand for water and forecast demand growth patterns, Owen says. "A lot of people don't think of [controlling demand] as an actual water source," she says. "If we can manage demand that actually puts off the need to develop a new supply because it structures your existing supply."

The utility is using alternative water sources, most notably seawater. Its 25-million-gallon-a-day desalination plant began functioning in 2003 and became fully operational in January. The plant uses reverse osmosis membranes to remove salt and minerals from seawater at high pressure, and has produced 2.5 billion gallons of drinkable water since March 2007.

However, the desalination plant and other alternative sources require more energy to operate. "What we want to be able to do is choose the right kind of processes, put them in the right order and places, so that we have the best life-cycle cost benefits," Owen says.

The New Growth Industry

While many cities want to take steps to protect the environment—evidenced by the more than 800 that have signed the Washington-based U.S. Conference of Mayors' Climate Protection Agreement—most officials lack the technical know-how to make the changes necessary to achieve sustainability goals. "If you asked most mayors a year ago 'How much carbon did your city produce in 1990, and, if you're going to reduce it by 12 percent, how are you going measure [the reduction?]' nobody knew how to measure it," Murphy says. "If you can't measure it, it's hard to figure out how you're doing in reducing it."

Today, consultants are expanding to fill those needs, such as carbon emissions measurement, which includes collecting data on local transportation, waste and energy consumption, according to Oakland, Calif.–based ICLEI, a nonprofit provider of emissions measurement software. Once communities know how much carbon they are producing, they can take steps to reduce that amount or trade with lower-producing communities for credit. Carbon trading allows cities to buy carbon "credits" from companies or cities that produce "surplus" emission reductions through new technology or the use of renewable energy. The credits count toward achieving overall emissions reduction goals.

America's Climate Security Act, proposed by Sens. John Warner, R–Va., and Joseph Lieberman, I–Conn., which seeks to reduce greenhouse gas emissions by 70 percent of the 2005 level by 2050, could feed the market for buying and selling carbon reduction credits by setting the rules and standards for carbon trading, Murphy says. "It will create a whole new market in carbon trading, and it will require calculations that [most local officials are not] going to be able to do," he says. "So, you're going to need lots of consultants to help."

ICLEI, formerly called the International Conference of Local Environmental Initiatives, presents a plan to its member cities about ways to reduce their emissions and make their communities more sustainable, says Annie Strickler, ICLEI communications director. The organization, which has 800 members worldwide and 375 member cities in the United States, offers its members "Clean Air Climate Protection" (CACP) software, which calculates the emission level in the community and by how much it needs to be reduced to meet a set goal. "[The emissions inventories] are different for every case," she says. ICLEI also offers member cities extra services, including performing emissions inventories, developing climate action plans and organizing training workshops.

For all the advancements in the field, today's sustainability consultants may not be going far enough, says Steamboat Springs, Colo.–based environmental consultant Bill Wallace, author of "Sustainability 101: The Basics Every Consulting Engineer Should Know," a presentation written for the Washington-based American Council of Engineering Companies. Trendy approaches to sustainability, such as energy efficiency upgrades for buildings, have a certain value but do not address the global issue of sustainability, he says. "Global warming has demonstrated to people that this is a bigger deal than this type of accessorizing will deal with," he says. "Most consultants seem to be helping their clients feel good about being green, but only a few are doing something substantively, [such as] projects that radically reduce [the clients'] consumption of resources."

Instead, sustainability consultants need to take a completely different approach to engineering, Wallace says. Consultants in different disciplines should find a way to work together to achieve maximum effect, he says, but an even more difficult challenge will be replacing the nation's current infrastructure. "To be sustainable in the truest sense, you need to change the way infrastructure is designed," he says. "[Local government planners must] step back and revisit the entire infrastructure and [ask], 'What do I have to have to reduce the use of resources and energy and really try to achieve super conservation?'"

24. The Green Standard

Connie Kuranko

Increasing numbers of environmentally friendly products are available-from office supplies to furniture, and technology products to lab supplies—and government purchasing professionals are looking at new contracts with a green lens. As local government leaders institute environmentally preferable policies and programs, purchasing professionals are boning up on their product knowledge and trying new purchasing methods to meet environmental goals while staying within their budgets.

Following the Money

Having increased by more than 400 percent in the last three years, green building programs are on the rise among the top 200 most populated counties in the country, according to a recent report from the National Association of Counties (NACo) and the American Institute of Architects, both based in Washington. The growth in greener building is attributed to local leadership and the sharing of ordinances and resolutions among counties and cities.

But, green buildings can do only so much to help reduce energy use and waste. They have to be augmented with renewable energy credits, hybrid fleet vehicles, biofuels, reduced garbage collection coupled with increased recycling, water use management, energy efficiency evaluations and more eco-friendly products and services.

The demand for greener products and services has prompted some cities and counties to hire sustainability directors and recycling experts, and has, in many cases, changed the government purchasing professional's role. Public purchasers are seeing a greater need for integration among departments and are looking for ways to work with other local and state agencies. They also have had to become versed in eco-labeling language to ensure the products they select have specific certifications and are not making false or misleading claims.

Buying in the Emerald City

Some cities and counties are taking the lead on sustainable purchasing and are becoming examples for others to follow. Seattle leaders, for example, have been "buying green" for years. "A series of local ordinances date back to the 1970s and provide the legal and policy framework to make green purchasing a priority and a

Originally published as Connie Kuranko (2008). "The Green Standard." *American City & County*, 122(9), September 2009. Reprinted with permission of the publisher.

mandate," says Nancy Locke, the city's purchasing manager. "Mayor Nickels and the city council have continued to renew and update the ordinances to stay up to date with the most current knowledge and best practices. Having such clear ordinance authority, established early on, gives us our strongest tool to ensure all departments pursue a green purchasing standard."

Seattle's Green Purchasing Program aims to promote goods, materials, services and capital improvements that help reduce greenhouse gas emissions. In addition, purchasing contracts include several mandates, such as using 100-percent recycled paper for city work, duplex document production, toxin-free chemicals in pesticide and facility management contracts and reduced Persistent Bioaccumulative Toxic chemicals (PBTs) in products the city buys.

In selecting from the top-rated bids or proposals, the city requires bidders to identify any PBTs in their products and may require them to describe environmental benefits of their products or services. The city also has used environmental scoring as a substantial part of the selection criteria for computer hardware, cleaning chemicals, paint, copier equipment and paper products.

The Seattle Purchasing Department taps into green experts who work with the city to help prepare strategies and bids. "Sometimes these are champions that work for different organizations or companies, but their personal knowledge or commitment makes them extremely valuable to our base of expertise. These experts encourage us and are often the ones who point out opportunities and help prepare strategies and specifications for the city's bids," Locke says.

In the last five years, Seattle officials have made more specific efforts to use cooperative purchasing as a tool to accomplish their environmental purchasing objectives.

It joined the Walnut Creek, Calif.–based U.S. Communities Green Purchasing Program to gain access to a broad line of environmentally certified products and services. The program identifies items in its contracts that meet third-party environmental certification standards, including EcoLogo, Green Seal and Energy Star, and public agencies can search the group's Web site to find products' environmental information. "Cooperative purchasing allows us easier access to environmentally preferable product lines. Sometimes the products are emerging technologies that don't yet lend themselves to an independent city bid; sometimes it allows us easy access to a wider share of green products," Locke says. "Our mayor has committed to serving as a model for our residents, companies and public agencies in our use of green products. Cooperative purchasing allows us to assist agencies with easy access to our own green contract bid results."

No Rules, Just Right

Hennepin County, Minn., instituted its Environmentally Preferable Purchasing and Green Building Program in 1997 and changed the name in April 2001 to the Environmentally Preferable Purchasing and Waste Reduction Resolution after county officials studied waste growth projections and disposal trends. The resolution is not guided by a specific ordinance, but is purposefully unspecific in nature. "We feel it gives our program more flexibility in a time of changing technologies, products, priorities, certifications, etc.," says Nathan Reinbold, environmentally preferable purchasing/recycling specialist. "Our resolution is written in general language to allow us to accomplish the most without being restricted. Hennepin didn't want certain certifications or a detailed resolution/policy to hamper what we set out to do in the first place: buy green and be green, while saving green."

Without a specific ordinance, Hennepin

County can choose the most appropriate products for its needs, rather than follow specific standards that can be restrictive. However, Reinbold says the county is moving to become more standardized to close loopholes that defeat the purpose of the green purchasing program.

Hennepin County purchasers look for environmentally preferable certifications, such as EcoLogo and Green Seal, when making purchasing decisions, and they consider the amount of waste that will be generated by the products they buy to help minimize the amount of toxic materials that are brought in and have to be disposed. They also aim to reduce the amount of packaging needed for products and often buy in bulk to limit packaging waste.

Hennepin County's Green Purchasing Program works with county departments to help purchase environmentally preferable products, create resolutions, lead workshops and report on green purchasing progress. "Being the largest county in Minnesota, we feel we have the role, responsibility and resources to pilot and implement green products and practices to show to the rest of the state that it can be done," Reinbold says. "Most importantly, purchasing can be done in a way that minimizes costs while still protecting the environment."

In 2005, the county established a Lead by Example Incentive Fund for county departments attempting to reduce waste or purchase green products. The fund offers $100,000 annually to be used on innovative waste reduction, recycling and environmentally preferable purchasing projects. The awards typically are between $5,000 and $25,000, and have helped with bulk computer purchases, using compost on roadway slopes to prevent erosion, and buying bulk dispensing supplies and chemicals to facilitate a switch to green cleaners.

To measure progress on green purchases, Reinbold receives reports from vendors detailing the lower toxicity rates of and recycled content in products. Hennepin County also measures its success by the number of buildings that are being cleaned in a "green" way.

Since the county instituted its environmentally preferable purchasing program, demand for guidance in sustainable purchasing has increased, creating an opportunity for the county to explore cooperative purchasing. "Being a part of a cooperative purchasing program like U.S. Communities, we realize substantial cost savings when we pool our purchasing powers," Reinbold says. "It is good business practice and common sense in the world of crunched budgets and trying to do more with less."

For local government purchasers in the early stages of instituting sustainable purchasing programs, Reinbold says, "Pick low-lying fruit first. Don't try to take on the world all at once. Going green is a never-ending, fluid process. You are always trying to do better over time with the resources you have to work with. When you understand this, environmentally preferable purchasing becomes a lot easier."

As Locke and Reinbold have found, creating partnerships and sharing information is key to the success of sustainable purchasing programs. Adapting to green purchasing policies and building a sustainable purchasing portfolio is not a task that can be done all at once, but is an exercise made easier and more effective when it is done cooperatively.

25. Solar Communities

Anna Read

Solar energy has received a lot of attention in recent years as communities look for alternatives to fossil fuels and as local governments, homeowners, and businesses look for ways to reduce increasing energy costs and reduce their carbon footprints. Investing in solar power can have a number of benefits for communities, including increasing energy reliability and security, reducing carbon emissions (by up to 23 million metric tons per year by 2030 nationwide), and creating jobs and promoting economic growth (U.S. Department of Energy, 2010).

Most communities in the United States are well situated to harness the power of the sun. As a result, solar power offers communities a clean, reliable, and renewable alternative to fossil fuels.

Solar power also offers another benefit to communities: job creation. The solar industry currently employs some 100,000 people across the country, and the Solar Energy Technologies Program in the Department of Energy (DOE) predicts that the solar industry will add an additional 250,000 jobs (Solar Energy Industries Association, 2010a). Many of the jobs created from increased investment in solar energy are local, including jobs installing and maintaining photovoltaic (PV) systems on homes, offices, and government buildings (see www.solarallianceofamerica.com and www.americansolarworks.com).

Industry Growth

The solar energy industry is growing rapidly. According to the Solar Energy Industries Association, installed solar capacity increased 37 percent, from 351 megawatts (MW) in 2008 to 481 MW in 2009, bringing total installed capacity of PV and concentrating solar power (CSP) to more than 2,000 MW, or enough to power 350,000 homes. Venture capitalists invested over $1.4 billion in the solar industry in 2009 (Solar Energy Industries Association, 2010b).

As installed capacity grew in 2009, the price of PV modules fell by more than 40 percent and the price of installed capacity decreased by more than 10 percent. DOE has indicated that PV and CSP have the potential to reach cost competitiveness with fossil fuels by 2015 (Solar Energy Industries Association, 2010a). As installed capacity increases and prices continue to decrease, solar energy becomes an increasingly viable renewable energy option for American communities.

Originally published as Anna Read (2011). "Solar Communities." *Public Management (PM) Magazine*, 93(2), March 2011. Reprinted with permission of the publisher.

Types of Solar Power

DOE identifies four main types of solar energy technologies:

- Photovoltaic (PV) systems. PV systems are made up of PV cells containing semiconductor materials (usually silicon) that directly convert sunlight into electricity.
- Concentrating solar power (CSP). CSP uses reflective devices, including parabolic trough systems and mirror panels, to convert solar energy into heat. The heat is used to power a steam turbine or heat engine, which generates electricity.
- Solar water-heating systems. Solar water-heating systems contain a solar collector that faces the sun. The collector absorbs energy from the sun and either directly heats the water or heats a "working fluid" that heats the water.
- Transpired solar collectors. Transpired solar collectors, also known as solar walls, use solar energy to preheat ventilation air for buildings.

Solar America Communities Outreach Partnership

ICMA, in partnership with DOE and ICLEI–USA Local Governments for Sustainability, is now working to increase awareness of solar energy and its benefits at the local level. Through the Solar America Communities Outreach Partnership, DOE, ICMA, and ICLEI–USA are working to increase the use and integration of solar energy technologies in communities across the country through a multiyear outreach effort.

Through this partnership, ICMA and ICLEI–USA teams are providing timely and actionable information to local governments, community groups, and other solar energy stakeholders in order to accelerate the adoption of solar energy at the local level. This outreach effort is focusing on three key areas:

- Reducing permitting, interconnection, inspection, and incentive processing time.
- Improving building and zoning codes by updating them to accommodate solar energy.
- Increasing access to local solar financing options.

The partnership is using a mix of educational workshops, peer-to-peer sharing opportunities, and web-based resources that help share best practices among communities. Through these outreach efforts, DOE, ICMA and ICLEI–USA teams, and participating local governments are working together to make solar a mainstream energy resource in U.S. communities by enabling local governments to replicate successful solar practices and quickly expand the adoption of solar energy.

For more information on the partnership and the benefits that communities are seeing from investing in solar energy, visit http://solaramericacommunities.energy.gov. Also on the site are *Solar Powering Your Community: A Guide for Local Governments* and other resources to help your community advance solar energy adoption. To see what other communities are doing, to ask questions, or to share information on solar energy in your community, visit the solar energy topic page on the Knowledge Network at www.icma.org/solar.

Solar America Communities is a DOE program designed to increase the use and integration of solar energy in American communities. ICMA and ICLEI–USA Local Governments for Sustainability were competitively selected by DOE to conduct outreach to local governments in the United States, enabling them to replicate successful solar practices and quickly expand local adoption of solar energy. For more information, visit www.solaramericacommunities.energy.gov.

References

Solar Energy Industries Association. (2010a). "About the Program" in *Solar Energy Technologies Program*. Washington, D.C.: SEIA.

Solar Energy Industries Association. (2010b). *US Solar Industry: Year in Review 2009*. April 15, 2010, Washington, D.C.: SEIA.

26. Privatization of Waste Water Treatment Plant

Ted Volskay

Since 1972, the U.S. Environmental Protection Agency (EPA) Construction Grants Program has invested more than $67 billion in federal funds into publicly owned (wastewater) treatment works (POTW) throughout the country. Congress initiated the phase out of the Construction Grants Program in 1987 and replaced it with the Clean Water State Revolving Fund (SRF) program which provides low-interest loans to communities for the construction of infrastructure projects involving water pollution control. On April 30, 1992, President George H.W. Bush signed Executive Order 12803, directing federal agencies to remove regulatory or procedural barriers to privatizing wastewater POTWs under their control. In addition, Executive Order 12803 required that privatized federally funded POTWs continue to serve their original purposes (EPA-832-B-00-002. Guidance on the Privatization of Federally Funded Wastewater Treatment Works; August 2000).

The first privatization agreement of a POTW under Executive Order 12803 was approved on July 21, 1995, when a private contractor purchased the Franklin, Ohio, POTW for $6.85 million. The Miami Con-servancy District owned and operated the wastewater treatment plant that served the residents of the cities of Franklin (Warren Co.), Germantown and Carlisle (Montgomery Co.), Ohio. The combined population of the three cities was approximately 22,000 (Coxson, 2011).

The contractor that had operated the Franklin Plant under contract since 1987 offered to purchase the POTW in 1992. The transaction took two years of negotiation between the Miami Conservancy District, which owned the POTW, and the private contractor. Subsequent to the negotiations was an eight-month state approval process, followed by a four-month federal (EPA and Office of Management and Budget) approval process. The Office of Management and Budget had to agree to the negotiated transfer price since the sale of assets was not competitively bid (EPA 832-R-97-001a. Response to Congress on Privatization of Wastewater Facilities, U.S. Environmental Protection Agency Office of Water, July 1997).

When agreement was reached on the terms, the City of Franklin, Ohio, became the first municipality in the nation to sell the public asset of a POTW that had been

Originally published as Ted Volskay (2011). "Privatization of Publicly Owned Waste Water Treatment Plant." *League of Women Voters Privatization Study*, Washington, D.C. Reprinted with permission of the publisher.

constructed with federal grant funds and enter into a public/private partnership agreement with the new owner.

Privatization Case Study: Franklin, Ohio, Wastewater Treatment Plant

Governmental Level: City (Franklin, Ohio) and County (Warren and Montgomery Counties)

Primary Privatization Mechanism: Asset Purchase and Operation

The Franklin POTW was accepted by the EPA as a privatization pilot project. Planning and negotiations between Franklin officials and the prospective buyer began in the summer of 1994. On July 14, 1995, the City of Franklin received word that the EPA had completed its final review and authorized sale of the POTW. The transaction was completed within two weeks and the contractor that operated the plant since 1987 purchased the POTW in July 1995 for $6.8 million.

Key to the success of this privatization initiative was 16 months of extensive planning and negotiations. A 20-year service agreement was signed that addresses the following key provisions:

- Unit rates the city will pay for sewage treatment;
- Acceptable conditions for rate increases;
- Operation and maintenance standards;
- Allocation of environmental liability;
- Protocol for prompt conflict resolution; and
- Renewal of the 20-year contract.

The three most pertinent fiscal considerations were the:

- Initial sale price of the plant;
- Annual rate and the amount and timing of any increases to the rate; and
- Repurchase price of the plant at the end of the 20-year contract or, as a

contingency, repurchase of the plant prior to that date.

A consultant with privatization experience was hired to advise and work with the three city managers during the evaluation and negotiation phase. An advisory board was established to represent the interest of the three cities and two counties, and to provide one voice for the buyer to negotiate with.

A matrix was devised that compared economic and noneconomic impacts of three alternatives:

Alternative 1—maintaining public ownership of the plant;

Alternative 2—creating a regional sewer district; and

Alternative 3—privatization.

The Miami Conservancy District retained ownership of the wastewater collection system that directs sewage to the POTW and a small part of the treatment process so that the treatment system could maintain the publicly owned treatment works classification and avoid the more stringent and costly requirements that would otherwise be invoked under the Resource Conservation and Recovery Act (RCRA). Similarly, the Ohio Environmental Protection Agency listed both the contractor and the Miami Conservancy District as being responsible for meeting POTW discharge requirements.

A 20-year agreement was signed that made the private contractor responsible for:

- Financing all plant upgrades and expansions;
- Operation and maintenance of the Wastewater Treatment Plant (WWTP);
- Administration of the municipal industrial pretreatment program.

The agreement gave the Miami Conservancy District the option to repurchase the POTW at the end of the 20-year term.[11] In addition, all plant personnel were retained under the contract.

The city of Franklin's rates for wastewater disposal were reduced by 23 percent during the first year of the contract and, with the exception of energy and chemical costs, future rate increases were limited to increases in the rate of inflation.

The pace of economic development in the area increased after sale of the treatment plant. Stabilized wastewater treatment fees were reportedly a primary incentive for expanding operations of three area paper industries and a subsequent increase in jobs. Increased economic development was closely followed by an expansion of the water distribution system from approximately 4 million gallons per day (gpd) to 10 million gpd.

The City of Franklin, Ohio, entered into its second public/private partnership on November 1, 1997, when it opened a new 5-million-gallon-per-day water supply treatment plant that was designed, built and financed, and is now operated by a private contractor.

Things to Consider

- The EPA must review and approve all proposals to sell POTW assets when Federal grants have been used to construct the treatment works.
- In addition to the EPA, the Office of Management and Budget (OMB) must also review and approve the sale of POTW assets constructed using Federal grants if the transaction price is not established using a full and open competitive bidding process.
- POTWs constructed solely using state revolving loans or local funding may be sold without EPA review or approval.
- EPA review and approval is not required when POTW operations are privatized (subcontracted to a private entity), even if the POTW was constructed using Federal construction grants.

References

Coxson, Samuel L. (2011). "Privatizing wastewater treatment in Franklin, Ohio." Government Finance Review accessed May 2011, http://www.allbusiness.com/finance-insurance/543487-1.html.

27. Enterprise-Wide Computerized Work and Asset Management System

Steve Klepper and *City Manager's Office Team*

In 2000, the City of Corpus Christi, Texas was at risk of utility privatization. Private utility operators were approaching the City Council with promises to reduce costs by over $200,000,000 over a 20-year period, while concurrently maintaining current levels of service.

On two different occasions, the City Council considered motions to immediately initiate Request for Proposals to contract-out all water treatment, water distribution, wastewater treatment, wastewater collection, storm water operations, and utility billing. Twice the City Council voted 4:4 (with ties resulting because at each vote one council person was absent). Because the motion to initiate the "privatization" process did not pass, the City Council directed the City Manager to take necessary actions to make the utilities more competitive. The City Manager initiated a utility re-engineering process with the objectives of reducing costs and improving levels of service to the citizens.

One of the first steps in this "re-engineering" process was to systematically assess existing management systems used in the utilities. At this time, there was no computerized work and asset management system in any City department with the exception of Fleet Maintenance. All citizen calls for service were taken by each department, using their own unique procedures and systems. Citizen calls were recorded on paper, without benefit of established city-wide call-taking or addressing standards. The City lacked the means to spatially analyze work done or work needed. There was little documented and systematic preventative maintenance, and minimal systematic planning of work in any of the utilities. The City lacked clear definition and measurement of actual service levels being provided. For many years the City collected performance measures. However, these measures were an ad hoc compilation, not tied to strategy, and not used for much of anything other than presentation in a budget book.

With the objective of transforming the city utility and public works operations, in 2002, the City of Corpus Christi started implementing a computerized work and asset management system (WAMS), one activity at a time. The idea was not merely

---

Originally published as Steve Klepper and City Manager's Office Team (2009). "Leveraging an Enterprise-Wide Computerized Work and Asset Management System to Improve Service Delivery in all Public Works and Utility Departments." City of Corpus Christi, Texas. TLG Case Study Submission. Icma.org. Reprinted with permission of the publisher.

to impose new technology over existing business practices, but rather to redesign business practices taking advantage of the new technology available.

By 2006, this system is now used to manage work and assets in all of City public works and utility activities: water treatment, water distribution, wastewater treatment, wastewater collection, gas distribution, park operations, street services, solid waste services, airport, and facility maintenance. This same system is also now used by the City's One-Call center to record citizen calls for service and to create work orders.

The City's computerized Work and Asset Management System is now integrated with the geographic information system. As a result, the City has a tool to spatially analyze infrastructure problems and citizen complaints. Maps of the City are routinely produced illustrating by geographical area such things as wastewater back-up calls, complaints of water quality, water main breaks or any other customer call for service. Maps help determine problem areas and are used to develop capital improvement and repair strategies. All traditional assets (e.g., a pipe segment or a manhole) have a unique location code and can therefore be mapped. Each customer is also regarded as a critical "asset" to manage, just as the traditional City assets like pumps, motors, mains and streets. The specific location where wastewater collection or water distribution service is provided is identified by a unique location code assigned to the "service premise" of the customer. These location codes enable the City to produce maps showing locations of complaints and work history.

Data from the Work and Asset Management System (WAMS) is used to help define and improve customer service. In most utility departments "good" customer service is specifically defined and is routinely measured to determine whether goals are being accomplished. Is it easy to assert an objective of "providing excellent customer service in the most efficient and effective manner reasonably possible." However, to provide real value, such statements of philosophy must be accompanied with specifics. The computerized system now provides the framework for the specifics.

The system also supports a City-wide balanced scorecard initiative, where actual real-time performance data for all City departments is displayed on a web site. For all of the utility and public works departments, most of the customer service, work process, and efficiency measures draw from the data available in the computerized Work and Asset Management System.

The City of Corpus Christi is one of the few mid-to-large cities to use a single computerized system to manage work and assets for all public work and utility activities, as well as recording citizen calls for service and creating the work orders for the line departments. While much work remains, the City now has the tools and management systems in place needed to continuously improve levels of service while concurrently monitoring efficiency and controlling costs.

Innovation/Creativity

Question: *How did you encourage creativity in order to generate solutions? How did your program/concept stretch or improve the boundaries of ordinary governmental operations? Were new technologies necessary and what methods and/or applications did you incorporate? Was an outside consultant used? If yes, indicate the level of involvement and identify the firm.*

Response: New technologies were essential to improving levels of service and systematically managing work and assets. A computerized work and asset management system was identified, and then implemented in each of the City's public works and utility departments, one department at a time. Significant work was needed to concurrently analyze existing business practices and consider re-designed practices necessary to achieving cost efficiencies and improving levels of service.

Although an enterprise-wide system was implemented, each department is provided flexibility to adapt the system to meet its own unique needs within the framework of established city-wide standards. One strategy used was to create within each user department a "power user" that understood the detailed work processes and management needs within their respective departments. The role of the Information Technology department is to provide the technical support to these "power users" rather than to drive the system design.

Extensive involvement was provided by EMA, Inc., as an outside consultant to help stand-up the system in each of the departments. Because the City initially lacked the technical expertise to implement the system, during the first year EMA essentially functioned as the IT "system administrator."

Citizen Outcomes

Question: *What customer needs and expectations were identified and fulfilled? How did your initiative improve access to your government? How has the health of your community improved as a result?*

Response: The health of the community has significantly improved because of the focus on providing better customer service. The first step was systematically defining what is meant by "good" customer service and then drawing upon existing data to measure and continuously monitor actual service levels.

This was the approach used in each department, where actually levels of service delivered were not previously well defined or measured. In the Wastewater collection activity, for example, "good" customer service was divided into two aspects: (1) timely response to citizen back-up calls and (2) the degree to which reliable (or continuous) service is provided.

All response and completion time data is an output of our computerized work and asset management system. "Timely" response is now measured by drawing upon information recorded on computerized work orders that record the elapsed time between when a citizen call was received and when the crew arrives. The elapsed time between when the call is received and when the work is completed is also routinely reported. This same approach is being used throughout the City.

"Reliable" service is measured by calculating the percent of customers with no service interruptions during a defined time period. For example, we now know the actual level of continuous wastewater service provided to our customers. During a one year period, 90 percent of all customers were provided continuous wastewater collection service (that is, they reported no back-ups). More than two back-ups were reported by 1.4 percent of customers during the year. These figures are based on distinct location codes, and therefore do not count the same customer more than once. With this information we now have a baseline against which we can benchmark changes over time and measure progress.

Applicable Results and Real World Advice

Question: *What are the applications you could share that would be of value to another local government? What are the results/outcomes? If performance measures were used, please describe those results.*

Response: Data from our system is routinely used to provide more efficient service delivery. For example, our analysis of wastewater back-up calls revealed during a one-year period, 1.4 percent of customers represented 33 percent of wastewater service responses. We now systematically develop repair strategies by focusing first on improving the service reliability to customers experiencing the most frequent problems.

All City utilities are moving towards more systematic planning of work and less reacting to the "crisis of the hour" by increasing over time the relative proportion of planned work and decreasing the reactive unplanned work. This is being accomplished by performing more preventative maintenance on infrastructure such as exercising water valves, flushing "dead-end" water mains, and cleaning wastewater mains known to regularly have blockages and cause service interruptions.

The ability to combine data from GIS and work orders provides a tool to help develop capital improvement strategies for the utilities. All City utilities and public works departments produce maps showing where work is needed and where work is performed. The Wastewater Collection division, for example, is now able to produce maps identifying areas of the city experiencing significant inflow and infiltration problems. We found an almost perfect correlation coefficient of 0.94 between monthly rainfall totals and the average time taken to respond to customer calls for back-ups. One might intuitively assume a high correlation between the number of back-ups calls and rainfall caused by inflow and infiltration. However, we found an extremely low correlation between rainfall and the number citizen back-up calls. This is because of there is a base level of call volume received regardless of rainfall conditions. Maps were then produced to identify those areas of the City with the basic infrastructure problems contributing to wastewater back-up calls even during extremely dry months.

28. Private Works

Robert Barkin

With the clock ticking last fall, Centennial, Colorado, officials had a tough decision to make. For the first time since it incorporated in 2001, the Denver-area city soon would be responsible for its own public works services, which previously were provided by Arapahoe County. City leaders had to make a choice: go it alone or hire out the operation to a contractor.

So, Public Works Director Dave Zelenok opened his spreadsheet and calculated the options. He could either build his department from scratch, buy all the equipment and hire staff, or he could outsource the whole operation to a third-party provider. After running the numbers, he and other city leaders decided to outsource. "I was pleasantly surprised," he says. "The outsource option was competitive against the public sector model in a large city."

On July 1, 2008, Englewood, Colo.–based CH2M HILL OMI began conducting all public works functions for the city of 110,000 residents, from water and wastewater system optimization and operation to community development and public works administration. "This is a turning point," Zelenok says. "Outsourcing has now moved into a major city of over 100,000 people. There's never been a conversion of this size."

Centennial is just the latest city to contract with a private firm to take on traditionally public responsibilities. While Centennial is contracting with a single provider, others have chosen to use a variety of vendors. But in all the cases, cities are motivated to consider the move in an effort to improve service and control costs through competition and reduced overhead. Whether more cities will outsource may depend on economics, community acceptance and potential political opposition.

Picking and Choosing Services

The trend toward outsourcing entire public works departments is more of a trickle than a gusher at this point. While acknowledging that there have been cities that have moved to the private sector model, Dennis Houlihan, a labor economist for the Washington-based American Federation of State, City and Municipal Employees, says that the number has been "tiny" and mostly among smaller communities. Public works remains primarily a municipal department, Houlihan says, because of conflicts between the goals of the private and public organi-

Originally published as Robert Barkin (2008). "Private Works." *American City & County*, 123(8), August 2008. Reprinted with permission of the publisher.

zations and lack of control of the public works function.

However, Richard Norment, executive director of the National Council for Public-Private Partnerships (NCPPP), says the concept of privately run public works departments is attracting increasing interest, nationally and internationally. "This started out popping up here and there," he says, "but now this is a serious emerging trend."

The model for outsourcing public works operations has been around for decades in the Los Angeles area. Lakewood, Calif., has relied on public works services supplied by outsiders for more than 50 years, ever since it incorporated in the early 1950s. Rather than allowing themselves to be annexed by Long Beach, homeowners in the development chose self-government. But that meant the new city could no longer rely on Los Angeles County to supply its services.

Initially, in 1954, the city contracted with the county for all of its services, including law enforcement, fire and public works. By 1957, the city had moved to a "hybrid" arrangement that meshed services from the county and private vendors, says Don Waldie, Lakewood's assistant to the city manager. "We learned early to mix services," he says. "We pick and choose which route is the most efficient and lowest cost. It depends on the character of the work."

The city of 83,000 residents has only 170 employees and a budget of $60 million. Rather than a large work force, the city has 20 people who manage vendor contracts. Waldie says that 25 percent of California cities now are organized following Lakewood's hybrid model. "I can't say whether this is a better way of performing these services or not," he says. "We have always done it this way. It would be impossible to change. We would be another kind of city."

Pleasant Ridge, Mich., a community of about 2,500 residents near Detroit, decided one year ago to end its 10-year public works contract with a single private company to move to a hybrid model that now depends on five different companies and services from neighboring municipalities. The city contracts with nearby Royal Oak for water and sewer services and with Oak Park for its curbside leaf pick-up. For landscaping and tree maintenance, it contracts with a local company. "After working entirely with one company, we realized there are strong areas and weak areas, as any other department under city auspices," says City Manager Sherry Ball. "This way, we have each provider's strong suit. We can capitalize on the best of the best."

Pleasant Ridge has no public works employees or legal costs, no overhead, no equipment or maintenance building; it just has to manage the contracts. The city is discussing with other communities the possibility of regionalizing public works services. "There's no reason not to form more of an alliance and share services," Ball says.

Going Solo

Given the same choice, though, Sandy Springs, Ga., leaders decided to hire a single provider when their city of 90,000 residents incorporated in 2005. Residents had been receiving services as an incorporated area of Fulton County, which includes Atlanta, but decided they could do better on their own.

The city hired one private firm for all city services-everything except police and fire, which the city provides. Since then, other nearby cities, including Johns Creek and Milton, also have adopted the sole-source model. Sandy Springs Mayor Eva Galambos says the ability to work with a single vendor has given the community "more flexibility than working through a civil service system."

One improvement has consolidated all city information on a single database that allows residents to expedite their permits.

An application for a home-owner to build a new deck can take 10 to 15 minutes, instead of the previous three weeks, and business permits are approved much faster. "We're sticking with this model," Galambos says. "It's definitely more efficient."

According to Norment, the Sandy Springs decision to use outsourcing for the whole city was a breakthrough for the model of providing public works services. Previously, he says, cities contracted just for pieces of their operation, like water systems. But difficult times are making cities rethink how they deliver services, he says, noting that renewal rates on contracts for private sector services are more than 95 percent.

In theory, nothing is preventing a much larger city from outsourcing its public works functions, Norment says. "The only impediment is developing the public consensus," he says. NCPPP has developed keys for successful private-public partnerships, and the list includes establishing the laws to allow such an operation, developing a receptive political environment and strong political leadership. "Cities are in a declining revenue stream," because of falling tax revenues, he says. "This allows them to maximize their revenue and maintain control."

Comparing Apples

Maximizing revenue and maintaining control were among the key objectives of Centennial, Colo., leaders as they debated whether to build their own public works department or hire an outside company to perform and manage the city's daily operations. Zelenok, the city's public works director and the key staffer behind the ultimate decision, came to the position from a unique perspective. Previously, as public works director for Colorado Springs, a city with about 375,000 residents, he had managed a department that performed everything from paving streets to operating a local toll road.

When Zelenok joined the city staff, Centennial had about eight months to figure out how to deliver public works services to the community. "I compared a fully burdened in-source model with an outsource model," he says, "and outsource won, but not by a huge amount." In comparing the two formats, Zelenok considered costs such as training, retirement plans and insurance. "Apples to apples," he says.

In the end, other considerations entered into the decision to use the private sector alternative. Zelenok points out that there is now a call center that will respond to residents' questions around the clock, seven days a week.

The final five-year contract, which includes a number of built-in penalties and performance incentives, is worth about $4 million for the second half of 2008 and about $8.6 million in 2009. The city will review the contract annually.

Most importantly, the outsourcing model gives the city more control, Zelenok says. "I don't have to worry about the budget for the next five years," he says.

For Zelenok, the outsource model allows him to spend less time on personnel issues, like hiring and firing, and more time crafting a strategic vision for the city. "It's what I really want to do," he says, "charting a way ahead for the community."

29. Why Wi-Fi? Why Not?

Kevin Fitchard

In 2004, when Philadelphia officials announced plans to build a citywide broadband network using a wireless technology called Wi-Fi, they fired the starter pistol in the race for the title of "Most Unwired City" and challenged the private sector to get in the game. Cities all over the country have since followed the City of Brotherly Love's lead, building wireless networks of their own, and private Internet service providers have become essential team members.

Cities' justifications for building the networks are as varied as the methods for doing so.

Philadelphia started its network to bring broadband into the homes of its poorest residents. Some remote communities view Wi-Fi as an economic development tool to attract and keep industry. Corpus Christi, Texas, has embraced Wi-Fi as a platform for city services, running public safety data networks and municipal applications. Still others see Wi-Fi as a great laboratory in the sky and are either launching or encouraging companies to launch wireless grids as technology test beds open to everyone. Whatever the reasons, the front-running municipal networks have clearly defined goals and operations designed to address community needs.

The Ways of Wi-Fi

While providing broadband Internet service with other wireless technologies is possible, Wi-Fi has particular appeal to cities because the equipment is relatively cheap, and unlike other wireless technologies, such as cellular, an operator does not require a spectrum license to use it.

The Wi-Fi airwaves are free. Even with those inherent cost savings, building a citywide Wi-Fi network can cost millions to tens of millions of dollars in capital investment depending on the size of the city. Implementing Wi-Fi is not a decision any government can make lightly, says Alan Shark, executive director of the Washington-based Public Technology Institute. "A city builds something because it does not exist and there is a public need for it," he says. A city may have broadband infrastructure, but it may not be accessible to everyone who needs it or provided in the ways that they need (i.e., wirelessly). It also may not be affordable to all residents. Those are all legitimate reasons to pursue a public Wi-Fi network or a public-private partnership, he says.

Philadelphia saw its poorest residents being passed by the broadband revolution

Originally published as Kevin Fitchard (2007). "Why Wi-Fi? Why Not?" *American City & County*, 122(3), March 2007. Reprinted with permission of the publisher.

and decided to bridge the digital divide between the rich and Internet savvy and the poor and unconnected. Philadelphia's broadband project is being built by Atlanta-based EarthLink, which is selling Internet accounts commercially directly to customers and wholesale to other ISPs. In exchange for access to Philadelphia's rights of way and utility poles, the company is providing the city discounted access accounts, which the city-created, nonprofit Wireless Philadelphia distributes to the technologically disenfranchised as part of a computer and Internet literacy program.

"EarthLink is building this thing at its own expense," says Greg Goldman, CEO of Wireless Philadelphia. "The mayor and the city just allowed it to happen. Now, it's up to us to do something with that network to address the digital divide. We want to make everyone understand how gaping that divide is in Philadelphia and the rest of the country, and what we can do to close it."

Corpus Christi officials decided to build a Wi-Fi network primarily to automate meter-reading tasks. Although cellular meter reading was available, the city found the cost too high and invested in its own municipally owned Wi-Fi network. It grew to blanket the 147-square-mile city, providing other services like voice over Internet Protocol communications and public broadband access. The city recently agreed to sell its assets to EarthLink.

Vail, Colo., officials opted for a public-private approach in which the local telephone company CenturyTel built a commercial Wi-Fi network with a dedicated spectrum for police and fire departments in exchange for use of the town's rights of way, utility poles and buried fiber-optics grid. Vail will be the anchor tenant of the commercial network, leasing capacity for city workers and city services. Eventually, Vail will share CenturyTel's revenues for commercial operations once construction costs are paid off, says Ron Braden, IT director

for Vail. And, as part of its agreement with the town, CenturyTel will offer Wi-Fi services free for the first hour to anyone who logs on, giving Vail a distinction among other ski resort towns in attracting seasonal visitors, Braden says.

Keeping It Private

Opting to stay out of the municipal Wi-Fi business, some cities are limiting their wireless broadband operations to hotspots on public property and leaving the rest to the private sector. As a high-tech city brimming with young professionals and home to one of the country's largest universities, Austin seems like an ideal candidate for a citywide network. But, city officials have had no inclination to expand on the first public hotspots established in 2002 in public squares, parks and the areas outside of municipal buildings.

There is simply no point for the city to invest in a citywide network when commercial industry has the expertise and willingness to do so, says Austin CIO Pete Collins. Almost every coffee shop in town has free Wi-Fi, and in May 2006, a free network using equipment donated entirely by San Jose, Calif.–based Cisco Systems came online in the southern half of downtown, coinciding with the World Congress of Information Technology held in the convention center. The downtown network serves businesses and visitors in the central business district and provides a test bed for new wireless applications.

Though their services are not free, cellular companies like Sprint, Verizon Wireless and Cingular Wireless have built advanced wireless networks—known as "3G" networks—that offer broadband connectivity well beyond the confines of Austin's public hotspots. And, even where mobility may not be an option, broadband still proliferates: DSL and cable modem connections are readily available from AT&T and Time Warner Cable. "I'm not against technology, I love technology," Collins says, but it is precisely because he loves technology, he adds, that he thinks government should leave it to the private enterprises that know it best.

"If I need broadband coverage for the city and county, it's a $20- to $50-million project, but by the time I actually complete it, a new technology will have come out," Collins says. "Given that this technology is moving at such a fast rate, it would be fiscally irresponsible to build one with taxpayer dollars knowing that once it was built something better would already be available."

Building a Backbone

While Austin is letting the private sector build out a wireless broadband infrastructure, Boston is choosing to construct a public wireless grid that any company or institution could use—just like the city streets. Boston officials are launching a nonprofit organization to build, maintain and run a municipal Wi-Fi network covering all 49 square miles of the densely packed city limits.

The nonprofit will not compete with for-profit Internet service providers, says Nicholas Vantzelfde, a director for Boston-based management consulting firm Altman Vilandrie & Co., the project manager for the city's wireless task force. Rather, it will build the backbone Wi-Fi infrastructure for the city and sell access to any and all comers, including any ISP. "[Wi-Fi is] the ideal technology for an open wireless network, one which encourages entrepreneurism and innovation," Vantzelfde says.

Vantzelfde says the private sector may be better at keeping ahead of the technology curve, but competition would drive most companies to restrict others from accessing their networks or not allow unproven applications from residing on it. By placing the network in the hands of the nonprofit, no application or idea would ever be denied access.

Old Enemies Become Friends

Ironically, the original opponents of citywide Wi-Fi-phone companies who screamed foul at the notion of a city using its tax-exempt status and taxpayer dollars to muscle into their highest growth market-are now some of its biggest supporters. San Antonio–based AT&T and Monroe, La.–based CenturyTel are competing with EarthLink for city contracts.

Companies in the municipal Wi-Fi business have their own reasons for playing ball with cities—they are not in it for civic reasons, says Roberta Wiggins, an analyst for the Boston-based Yankee Group covering the municipal wireless industry. EarthLink, for instance, is trying to build up a critical mass of city contracts so it can bill itself as a nationwide ISP that is not dependent on other companies' broadband lines to do business. AT&T and the other telcoms see citywide Wi-Fi as a way to supplement their existing DSL businesses rather than a DSL alternative, Wiggins says.

As more companies court cities to build and run Wi-Fi networks, local officials are growing spoiled by favorable terms and are sometimes overreaching, Wiggins says. If cities get too greedy, the competitive motivation for companies to enter into partnerships will disappear. "One city put out an RFP that was essentially every other municipal Wi-Fi RFP combined," Wiggins says. "They asked for everything, and they asked for it all for free. They didn't get a single response."

Riverside, Calif., is going for it all. It contracted with AT&T to build a wireless network with a dedicated public safety overlay, free ad-supported Wi-Fi for all residents, municipal applications and even a digital inclusion program giving families making under $45,000 a year discounted broadband service. But, Riverside also has to fork over some of the costs. As part of its deal, it has committed $2 million over the next five years in service fees. Riverside's new Wi-Fi network may not be gratis, but it is getting a lot for a bargain, says Steve Reneker, the city's CIO. "We realized you can't get everything for free."

As more cities join the wireless pack, a bandwagon mentality is developing. "The problem with Wi-Fi is that there are not enough people asking, 'Why?' They are only asking, 'How?'" Shark says. "Many places have pre-determined that they need Wi-Fi. There is an irrational piece to this. They want Wi-Fi because they don't want to be left behind."

How Municipal Wi-Fi Works

Wi-Fi is a globally adopted technology based on a standard called 802.11. That mishmash of numbers contains the core specifications for wireless local area networks around the world, and, consequently, a Wi-Fi-enabled laptop or personal digital assistant will work pretty much any place with a Wi-Fi access point.

The typical Wi-Fi hotspot in the local coffee shop or copy center has a range of only a few hundred feet and uses a wireless router that has to be connected to the Internet through a DSL line or fiber connection. A citywide network, meanwhile, calls for hundreds of access points per square mile, and linking each one of those to a broadband connection is costly. Mesh networks, however, solve that problem by using Wi-Fi routers not only to connect to the end-users' laptops, but also to transmit data between routers. The end result: the mesh network forms an overlapping chain, requiring only one in every several access points to connect to the Internet.

30. Examining Parking Privatization as a Fiscal Solution

David Taxman

Most cities are facing fiscal difficulties and significant budget deficits, and many are instituting hiring freezes or layoffs, delaying or canceling infrastructure projects, or implementing cuts across the board in an effort to improve their situations. Cities are also trying to raise revenues by increasing charges for services, property taxes, and sales taxes. These bailout methods either reduce a city's resources or place a greater financial burden on citizens. However, cities have also begun finding new, creative ways to generate money to finance projects, pay off debt, and secure employee pensions. This has led to numerous cities considering public-private partnerships that involve leasing their on-street or off-street parking assets.

A public-private partnership involves the long-term lease of a city's parking assets to a private operator in exchange for periodic payments, or an upfront lump sum. The private operator receives the revenue generated by the parking system over the course of the lease and is responsible for the management, capital repairs, and maintenance of the parking system. Public-private partnerships are not a new concept in the United States; cities have outsourced the operation and management of toll roads, wastewater management, urban development, utilities, financial management, and the operation of schools.

But the United States has lagged Europe, Australia, and Canada in privatizing parking assets. This is not because of a lack of private investors-large financial investment firms have both available capital and interest in parking investments, viewing them as a safe spot in an otherwise risky market. The question for a city, then, is whether privatizing its parking systems is an effective solution to help raise capital and improve its financial situation.

Making the Decision

In a public-private partnership, a city still has some rights in the management of the parking system. To set the parameters and guidelines of the deal, a concession agreement is designed with input from both the seller (the city) and potential buyers (investment firms or a parking operator). The concession agreement is formulated to

Originally published as David Taxman (2010). "Examining Parking Privatization as a Fiscal Solution." *Government Finance Review*, June 2010. Reprinted with permission of the publisher.

determine points including who will collect enforcement revenue, what happens if meters are removed, and how new meters are installed. Many issues need to be considered, and the city should have a plan that promotes development and allows for checks and balances. Some cities seek a parking consultant to assess future issues that need to be addressed in the concession agreement.

Other than assessing issues that might arise regarding the management of the system, the city should also understand the potential value of the asset before placing it on the auction block. The organization needs to perform the proper due diligence by assessing the system's revenue potential, future capital expenses, and necessary technology upgrades. This helps avoid selling the asset below its market value and short-changing residents—a government needs to understand the full revenue potential of the parking system to insure that it is sold at a fair amount of money. The assessment should consider the following major factors: rate increases, future demand, capital expenses, new revenue collection equipment cost, and elasticity of demand.

The Downside

Even after the value of the parking system has been estimated, a number of pros and cons need to be considered. Cities need to carefully weigh the disadvantages, as well as the advantages. Potential disadvantages of privatizing a city's parking system include: losing the existing parking management labor force, upsetting residents and parkers due to increased parking rates, and losing control of the parking system.

Staff. A private-sector operator might require that its staff operate the system. In that case, the city could require in the concession agreement that all current employees maintain their positions. This stipula-

tion can reduce the overall value of the system, however, since the city employees might have more generous pay and benefits packages than those offered by the private vendor.

Citizens' Concerns. A market analysis of the parking system might reveal a potential to substantially increase the parking rates, in which case the government could experience a backlash from residents. If the parking system being considered for privatization has a monopoly on the market, the city needs to set a rate increase schedule to prevent the private operator from exploiting parkers.

Control. The city needs to feel comfortable with the experience and qualifications of the parking operator. The concession agreement should include language that addresses the city's role in overseeing management of the system and gives the city the power to intervene when necessary.

The Upside

There can also be a number of advantages to parking privatization. These include immediate revenue, the ability to free up capital, and the opportunity to get out of the parking business, which can allow a government to focus on more important issues.

Revenue. The city receives an upfront, lump sum payment that can be used for government projects and programs. This payment can also be used to address the city's current debt, although governments will want to be careful about using this money for a one-time budget fix. In addition, the buyer's bid will be based on an aggressive rate schedule; this proposed rate schedule may be unrealized revenue for the city, as it is can be difficult for a government to pass parking rate increases.

Freeing up Capital. The city can use a parking privatization agreement to free up capital and make the private operator responsible for capital repairs to the aging infrastructure (off-street facilities), and for installing a newer revenue collection technology (on-street and off-street parking). Updating the on-street revenue collection equipment to support multiple payment options is necessary once parking rates are increased to more than a dollar an hour, as single space meters become obsolete and inefficient. Once the lease has expired, the city then receives a parking system that has upgraded revenue collection technology and parking rates that are aggressively aligned with the market. The city has also hedged the risk involved with operating a revenue system that could potentially become obsolete or less-used due to increased public transportation ridership, high gas prices, or even the trend toward more free parking facilities.

Business Focus. Privatizing a city's parking system allows the government to get out of the parking business and instead allow a specialized private operator to handle the system. A private operator does not manage other public assets; it is specifically concerned with managing the parking system effectively and providing upgraded amenities and customer service. Freeing the city from managing the entire parking system will also allow it to concentrate on other programs and assets that might be of more strategic importance. Also, the monies they receive from privatization could be utilized in financing more vital programs.

The City of Chicago

The City of Chicago, Illinois, considered the benefits and disadvantages of privatizing parking and decided to lease both its 36,000 metered spaces and four Grant Park/Millennium Park garages. The city received $1.15 billion dollars for the 75-year lease of the meters and $563 million for a 99-year

lease of the garages. The money received from these deals has been used to pay off debt associated with building Millennium Park, improving the infrastructure of neighborhood parks, funding programs for low-income residents, settling budget deficits, and establishing a long-term reserve fund.

Privatizing the Grant Park/Millennium Park garages allows Chicago to avoid capital repairs. Before bidding, the investment firms in the Chicago deal hired consultants to conduct a conditions assessment of the garages and determine future costs associated with maintaining the structural and architectural integrity and the mechanical, electrical, and fire protection maintenance costs. Based on the city's consultant, the estimated cost to renovate the East Monroe Garage alone would have been more than $63 million dollars. In addition, significant costs could be anticipated for ongoing maintenance and repair of the other parking facilities, even though they had been recently constructed or renovated. Underground garages typically require substantial capital expenses associated with replacement of the membranes and concrete slabs, and other recurring repairs over a 99-year period. Maintaining these garages would have become a significant financial burden on the city. Leasing the garages allowed Chicago to place the repair obligations on the private operator and free up capital for other projects.

The main lesson learned from the privatization of the Chicago metered parking system was that governments must have an effective process in place to introduce users to new rates, hours of operation, and revenue collection technology. Also, the parking operators must have adequate revenue collection technology in place to support the new hourly rates. Chicago's parking meter rates were quickly increased from twenty-five cents an hour to a dollar an hour in many neighborhoods, but many of the single space meters could not effectively support the quantity of coins placed in them, and the operator underestimated the resources required to make timely collections. This led to jammed meters and people receiving tickets for parking at inoperable meters. There were also issues with the incorrect labeling of the hours of operation and parking rates. Overall, this became a public relations liability that gave residents a negative opinion of the privatization of the meters. These issues have mostly been corrected, but cities can avoid these problems by putting an effective implementation process in place before making changes.

Conclusion

Since Chicago has privatized its parking system, a number of other cities—including Los Angeles, California; Harrisburg, Pennsylvania; Pittsburgh, Pennsylvania; San Francisco, California; and Indianapolis, Indiana—have started evaluating privatization of some or all of their on-street and off-street parking systems. It is a viable option to generate immediate capital, but cities need to weigh the pros and cons before making a decision.

31. Determining the Role of P3: Building Inspections

Kyle Steitz

Imagine that you are a child selling lemonade in your neighborhood. During the summer months, when business is good, you have a hard time finding enough staff to keep up with the demand. Your current staff is overworked, taking extra trips to the store to buy supplies, squeeze the extra lemons, and deal with longer lines. As a result, the quality of your lemonade is suffering. Worse yet, several of the neighbors have filed complaints about the customer service at your stand. If you hired additional staff, you would have little for them to do during colder months and you don't want to deal with letting anyone go. This fluctuation makes staffing difficult and you find yourself running at a substantial financial deficit while you wait for the warmer months to return.

Now imagine that there was an opportunity to bring in a group of neighborhood kids you could partner with to increase production capacity and help with customer service, only when you needed them—or if by working with lemonade experts, they could introduce you to equipment that would make your stand more efficient. It would still be your stand, but the extra help gives you more time to focus on what your staff does best.

For a kid's lemonade stand, this kind of outsourcing is pretty obviously a good idea. Other kinds of outsourcing are a bit more complex. Still, the ideology and concept behind this analogy is useful when approaching the way a jurisdiction's building department operates.

Defining Privatization

Historically, public-private partnership (P3) agreements have been focused on economic development projects proposed by developers who are looking for financial assistance from a jurisdiction that stands to benefit from the project. But these agreements have evolved to include a wide range of potential uses, and the term "P3" now implies any agreement that involves a contract between the public sector and the private sector that has the private sector providing public services or public benefits.

Governments that are considering a P3 need to fully understand the risks and long-term financial implications. When deciding

Originally published as Kyle Steitz (2014). "Determining the Role of P3s." *Government Finance Review*, 30(4), August 2014. Reprinted with permission of the publisher.

to move forward with a P3 deal that is in the best interest of the public, a number of general considerations need to be evaluated. Some of these are generally applicable to all such contracts, such as the need for public participation, sound financial negotiations, and monitoring of performance and results. Others concern issues specific to P3s: preliminary evaluation, retaining advisors or experts, economic and fiscal impact analysis, service level implications, and risk assessment.

Evaluating the Options

P3s are a tool that can be effective when used well and ineffective when used incorrectly. Many communities have relied on contracted providers for services such as solid waste collection and disposal, street repairs, and utilities for years, and with the budgetary issues many local governments still face after the Great Recession, communities are evaluating whether it makes sense to privatize or use alternative delivery options for other services as well.

The GFOA has recognized that the need to provide cost-effective options while maintaining expected levels of service can cause governments to search for alternative service delivery options, and that with the proper research and due diligence, it can provide numerous advantages. Benefits can include service improvements, a reduction or transfer of risk, a means of accommodating fluctuating seasonal peak demands, access to outside expertise, and new insight into innovations. Entering into a P3 can mean having the right numbers of employees, with the right expertise, when you need them. Outlining clear performance metrics in the contract allows a government to make sure that quality thresholds and expectations are met, including outstanding customer service.

The New Jersey Privatization Task Force published a report in May 2010, concluding that "through sensible planning and implementation, privatization offers a variety of benefits to governments and taxpayers, including lower costs, improvements in the quality of public services, and access to private-sector capital and professional expertise." The task force noted numerous examples of projects that were done well, but it also gave examples of failures. The issues were similar for each of these unsuccessful initiatives: poor conception, unclear goals, superficial due diligence, inexperienced and/or undercapitalized contractors, lax oversight, and, on occasion, conflicts of interest. Other significant concerns are the possibilities of creating monopolies, of situations that are counter to the public interest (for example, if important services like health care are sold off and the private entity cuts back on them because of the cost), and opportunity cost.

To ensure that P3s work in the best interest of all parties, governments need to go into any such deal with a thorough understanding of the potential cost savings, service quality improvements, and most importantly, risks. One of the most important safeguards is to effectively manage the process, continually evaluating performance to ensure that P3 deals are performed consistently, according the government's carefully considered policies, and followed by the private agent. This includes requiring a firm business case and a rigorous cost-benefit analysis for any proposed P3. Effective management and monitoring includes continued communication and reporting with interested parties throughout the privatization process. Governments need to consult best practices regarding project analysis, vendor selection, contracting, and performance monitoring and oversight.

P3 in Troy, Michigan

One potential outcome of a well-executed P3 program, and the focal point of this case study, is cost savings. Financial savings are often realized through economies of scale, access to cutting-edge technology the government wouldn't have been able to afford or support on its own, innovations, or simply a different way of completing the job. Reduced labor costs can also help a jurisdiction better manage its financial burdens. Following is an example of a community that privatized its building department services—a change more and more jurisdictions are considering.

The changes saved the building inspections budget $1 million in fiscal 2010-11, the first year of the P3 contract. The City of Troy, Michigan, is the largest city in Oakland County, with a population of 82,212. Before 2010, Troy's building services department was not meeting its budget; the city's comprehensive.

The annual financial report from June 30, 2010, reported a cumulative shortfall of $6.6 million, caused by years of increases in employee costs, pensions, and related operational costs. Troy had grown quite a bit in previous years, and that expansion had required additional full-time staff, all union positions. When the economy and construction slowed, staffing could not be adjusted in the same timely manner, so the city was now overstaffed. The situation was not sustainable for the long term.

Recognizing that there were areas where improvements could be made, city officials hired a consulting service that specializes in the areas of municipal organization, management, and process analysis to evaluate all departments and make recommendations. The consulting company suggested a number of options for the building services department, and city officials decided to hire a private firm to run the building inspections department.

The private firm manages the daily operations of the building department, performs inspections, plan reviews, staffs the front counter, archives city records, and works with city officials on departmental budget. The firm also works with the economic development department to encourage growth and promote business opportunities within the community. In return, the firm receives a percentage of the city's permit fees.

An important concern for any government entering into a P3 agreement is making sure the contract contains performance measures to ensure the jurisdiction remains in control. In this case, the primary measure for gauging the effectiveness of the private firm's systems and the efficiency of its staff is review and inspection of turnaround times, which are tracked and reported on monthly in a format agreed to by the city's staff. Additional techniques include customer satisfaction surveys and community meetings/educational seminars. Staff members provided by the firm are an extension of the city's staff, so the contract includes a clause allowing the jurisdiction to terminate the agreement with cause. The firm is responsible for fixing the situation if Troy is unhappy with the performance or general personality of any individual.

The private firm also introduced process improvements, creating efficiencies—a benefit that could be achieved without the private firm's involvement with the city. For example, reconfiguring the department's office space within city hall has improved its workflow to the point that it is now using half the square footage to accomplish the same amount of work. Thousands of paper records were scanned for more efficient archiving and retrieval. Inspectors were equipped with wireless laptops so they could access and enter information in the field.

Conclusions

While the lemonade stand run by the neighborhood children may not actually be turning to privatization, jurisdictions across the country are finding P3s an effective and efficient way of dealing with financial challenges. P3s are certainly not for everyone, but many organizations could potentially benefit from asking themselves if there is a better way to operate. When done correctly, P3s can be a tool for improving service levels, realizing cost savings, and dealing with fluctuating activity levels and demands.

32. Arts Mean Economic Revitalization

Robert Lynch

Picture a perfect evening out. You jump in your car and head downtown to go see the regional theater's latest production. Before the show begins, you pay to park your car in a municipal garage and take advantage of a pre-theater dinner menu at a local restaurant.

Then you walk to the show, possibly making a stop along the way to shop when a local storefront catches your eye, and you proceed on to enjoy the performance. Afterward, you're not quite ready to end the night so you drop into a nearby restaurant for coffee and dessert. Depending upon how far you drove from home, you might even spend the night in a local hotel.

Sounds like a wonderful evening, right? If you're a local government manager, it also sounds like a great night for your local economy. This scenario is a fairly typical description of what happens when arts patrons attend cultural events. As it illustrates, the investments made in local nonprofit arts and culture organizations provide tremendous support to other sectors of the local economy. Arts and culture organizations leverage additional event-related spending by their audiences that pumps revenue into the local economy.

Any time that money changes hands, there is a measurable economic impact. Americans for the Arts' latest report Arts & Economic Prosperity IV studied the economic impact of nonprofit arts and culture organizations in communities across the United States, representing all Southern states and the District of Columbia.

Survey data was collected from 9,721 organizations and 151,802 of their event attendees. According to the study, the nonprofit arts and culture industry generated $135.2 billion dollars of economic activity—$61.1 billion in spending by nonprofit arts and culture organizations, plus an additional $74.1 billion in spending by their audiences, resulting in $22.3 billion in revenue to local, state, and federal governments. This is a yield well beyond their collective $4 billion in arts appropriations. It is estimated that 25 to 30 percent of this pie is local governments' appropriations.

What makes the economic impact of arts and culture organizations unique is that, unlike many other industries, they induce large amounts of event-related spending by

Originally published as Robert Lynch (2013). "Arts Mean Economic Revitalization." *Public Management (PM) Magazine*, 95(2), March 2013. Reprinted with permission of the publisher.

their audiences. Local merchants reap the benefits of your city's investment in the arts. In fact, the typical arts attendee spends $24.60 per person, per event, beyond the cost of admission on meals, local ground transportation, shopping and souvenirs, overnight lodging, and even babysitting.

Arts organizations fundamentally support locally based businesses. They operate as small businesses, employ people locally, and purchase goods, which can be grown locally.

A Story of Revitalization

Most everyone is familiar with the Louisville Slugger Factory and Museum in Louisville, Kentucky. But, what you might not know is how the factory came to its current location at 800 W Main Street in downtown Louisville. Going back 20 years, Main Street was composed of empty storefronts and run-down businesses and contributed little to the city's tax base.

Then something transformational occurred. A small theater decided to open on Main Street, likely because the rent was so cheap. Then a small coffee house opened, and restaurants and art galleries soon followed. Eventually, Louisville Slugger moved from across the river to Main Street, and it now serves as an anchor for what is known as "Gallery Row." Currently, Gallery Row generates hundreds of thousands of dollars in tax revenues for the city, and it all started because a little theater moved in.

This story has repeated itself countless times across the country. Businesses, especially those in the service arena, are drawn to neighborhoods where the arts are happening. Local government managers know that the arts and culture are great for economic revitalization.

Paducah, Kentucky, took this concept to the next level by actually using the arts and culture as the centerpiece of a program designed to revitalize an entire area of that city. The Artist Relocation Program uses city funds combined with strong public partnerships with local businesses and banks to create incentives for artists to move into the city.

Benefits to relocating artists include financial incentives, lower-than-market interest rates, discounts on all closing costs, and a full array of products and services. Business incentives include free lots for new construction; free web page and other joint marketing programs and promotional options; and preservation tax incentives.

As a result of this program, the neighborhood has been transformed from dilapidated housing and warehouses to an area that is now a hot spot to live in the city. In addition to artists, other professionals have moved in, cementing the program's success.

Not only are your own residents attracted to the arts and cultural events in your area, but visitors from other regions are, too. Communities that draw cultural tourists experience an additional boost of economic activity. After all, no one travels to simply stay at a hotel; they travel to attend an event, view an attraction, or participate in an activity.

Case Study

Wichita, Kansas, is one of the 50 largest cities in America with a population of nearly 400,000 and a regional draw of 800,000. Known as the "Aviation Capital of the World," 60 percent of all general aviation manufacturing occurs here. Most people are unaware, however, that Wichita has another economic powerhouse: the arts industry.

Wichita was one of 186 cities included in the Americans for the Arts' Arts & Economic Prosperity IV study. It revealed that the arts in Wichita generate $66.2 million in economic activity and support 2,006 jobs.

The arts are a business in Wichita, and there's no better example than Disney's *The Lion King*. This touring Broadway show sold 60,000 tickets over a four-week run in September 2012, generating $4.3 million. Forty-three percent of ticket buyers were from outside Wichita.

The arts are so important to Wichita that we are considering the creation of an art district, to nurture and grow our cultural community.

Look at the Numbers

In fact, 32 percent of arts attendees live outside the county in which the arts event takes place. Why are they there? Nearly 60 percent of nonlocal arts attendees report that the primary reason for their trip was specifically to attend that arts event.

And, their event-related spending is more than twice that of local attendees ($39.96 versus $17.42). Arts and culture organizations provide these types of opportunities, which in turn attract and promote other business interests such as the hospitality industry.

Cultural tourism is an important piece of your economy. According to the U.S. Travel Association and the U.S Department of Commerce, research has consistently shown that arts tourists stay longer, spend more than the average traveler, are more likely to spend $1,000 or more, and are more likely to stay in a hotel or other lodging.

Among "nonlocal" arts attendees, nearly 30 percent spent at least one night away from home in the community where the cultural event took place. With those "heads in beds," the cash registers are ringing-those overnight attendees spent an average of $170.58 per person. A vibrant arts community not only keeps residents and their discretionary spending close to home, but it also attracts visitors who spend money and help local businesses thrive.

One might think that tourism is only a factor for the big communities with attractions like Disney World or the Grand Canyon. But savvy managers know that tourists actively seek out events in every state and in every size city or county. More times than not, especially in small towns, these tourists are there solely for some arts or cultural event, which greatly adds to tax revenues.

Just look to New Orleans, where jazz and the culinary arts draw hundreds of thousands of visitors annually. Furthermore, New Orleans and many of the smaller towns in Louisiana realized it was a smart move to use the arts and culture as a rebuilding tool after Hurricane Katrina.

Takeaways

- Arts and culture organizations, unlike other industries, induce event_related spending.
- Arts and cultural organizations can assist in the revitalization of blighted areas.
- Cities benefit when they can attract cultural tourists who stay longer and spend more money.

33. Retirees: A New Economic Development Strategy

Christen Smith

A promising future clean-growth industry is advancing economic development in communities across the country. All forecasts indicate that the industry will offer significant short- and long-term growth. The industry: retirees.

Communities that provide a high quality of life, including broad-based, innovative park and recreation opportunities for their residents age 50-plus, are attracting seniors to relocate to their communities for retirement, and these migrating seniors are providing a significant stimulus to their local economies.

How much value do retirees add to a local economy? A quick glance at the numbers demonstrates the revenue potential. If 25 retiree households with an average annual household spending of $40,000 per household move into a community next year, the resulting economic impact of those households on the community would be an estimated $1,000,000 per year.

From the perspective of economic development investments, targeting recruitment efforts on retirees rather than corporations has a number of major advantages. Retirees do not require economic incentive packages to attract them to relocate. Capital improvements, such as remodeling to enhance accessibility of public buildings that take place as a part of a retiree recruitment effort are likely to focus on community support services that also benefit existing residents.

Retirees' incomes from Social Security and pensions are stable and are not subject to the fluctuations that are experienced in the business cycles. A recent survey found that more than half of 60-year-olds are revamping their retirement plans due to the recent downturn in the economy. While these pre-retirees may be delaying their retirement dates, people continue to anticipate that they will retire.

Although the retirees' income sources are outside the community, a significant portion of their expenditures are local and directly benefit the local economy. Further, retirees are likely to transfer significant assets into local investment and banking institutions.

Retirees increase the local tax base, and they tend to be contributing taxpayers. Their taxes can be expected to support services they will not use. Seniors, for example, are not likely to enroll children in the school

Originally published as Christen Smith (2009). "Retirees: A New Economic Development Strategy." *Public Management (PM) Magazine*, 91(4), May 2009. Reprinted with permission of the publisher.

system or strain the local criminal justice system.

Retirees often become a rich pool of volunteers in the community. The average value of an active adult volunteer is nearly $20 per hour. More than half (51 percent) of baby boomers say they expect to devote more time to community service or volunteering after retirement.

When boomers were asked to identify the community services and programs that they currently use and that they will want to use more in their future retirement years, they identified four categories of services: social, cultural, and leisure activities; parks and recreational services and facilities; senior-designed community and social services; and education and library services.

The population projections for 2010 to 2030 indicate that younger seniors, those ages 50 to 75, will migrate to Las Vegas, Denver, Dallas, and Atlanta—communities that have traditionally been recognized for their youthful profiles. Smaller, non-metropolitan areas are also experiencing rapid senior growth, including Santa Fe, New Mexico; Bend, Oregon; Coeur d'Alene, Idaho; St. George, Utah; Olympia, Washington; and Loveland, Colorado. These choices indicate that factors other than climate are involved in decisions about retirement destinations.

Younger, more affluent retirees are migrating to areas that are rich in amenities, and community services are prominent among the amenities that are attracting them. The availability of these opportunities in the community is second only to family location as factors influencing retirees' decisions about where to live during their retirement years.

Enhancing local social, cultural, and leisure activities, parks and recreational services and facilities, and education and library services for adults over age 50 is an economic development strategy that will result in a high rate of return on the community's investments.

Resources

"Baby Boomers Envision Retirement II: Key Findings." Washington, D.C.: RoperASW for AARP, May 2004.

Crompton, John L. (2007). *Community Benefits and Repositioning: The Keys to Parks and Recreation's Future Visibility*. Ashburn, Va.: National Recreation and Park Association, 2007.

Frey, William H. (2007). *Mapping the Growth of Older America: Seniors and Boomers in the Early 21st Century* (Living Cities Census Series). Washington, D.C.: Brookings Institution.

"How Well Do You Know Boomers? Counting Down the Top 10 Boomer Myths." Washington, D.C.: Focalyst Insight Report for AARP, 2008.

34. Social Impact of Bonds to Fund Human Services

Charles Taylor

Two counties more than 2,100 miles apart—Santa Clara County, California, and Cuyahoga County, Ohio—are among the first counties in the nation to explore a new financing model to address some of their thorniest social problems.

The Santa Clara County, California, Board of Supervisors recently voted to put financial skin in the game, allocating $75,000 toward hiring a consultant to structure two Pay for Success pilots aimed at improving services and outcomes for the mentally ill and homeless populations. It's the county's share of $225,000, the balance of which will be paid by foundations and non-profits.

Pay for Success uses performance-based contracting to address human services needs that typically are the responsibility of government by securing up-front funding from philanthropic investors. It's also known as social impact financing or, commonly, social impact bonds (SIB). Investors are repaid only if predetermined targeted outcomes are achieved-as judged by an independent evaluator.

"We determined not only did it make enough sense on paper, but there was enough of a start in a couple of other places that we're not completely alone in this," said Dave Cortese, the Santa Clara County supervisor who has been one of the leading proponents of pay for success.

Cuyahoga County is evaluating responses from agencies and organizations interested in partnering with the county on Pay for Success projects and is close to announcing which social issues are to be addressed, according to David Merriman, the county's deputy chief of staff for health and human services. The Santa Barbara County, Calif. Board of Supervisors recently approved a feasibility study of a pilot program to reduce recidivism.

The largest-scale SIB project to date, started in 2010 at Peterborough Prison near London in the United Kingdom, targets recidivism. Early results have shown a slight drop in reconvictions of released short-term inmates, according to a U.K. Ministry of Justice report. Social Finance UK, which is managing the pilot, said the first data for evaluation of the pilot is expected in early 2014.

"Because the concept of SIBs is so new … information about how—and how well—

Originally published as Charles Taylor (2013). "Counties Eye Social Impact of Bonds to Fund Human Services Needs." *NACo County News*, 45(19), October 7, 2013. Reprinted with permission of the publisher.

they could work is currently very limited," according to a May 2012 report by McKinsey & Company, From Potential to Action: Bringing Social Impact Bonds to the U.S., which analyzed the feasibility and potential of SIBs.

Despite the newness of SIBs, the counties interviewed for this chapter see enough potential-with little risk to themselves—to try this prevention-based approach to social problems.

George Graves, Santa Clara County's chief operating officer, said if there is risk, it appears to be minimal. "I don't know that I'd describe it as a risk other than the $75,000 that we're putting up," he said. "I think that at this point in time, considering the economic circumstances, I think it's our responsibility to fully explore any option that has the potential of bringing resources to address the kinds of problems we're talking about, whether they are homelessness or recidivism or how to better provide options for step-down [mental health] services."

Cuyahoga County was also approached by the local philanthropic community with a concept that fit into County Executive Ed FitzGerald's new results-oriented approach to county government. The George Gund Foundation is supporting the work in Cuyahoga County.

Caroline Whistler is a co-founder of Third Sector Capital Partners, Boston-based consultants working with Cuyahoga and Santa Clara to help structure their pilots. "In some cases, nonprofits are absolutely driving this," she said, "but it's also something that private foundations are pushing forward as well as, in some cases, governments themselves."

Third Sector is serving as what's known in SIB parlance as an "intermediary." The role varies, according to Rebecca Leventhal of Social Finance U.S., another social finance consultant and sister organization Social Finance UK. Intermediaries work with governments on social impact pilots in roles that range from identifying potential funders and evaluating which social issues to tackle, to structuring the financing and choosing agencies to provide services.

Though Graves is a bit skeptical about the county's realizing "cashable" savings through pay for success pilots, he said there may be value if service providers who receive social innovation funding can achieve desired outcomes more quickly or at no greater cost than if there county were providing the service. Cortese, the Santa Clara supervisor, agrees.

"The good news is that we're structuring these two pilot projects, and that's exactly what they are, let's see if they work," he said. "These are the ones that are the lowest hanging fruit. And it's going to get harder from here on out in terms of finding projects where we can really expect to see any kind of savings to be shared."

How "Pay for Success" Works

Santa Clara County, Calif. provided the following example of how a Pay for Success might be structured:

- A foundation or private investor agrees, for example, to pay upfront $100,000 to contract with a nonprofit or community organization for health services for homeless individuals and families.
- The contract spells out outcomes that must be reached before the county reimburses the investor or foundation. For example, the nonprofit must provide basic health care for 100 clients in a year.
- A health clinic is set up and the nonprofit works with other agencies and nonprofits that help the homeless to bring in clients to receive the care.

- The county pays only when outcomes are reached as determined and evaluated by an independent partner. The investor or foundation recovers the $100,000 with interest, or reinvests it in the program so more homeless can receive health care.

35. Public Library Privatization

Muriel Strand

Public libraries are caught in the wake of budget meltdowns at all levels of government. Previously, relatively few libraries have privatized certain functions, whether temporarily or permanently. But with revenues declining, more jurisdictions have recently considered subcontracting certain, usually limited, library tasks to the private sector, notably Library Systems & Services, LLC (LSSI) (Streitfeld, 2010). Library Associates Companies (LAC Group), Informational International Associates, and Book Wholesalers, Inc. (BWI), are other possible vendors, but public libraries seem less aware of them.

LSSI got their start in 1981, with the Library of Congress and other government agencies. "Founded by library professionals," it is nonetheless a privately-held, for-profit limited liability corporation. Islington Capital Partners is the private equity investor that offers them access to additional capital, allowing LSSI to grow their operations quickly, and to keep up with the information technology that appears to be one of their strong points.

Over the decades, LSSI has contracted with a number of local libraries across the nation, with results that seem to have been generally agreeable and convenient. Of the handful of libraries which have terminated contracts with LSSI, one library director said it was a combination of LSSI accounts-payable tardiness and the local library board feeling sufficiently recovered from an ineffective library director who was the reason for LSSI's presence in the first place. Another system's library director said LSSI had been brought in to help a branch of the Los Angeles County Library become an independent city library, and after the new library was stable the city took over. The long-term LSSI staff, who had been working there, was able to become city staff and acquired pension benefits.

However, California State legislative staff refers to several instances when local governments (in Linden, NJ, Fargo, ND, and Hemet, CA) decided it would be cheaper to bring the work back in house. Decisions about fines and fees, handling cash and acquisitions all require more responsibility and accountability, no matter who performs them (privatizationbeast.org/2011/02/28/the-beasts-business-model-what-it-means-for-your-library).

Public libraries in Jackson County, Oregon, which had been closed due to budget constraints were reopened recently under LSSI contracts. The city of Santa Clarita,

Originally published as Muriel Strand (2011). "Public Library Privatization—A Case Study." *League of Women Voters: Privatization of Government Services, Assets and Functions Study*, Washington, D.C. Reprinted with permission of the publisher.

with three libraries, decided to subcontract various operations to LSSI rather than continuing to participate in the LA county library system, and by some accounts is now offering more to readers (www.ameri canlibrariesmagazine.org/news/07272011).

At the time of the actual changeover, their contract with LSSI was publicly posted on their website: www.santaclaritalibrary. com. According to California legislative staff, Santa Clarita has budgeted $8 million to $12 million for transition costs.

Riverside County, CA, Library decided to contract with LSSI to operate the library, while reserving the right to set policies, rather than continue as a subset of the Riverside City Library (Christmas, 2010).

Recent tentative proposals to bring in LSSI as a way to buffer budget cuts have caused concerns and have been rebuffed in several places, including Stockton, California (Johnson and Siders, 2010; Johnson, 2010; Goldberg, 2011). However, the issue of public pensions and unions, while very important, is not the same issue as the independence and accountability of local libraries, and the protection of free speech. Grappling with the former issue is more difficult when people believe the latter may be threatened thereby, so calmness and clarity are crucial.

In California, legislation that would raise the bar for local cities and counties wishing to contract with companies like LSSI is in a state senate committee as of June 2011. Libraries which decide to privatize would be responsible for financial audits. Previous legislation allowed existing California local library systems to retain the per-capita library revenues from property taxes when a portion of the system seceded, rather than requiring the per-capita money to go with the seceding population. The requirements in Assembly Bill (AB) 438 would apply to nonprofits, mostly because many for-profits have nonprofit associates.

REFERENCES

Christmas, Gary (2010). "The Riverside County Library System: Thirteen Years of Innovation, Experimentation, and Progress." http://www.countyofriverside.us/export/sites/default/government/docs/Library_White_Paper_June_17_2010.pdf.

Goldberg, Beverly. (2011). "Privatization-and Pushback-Proceed in Santa Clarita." *American Libraries Magazine*, July 27, 2011. www.afscmeinfocenter.org/privatizationupdate/library/.

Johnson, Zachary K. (2010). "Details released on library proposal." www.recordnet.com/apps/pbcs.dll/article?AID=/20100814/A_NEWS/8140319&cid=sitesearch. August 14, 2010.

Johnson, Zachary K., and David Siders. (2010). "Officials consider privatizing libraries to cut costs." www.recordnet.com/apps/pbcs.dll/article?AID=/20100413/A_NEWS/4130324&cid=sitesearch. April 13, 2010.

Streitfeld, David. (2010). "Anger as a Private Company Takes Over Libraries." *New York Times*, September 26. 2010.

36. Does Government Work Require Government Employees?

John Buntin

"Stop! Taser, Taser, Taser!"

Triggers pull, nitrogen canisters pop and barbed darts clatter against body silhouettes taped to a wall. If the silhouettes had been people, five-second pulses of electrical current would have flowed into their bodies, toppling most of them to the ground.

"Don't aim too close to the heart," says Sgt. Jeremy Floyd. If someone's coming at you, he says, shoot for the lower abdomen.

Floyd, the training instructor at a Wednesday evening Taser recertification class in Redlands, Calif., is sharing the fine points of stun gun use with a small group of men and women, all of them outfitted in blue trousers and white shirts with police badges. The badges identify them as members of the Redlands Police Department, but things are not what they seem. For starters, Taser target practice isn't taking place at a police firing range. It's happening on the porch of the Joslyn Senior Center. And in a state where many sworn law enforcement officers retire in their 50s, most of these officers look, well, older. White hair is the norm here rather than the exception. There are other oddities, too. Police department physical fitness requirements often exclude individuals with disabilities, yet one of the men is firing from a motorized wheelchair.

That said, the men and women gathered on the porch are members of the Redlands Police Department, as their badges denote. But they are not sworn or paid officers. They're volunteers, part of the city's Citizen Volunteer Patrol (CVP) unit. And they're at the forefront of the one of the country's more ambitious efforts to integrate volunteers into the workings of local government.

At a time when most city and local governments are preparing to do less with less, officials in Redlands are taking a different approach: They're attempting to maintain current levels of service through other means. Ramping up the use of volunteers is one of them.

It's easy to see why. Three years ago, the police department in Redlands, a city of 71,000 people east of Los Angeles, had 98 sworn officers, 208 civilians and about two dozen volunteers. The police budget was $23.8 million, nearly half of the city's operating budget. Today, the department employs 75 sworn officers and 138 civilians and relies on 291 active volunteers, who last year

---

Originally published as John Buntin (2011). "Does Government Work Require Government Employees?" *Governing*, April 2011. Reprinted with permission of the publisher.

contributed more than 31,000 hours of their time to the city.

The volunteers are not just answering the phones at police headquarters. They cordon off crime scenes, direct traffic, patrol the city's 14 parks, write parking tickets, assist with animal control and provide crowd control at special events. They are also trained to check in parolees, assist with records processing, help staff DUI checkpoints, take reports on routine property crimes, serve as the liaison with the local San Bernardino County district attorney's office, provide counseling to crime victims and monitor sex offenders remotely. In addition, they serve more traditional functions as volunteer reserve officers. Two volunteer reserve officers even conduct investigations alongside the city's detectives. One has his own caseload. Some of the volunteers—those who go through the special training session—are allowed to carry Taser guns for their own protection.

It isn't just the police department that's assigned volunteers to important duties. Eighteen months ago, when Les Jolly took over the city's Quality of Life Department, he started to develop a program that will soon field volunteer code inspectors. "Our staff was cut by over 10 percent this fiscal year," Jolly says. "If you don't think of creative ways to supplement what you do, then you are going to fail." Redlands also employs a part-time volunteer coordinator, Tabetha Johnson, who routinely works with local civic clubs to mobilize hundreds of volunteers for events such as Redlands' annual professional bicycle race.

"We have fewer resources," says City Manager N. Enrique Martinez. "We had to cut staff. My challenge is to maintain the same service level if not better. The public is not interested in whether you have 15 fewer people than before or not."

Nor should they be. At least that's the argument Police Chief Jim Bueermann makes. "The fallback position for most local government bureaucrats like me," he says, "is that it's so much easier to say, 'We have $3 million less so you are going to get fewer services.' But there are multiple ways to get to the outcomes that taxpayers expect their police department is going to deliver." Prominent among them are a greater reliance on technology and a greater use of volunteers. Call it do-it-yourself government. But can volunteers really put in the hours and perform sensitive, highly skilled jobs that take more than a friendly smile? Can they enable a government to do more with less? A close look at Redlands' experience suggests that under some circumstances, the answer just might be yes-although that might not translate into taxpayer support.

Jim Bueermann took command of the Redlands Police Department in 1998. A lifelong resident of the city and a 20-year veteran of the force, he knew his community well—the rough neighborhoods as well as the affluent enclaves where, starting in 1870, wealthy visitors from the Midwest and the East found an ideal retreat in Redlands' fragrant orange groves and snow-capped San Bernardino Mountains. Over the years, the visitors endowed their new community with such gifts as a symphony, a magnificent Moorish-style library, and perhaps most importantly, the University of Redlands. The city soon became known as "The Jewel of the Inland Empire."

That phrase is not heard much anymore. Today, the Inland Empire is defined more by foreclosures than orange groves. The problems of neighboring communities, such as gang-plagued San Bernardino, with which Redlands shares a border, have crept in. And, despite its relative affluence, Redlands has suffered through three years of declining revenues, which have resulted in budget cuts to city departments, including the police.

When the police department's workforce fell by a third, Bueermann turned to a city tradition: volunteerism. He accelerated volunteer-recruitment efforts and hired a volunteer coordinator to oversee his department's initiatives. In the process, Bueermann discovered something surprising. Volunteers are not deterred by requirements that are demanding and responsibilities that are real. They are attracted to them.

Veteran police officers discovered something too. When the volunteer program was starting out, says Lt. Chris Catren, "we were filling the gaps with volunteers." But as police came to realize that volunteers could do many of the routine tasks that had once constituted a significant part of their workdays—directing traffic, taking reports, delivering evidence to the district attorney's office, providing crime-scene control—they came to depend on them. "They are," Catren says, "as much a part of our service delivery model as the person in a black-and-white uniform with a badge and a gun."

The department has used volunteer officers to take on specific, new tasks, such as patrolling parks, municipal orange groves and desert areas that stretch across the 40-square-mile city. One such area is the Santa Ana river basin, known locally as "the wash."

The Santa Ana River, Southern California's largest, begins in the San Bernardino Mountains and ends in the Pacific Ocean at Huntington Beach. Once upon a time, mountain storms would send deluges of water coursing through the river's channel and into the sea. Today, subdivisions in Orange County occupy many of those floodplains, and the Seven Oaks Dam holds back the waters that would otherwise sweep those subdivisions away. But dams silt up. To maintain them, authorities must occasionally release water into the wash. That poses a problem because the wash also serves as home for the homeless.

In the past, police officers alerted encampments of the homeless to the coming water release so they could move to safer grounds. Now, the city relies on a group of volunteers known as the Citizen Volunteer Park Rangers to make sure the homeless are out of harm's way.

On a recent Friday afternoon, two uniformed rangers, Lee Haag, a retired Air Force officer, and Sherli Leonard, the executive director of the Redlands Conservancy, descend on their horses into the wash. A few weeks earlier, they had distributed fliers warning of the water release at two recently spotted encampments—one north of the Redlands Municipal Airport, the other in the lee of the Orange Street Bridge. Now they're checking the encampment near the bridge. As they approach, it is deserted except for a stray dog. As the horses climb out of the wash, the rangers encounter a woman out for a walk. She stops to pat the horses. Knowing that rangers are out patrolling the wash, she says, has made her day.

The creation of the Volunteer Park Rangers says a lot about how the city interacts with its volunteers. The ranger program started almost accidentally. Three years ago, retired audiologist Brad Billings read an interview in the local paper in which Police Chief Bueermann expressed a desire to organize a volunteer patrol to tackle problems of graffiti and disorder in the city's parks. Billings e-mailed the chief and two hours later got an e-mail back inviting him to a meeting. Their discussion was brief.

"Brad, it's yours," Bueermann told him. "Go for it." Bueermann appointed a sergeant to supervise the program but left it to Billings to organize, raise funds and run the initiative, which now numbers more than two dozen volunteers. Like the Citizen Volunteer Patrol, rangers received training, uniforms, iPhones (to mark the location of graffiti and other problems) and access to city equipment. Sending volunteer rangers into the wash is something many cities wouldn't do—even if the volunteers were trained and well equipped. Bueermann says such risk-taking is essential. "Too often we accept a lack of money as a reason not to do things," he says. "There are so many ways to get around that if we just accept a level of ambiguity, develop a tolerance for risk-taking and realize that sometimes failure is about learning."

As for Haag and Leonard, they say they have never felt unsafe.

Redlands is unusual for the depth and breadth of its volunteer activities, but it isn't alone. Confronted with the challenges of the Great Recession, cities across the country have begun to reconsider what can be done with volunteers. In December 2009, New York City Mayor Michael Bloomberg assembled 15 mayors to announce the launch of a new initiative, Cities of Service. Underwritten by both Bloomberg Philanthropies and the Rockefeller Foundation, the initiative provides cities with $200,000 grants to hire "chief service officers" to identify local priorities and develop plans to address them, using volunteers.

One of the mayors who appeared with Bloomberg was Nashville's Karl Dean. In January 2010, Nashville received one of the first $200,000 Cities of Service grants. Dean tapped Laurel Creech to run the program. Her first day of work last May coincided with the 100-year flood that submerged parts of downtown Nashville as well as several residential neighborhoods. From the city emergency command center, Creech worked with a local volunteer group, Hands On Nashville, to text thousands of volunteers with a request for help sandbagging downtown against the rising Cumberland River. Within three hours, more than a thousand volunteers were on hand.

Since then, Creech has developed a service plan that focuses on two issues—education and the environment. According to Creech, working with the heads of city agencies has been challenging. Although quite a few departments utilize volunteers in many ways, a lot of them don't use volunteers as effectively as they could or, she says, they "don't really know what suitable volunteer programs are and what volunteers can do and can't do. The challenge is getting them to recognize that there are opportunities for improvement."

Still, Nashville's chief service officer believes that volunteers will take on more and more tasks once performed by government employees.

In Redlands, that moment has already arrived. When budget cuts nixed the Redlands Police Department's plans to lease a helicopter from the county (at a cost of $500,000 a month plus operating costs) to provide air support, the department used drug forfeiture funds to purchase a 1967 Cessna 172, which it then kitted out with a $30,000 video camera that could be operated by a laptop in the back of the plane. To operate the plane, the department turned to volunteer pilots like Bill Cheeseman, age 70.

Cheeseman is a retired engineer who describes himself as "a gentleman acrobatic flier." On a recent sunny afternoon, he takes the plane up for a patrol shift. A police officer, Sgt. Shawn Ryan, sits in the back, along with his electronic equipment: image-stabilized binoculars, a laptop to monitor the police dispatcher and operate the video camera, as well as a LoJack system for detecting stolen cars. As the plane lifts off the runway of the Redlands Municipal Airport, a police dispatcher reports a recurring alarm in a neighborhood of mansions between Caroline Park and the Redlands Country Club. Two patrol cars arrive at the scene just minutes before the Cessna, which circles overhead.

Two officers from the patrol car have entered the house. They have silenced their radio. If there's a burglar inside, they don't want its squawk to announce their presence. Two thousand feet overhead, Ryan focuses on the house. "If someone runs out," he says, "we'll see them."

No one makes a run for it. The officers on the ground report that the wind was opening and closing an unlocked door. But even when the plane responds to a false alarm, it serves a useful purpose. One of Bueermann's first and most controversial actions as chief was to disband a "beat" system that assigned police officers to various sectors of the city, with little regard for actual crime rates. Needless to say, affluent low-crime neighborhoods were unhappy with the change. By putting a plane in the air—and highly visible police vehicles on the ground (albeit ones often driven by volunteers)—he's been able to assuage their concerns and free up his officers for the proactive police work of targeting gangs, guns and violence in the most dangerous parts of town.

It's the kind of creative problem-solving that has allowed the city to cut personnel by 16 percent without damaging city services, says Redlands City Manager Martinez. Last spring, San Bernardino County and the city of Redlands commissioned a polling firm to gauge public satisfaction with city services. Even though citywide staffing and funding have been cut and cut again since 2007, 81 percent of respondents said services were at least satisfactory—and 30 percent of that 81 percent actually rated services as better than satisfactory.

To Martinez, it was a testament to the creativity of city staff and the partnerships they have been able to build. "Less is not less," he says. "The way services have been delivered for the past 20 years is very labor intensive."

But the city's approach may also have lulled the citizens of Redlands into thinking that city leaders have solved the problem of doing more with less and that the city doesn't need more money to keep providing a top-notch level of service. Last November, when a measure to impose a half-cent sales tax surcharge to shore up city services went before the voters, it failed. In Redlands, the voters have spoken. Do-it-yourself government is here for good.

37. Is Public Safety Exempt from Managed Competition?

Tom Guilfoy

One of my favorite singer-songwriters from the early 1970s was Jim Croce. Between 1966 and 1973, Croce released five studio albums and 11 singles. One of those singles was "You Don't Mess Around with Jim." That song serves as an appropriate backdrop for this chapter.

The unwritten rule in most government circles, especially in Texas, is that you don't mess around with Managed Competition in Public Safety. I've often wondered why the vast majority of local governments exempt Public Safety–related departments (i.e., Police, Fire/Rescue, Municipal Courts, Legal, Environmental Services, etc.) from managed competition. I know that Public Safety is an essential government function and should not be privatized, but does that mean that it should not be managed like any other high performance service business?

Public Safety is a top priority in our community, as it should be. As City Manager Leonard Martin has often stated, "No one wants to live in a place where you don't feel safe." Carrollton spends approximately $50 million annually (65 percent of the General Fund) on public safety-related operations and support functions.

In Carrollton, Public Safety is not exempt from managed competition. There are examples in all of our Public Safety departments of offering services cheaper, better, faster and friendlier. Because of the unique laws that govern each of the operations, the managed competition efforts are not as apparent to outsiders but they do strive to be as innovative as possible.

Like most City employees who don't work in Public Safety, I'm not aware of much of what goes on in the Carrollton Police Department, but I've always been curious about what police work is really like. I recently learned of a program that Chief Redden and his management team have introduced that is changing the culture from within the department. The more I learn about it, the more I can appreciate how closely it parallels the philosophy and principles of managed competition and our City's strategic goal of operating like a competitive service business.

"I get questioned about how public safety is participating in managed competition. While we are not going to outsource them, this is a prime example of how they are a part of our overall effort. Chief Redden's

Originally published as Tom Guilfoy (2012). "Is Public Safety Exempt from Managed Competition?" *Managed Competition Newsletter*, March 20, 2012, Carrollton, Texas. Reprinted with permission of the author.

memo lays out how the Police Department is getting more productivity out of the operation without spending more money. That is becoming a more competitive business unit."—Leonard Martin

And so, with Chief Redden's permission, I wanted to share the following excerpts from his recent internal communications regarding CPD's new Patrol Performance Program (IPI). I think his message is educational and inspirational.

"The mere presence of a police officer has been found to not deter crime as suspected, as proven in the Kansas City Experiment in the 1970's (policefoundation.org/docs/kansas.html). While officer presence can possibly deter crime, even though it is not supported by research, it may make citizens feel more comfortable, but even before starting this program, we heard from citizens that they never saw officers in their neighborhood.

"My response to those citizens was usually that we officers don't see them either when we drive through, and that just because we don't see each other doesn't mean that neither of us were there.

"So, if the mere presence of a police officer in a neighborhood has been proven not to deter criminal activity, then what does? In order to effectively address crime, three factors must be addressed (called the Crime Triangle). It's like a three-legged stool. If you remove any one of the legs, the stool won't stand. Therefore, if you remove any one of the factors in the crime triangle, no crime will occur. The three factors are:

1. **The victim of the crime cannot be present**. If the victim of the crime is not there, there cannot be a crime. This either equates to a victim not being in a location that is unfamiliar to them, for them to be aware of their surroundings and do their best to avoid a crime for the business, building or vehicle that is the target of the crime to not be present. This is certainly beyond the control of the police department.

2. **The opportunity for a crime must be removed**. This is accomplished by removing known dangerous locations, improving lighting, removing graffiti, not allowing a neighborhood to degrade which could invite crime and show that there is a general concern for what is going on in the area. Criminals are basically lazy, so any inconvenience will generally deter them. Also included is heightened security measures for belongings, such as locking cars, taking belongings and taking measures to secure homes and businesses (alarms, dogs, lighting).

3. **The criminal must not be present**. In other words, if the criminal isn't there, then no crime will be committed. Criminals are opportunistic and take advantage of weakness. If they sense a weakness in the security of a business or residence then they will break in. If they sense a weakness in an individual then they will take advantage, and rob or assault them. This statement isn't always true and we will never be able to curtail all crime. Crimes that occur within the home are very difficult to detect and no matter what we do we cannot always prevent all of these. Some criminals get desperate and commit crimes that seem unreasonable, such as bank robbery where they know their picture will be taken, but they do it anyway.

"But for the most part, if we can remove the criminal we have no crime.

"Of all three of these there is really only one factor that the police can affect. We cannot remove the victim of the crime. This is a free society where people can go anywhere they want. We can't keep them from going anywhere they please, even in an 'unsavory' neighborhood or situation. But they are unsavory because someone is there already.

"The Police Department can have some effect on removing the opportunity for a crime. But we can only have a small effect.

We cannot make people secure their belongings. We've been trying for decades to get people to lock their cars, not leave belongings out, and not leave their car running at the store, to get an alarm, better locks, better lighting and such. It's up to them to do this, and unfortunately they usually don't do anything until a crime has already occurred. We can report property that appears to be a problem area. We can go to locations that appear to be a problem in hopes of deterring crime, we can help set up Crime Watch groups, speak about crime prevention and help remove graffiti and even make roadway engineering changes in some cases to address problems.

"However, much of this is outside of our jurisdiction. Some of it is Code Enforcement and building standards (Crime Prevention through Environmental Design: ncjrs. gov/pdffiles/crimepre.pdf), but most of it falls on individuals, businesses and private property owners. They must be willing to make wise choices or put money into their properties to remove sometimes obvious problems, but usually they won't.

"The one aspect that the Police Department has the most effect on is removing the criminal. And, it is the basic tenant of our job. We are the only profession given the authority by the State to arrest people and put them jail. In order for police officers to make an arrest we have to make contact with people, identify them, and establish probable cause to make an arrest. Officers can drive around empty streets all day long and look at houses and never make contact with anyone.

"However, nearly all criminals have to travel to and from the location of the offense. They do this by driving there most often, but can also walk and ride a bike. But if they expect to make a timely get-away or haul what they've taken, they travel by vehicle. By officers stopping cars and identifying people, they are more likely to make contact with those that are out committing a crime.

A traffic stop not only has an effect on just the person being stopped, it also affects everyone who drives by and sees that officer. It either slows people down, or if they are a criminal, it could send a message that the police are active here and they may get caught.

"Criminals usually only commit a crime when they are comfortable to do so. They thrive off of anonymity and when they have been stopped and identified in a certain part of town they may not feel as comfortable committing a crime there. And, if they are in jail then we know they won't be committing any crimes. Therefore, in order to effectively address crime, officers must be actively, aggressively looking for criminals. As shown, the most productive way of doing this is by contacting them on traffic stops or while walking.

"Let me explain the reasoning behind our Patrol Performance Program (IPI). In the past, the crime rate in Carrollton rose and fell along with many of the other cities around us. We basically floated along, doing our fair share of enforcement and community projects with a goal of reducing crime. We weren't the most crime ridden City, but we weren't the safest either. The efforts taking place were good, but not excellent. One of the things I promised when I came to Carrollton was that we were always going to strive for perfection. I want this department to be a trend setter, to be on the cutting edge of policing and willing to try something new. I want other departments to look at us and be envious of our accomplishments. I'm sure you've all heard the definition of insanity as doing the same thing over and over and expecting different results.

"Well I'm not satisfied with that and I certainly hope none of you are either. I want criminals to be afraid to come to Carrollton. I want us to have the reputation as a department that 'takes care of business' when it comes to addressing crime and criminals. After all, that is our job. We all swore to the same oath which says that we will safeguard lives and property and enforce the laws. I want to reiterate though, that the vast majority of officers were already doing this at an acceptable or superior level. This program was only initiated to ensure that the 20–25 percent that weren't were doing their fair share. Another one of my promises was that everyone would be treated in a 'fair and equitable manner.' This means that everyone will be held to the same standard, that everything we do will not be done maliciously, but instead for the betterment of the department, the City and citizens and the employees that work here.

"We are striving for improved efficiency and productivity using the amount of resources we already have. I have moved as many officers back into Patrol as I can afford at this time, so if the officers that we have are staying busy, we have effectively increased our patrol force. Our model is being looked at currently by Grand Prairie Police Department, and I suspect it will be modeled by many others in the future. Most importantly I am comfortable telling the public that their police officers are working hard, doing everything to help make Carrollton a safer place. It will take time to reap the benefits of this level of activity. However, if you hold the line and maintain a strong presence I guarantee that the criminal element will get so uncomfortable that they will go somewhere else.

"I do respect and appreciate every one of you. I've heard people say that they dislike this program so much that they either want out of Patrol or are looking to leave the department. I hope this isn't the case, but if the reason is that you aren't comfortable with this level of activity then maybe another slower-paced department is a better fit. I'm not saying this to be cold or demeaning, because I hope everyone will stay. Life is too short to be unhappy, so if you're unhappy then maybe you need to change something. I had one officer tell me, 'Chief you can't buy officer's happiness with Tasers and Tahoes.' The purpose of purchasing those was not to make you happy, it was to improve your safety, reduce lost work time due to injuries and basically make us more efficient.

"Happiness is a state of mind that only you control. If you choose to be unhappy there is nothing that I can do to improve that. I want your work experience to be enjoyable, but I hope that your sense of happiness comes from your personal life and not work. All I want from you is your commitment for the 12 hours you are here working. The rest of your time is your time, and that is where I hope you find your enjoyment."

38. Public-Private Partnerships in Higher Education

Frank Woodward

Woodward Jon Nixon wrote in 2011 in *Higher Education and the Public Good: Imagining the University* that, although universities are natural forums for social engagement and public dialogue, in the contemporary economic climate they have increasingly needed to prove their value as commodities in the public interest. Faced with increasing costs, skyrocketing tuition and rapidly shifting technology, higher education finds itself reframed as a commodity whose future rises or falls on the degree to which it is good for something.

In this light, a number of university systems have sought innovative policy initiatives that attempt to bridge the gap between public service and private delivery. These initiatives can potentially offer economic efficiencies for states, but they often raise important questions about the value and character of traditional forms of higher education as well. As this chapter will explore, such initiatives can lead both to new interpretations of education policy and to broad challenges to existing economic models.

In the mid–1990s, a group of governors from 19 western states looked to the newly emerging World Wide Web as a platform for higher education delivery. Their initiative launched Western Governors University (WGU), which according to their website was developed as a way to address "rapid population growth confronted by limited public funds for educational services." Today, WGU is a private, regionally accredited, nonprofit online university enrolling over 40,000 students from all 50 states. One of its most distinctive—if not controversial—elements is its implementation of a competency-based model. This model was endorsed by WGU's founders to provide what they saw as a focus on concrete, practical outcomes built directly around job market needs.

"Who Wants to Sit through Classes…?"

Competency-based models offer credit for the demonstrated achievement of defined subject outcomes, and are not tied to traditional term-length courses or programs. In the WGU model, traditional tuition charges are replaced with a flat fee

---

Originally published as Frank Woodward (2014). "Public-Private Partnerships in Higher Education: The Western Governors University Initiative." *PA Times*, July 22, 2014. Reprinted with permission of the publisher.

structure, allowing students to attempt as many competencies as they wish within a six-month period. *U.S. News* recently quoted WGU's President Robert Mendenhall who characterized the competency-based model by asking this question: "Who wants to sit through classes when you already know the stuff?" Academicians might well argue that "the stuff" to which Mendenhall refers is indeed worthy of reflection and discussion in a classroom setting. However, state governors and policymakers have found his analysis hard to argue purely from an economic perspective.

The full academic implications of WGU's model remain to be seen. It is clear that while WGU has soared in popularity, its completion rates remain very low. According to the *Chronicle of Higher Education*'s College Completion report based on 2010 data, WGU's six-year graduation rate was only 6.5 percent, placing them in only the second percentile among four-year private nonprofit universities (the data file is available from the *Chronicle of Higher Education*). This fact alone should give state policymakers pause in their rush to establish partnerships and implement changes to traditional public education models.

From a policy perspective, Western Governors University's model has already challenged a number of traditional policy interpretations. Because WGU is online only, the competency-based model has demanded considerable political support in order to maintain Title IV eligibility for financial aid. According to Doug Lederman writing for Inside Higher Ed in 2014, WGU originally qualified to receive and distribute Title IV financial aid funding through its classification as a "distance learning demonstration program."

However, Lederman reports that in 2006, this U.S. Department of Higher Education exemption ran its course. As a result, Section 8020 of the Higher Education Reconciliation Act (HERA) of 2006 revised the definition of 'eligible program' in order to include institutions that use a "direct assessment of student learning...." Interestingly, as Lederman observed, WGU chose not to take advantage of this direct assessment categorization, instead relying on a technical definition equating their competency-based units to credit hours. However, the HERA reauthorization has certainly opened a door for other direct assessment programs to take advantage of Title IV funds as they develop and implement alternative delivery systems.

Growing State Partnerships: WGU–Tennessee

WGU's regional accreditation and flat-rate tuition model continue to fuel its appeal among states and its expansion into new markets nationwide. Early in 2014, Tennessee Governor Bill Haslam launched the "Tennessee Promise" initiative, promising to supplement any remaining tuition and fees costs not already covered by financial aid for two years of community college education for Tennessee students. This initiative partners with Western Governors University in the establishment of a branch called WGU–Tennessee. In Governor Haslam's view, "WGU Tennessee fills a critical need in our postsecondary landscape." This public-private partnership serves as a component of Tennessee's "Drive to 55" initiative, which seeks to raise the percentage of Tennessee residents with at least a two-year degree or certification to 55 percent by 2025.

Governor Haslam's initiative reveals the extent to which public-private education partnerships potentially reframe a state's educational values in largely economic terms. However, WGU's extremely low graduation rates and its controversial academic delivery model deserve critical attention and analysis on the part of state policymakers before significant investments and partnerships are established. While the potential for creative and innovative state partnerships certainly exist, these initiatives must be based on a more substantive evaluation of competency-based delivery. In the meantime, states would do well not to forget the many thousands of students, faculty and staff who are part of existing, "traditional" universities throughout each state. These traditional universities still have a great deal to offer, and although the economic challenges are significant, they can also remain a source of innovation and increased efficiency in public higher education.

39. Privatization, Efficiency and the Public Interest

Michael Abels

Analyzing privatization's impact requires public administrators to consider a fundamental value that often has been sacrificed in the quest to reduce the cost of government. The question? How can the drive for efficiency through privatization negatively impact ethical values, including those outlined in ASPA's own code of ethics? In particular, the code's first tenet states that public administrators must serve the public interest while the fourth instructs us to strengthen social equity.

Heavily influenced by capitalism, U.S. public administration historically has treated efficiency as a principal value. In the 1980s, efficiency was incorporated as an overriding value by a political philosophy that emphasized individualism as a paramount value at the expense of the state. For 35 years, this philosophy-an anti-tax, anti-government agenda-has dominated the nation's political leadership. Supporting this political movement was an administrative paradigm that called for individualizing services, viewing citizens as customers and reducing cost by focusing government's mission solely on setting policy. The primary vehicle is privatization of public services. These principles, incorporated in the "reinventing government" model, have served as a foundation for American public administration.

Today, we experience the negative outcomes of this movement. The U.S. Justice Department's 2014 report on the operations of the Ferguson, Missouri police department serves as a clarion call for public management. It concluded that prioritizing revenue generation over enhanced community safety was an aberrant practice of one city. However, the conclusion means much more to the profession of public administration. The drive to generate revenue by any source other than taxation is not an outlier in local government finance. It is a direct outgrowth from the notion that privatization is a primary tool for maintaining low taxes. As conservative columnist Michael Gerson wrote earlier this year, some municipalities squeeze money from citizens through fines and fees because they want to spend money without the inconvenience of taxation. He noted that this causes the burden of supporting government to fall heaviest on those with the least ability to pay.

Public administrators must reassess the

Originally published as Michael Abels (2015). "Privatization, Efficiency and the Public Interest." *PA Times*, October 9, 2015. Reprinted with permission of the publisher.

tools we have implemented to make government more efficient. Has reinventing government negated our proclaimed values of advancing the public interest and strengthening social equity? Accepting as fact that privatization makes government services more efficient, does efficiency define the keystone attribute of the public interest?

Another outcome of this era is that public administrators have become inculcated with the conviction that taxes must not be the mechanism to fund new or increased public services. To comply with this philosophy, we innovatively design new forms of privatization with fees targeted toward those who receive distinct benefit from a service.

As professional managers, we encourage innovative methods for financing community development. Gated communities and community development districts may offer new techniques for financing infrastructure and community services. But, they exacerbate the sense of individualism and the attitude that "I will take care of mine." A "you take care of yours" philosophy is sweeping our local communities and destroying government's focus on the public interest.

Also seen in the drive for efficiency is increased privatization of public services and paying for them through user fees that supplant shared responsibility where all pay through general taxation but-because of need-some parts of the community may benefit more than others.

With the increase in U.S. income inequality, the privatization movement has troubling dimensions. Wealthy individuals assume government's responsibility by contracting for private services in cities that do not have the resources to deliver them in a way that satisfies those individuals. David Amsden this year reported in *The New York Times Magazine* that a New Orleans entrepreneur paid for private police to supplement city public safety and private sanitation crews to service the district where he lives. This may seem similar to a service enhancement supported through a community development district, but it is much different.

Where the former are paid for by taxes and targeted at community identified deficiencies, in this case one individual decides to address service deficiencies in a small area of personal concern to him. Public services contracted through wealthy individuals may become the catalyst that further balkanizes our communities into distinct economic zones.

Privatization of public services is steadily replacing traditional government-provided services. As a profession, we must ask whether the value of reducing the cost of government a superior value to that of advancing the collective welfare of the citizens we serve. What *is* the public interest? Is it primarily reducing the size and cost of government? What does the first tenet of ASPA's code of ethics demand and what does "advancing the public interest" mean to our field?

40. Large Questions

Paul Farmer

What Money Can't Buy: The Moral Limits of Markets is Harvard Professor Michael Sandel's latest book. Sandel, author of *Justice: What's the Right Thing to Do?* and the keynote speaker at the 2011 National Planning Conference in Boston, again raises questions of great interest to planners. Even conservative columnist George Will praises Sandel and his latest work. The blurb that Will wrote for the cover of the book says this: "Michael J. Sandel, political philosopher and public intellectual, is a liberal, but not the annoying sort."

His aim is not to boss people around but to bring them around to the pleasures of thinking clearly about large questions of social policy planners, in fact, confront many of the large questions that Sandel addresses. Do high-occupancy toll lanes raise moral issues? Should Yosemite campsites be allocated to the highest bidders? Should corporations be able to pay for the right to pollute? Should publicly financed ballparks sell private naming rights? Of course, Sandel also raises questions about broad societal issues, such as bribes to lose weight or cash for sterilization. Or the sale of kidneys or even children for adoption.

Sandel's book expands on ideas that I encountered in a graduate planning class at Cornell University in the 1970s. In his seminal 1970 work, *The Gift Relationship: From Human Blood to Social Policy*, Richard Titmuss, who taught social policy at the London School of Economics, examined the blood bank systems of the U.S. and Great Britain. He used his study of blood to generalize, asking broader questions about society. The book later came into play when I organized the Social Policy Planning Option in the new graduate planning program that we were creating at the University of Wisconsin–Milwaukee; it became required reading.

Titmuss's data-driven study led to his conclusion that the British system, based on altruism, was superior to the U.S. system, which relied more on market mechanisms. The U.S. system produced wasted blood, chronic and acute shortages, higher costs, and a much greater probability of contamination. It cost five to 15 times what the British system cost. And ours was the "efficient" market system. Titmuss also found that the U.S. market system led to a redistribution of blood—from the poor who needed cash to the wealthier who needed blood.

He also asked questions about the sale of body parts, such as kidneys and eyes. Why

Originally published as Paul Farmer (2012). "Large Questions." *Planning*, 78(6), July 2012. Reprinted with permission of the publisher.

shouldn't a poor person be able to sell an eye to someone who could afford to buy one? After all, perhaps the recipient would otherwise be blind. Titmuss didn't stop there. He also explored altruism, as the title of his book implies. As planners, we constantly struggle with this question of markets versus other societal values.

How many books have made an impact on the way we think, whether about planning matters or broader issues of society, morals, or choices? C.P. Snow's slim but provocative book, The Two Cultures and the Scientific Revolution, which grew from his influential 1959 Rede Lecture at Cambridge University, was one of about half a dozen books—and the only one that I remember—from our required Freshman Week reading list at Rice University. Why return to Snow's work almost half a century later and why reference it alongside the Titmuss and Sandel works? From his vantage point in 1950s Britain, during the height of the Cold War, and from his own 30-year career as both a scientist and a novelist, Snow articulated the separation of the two cultures. At one pole, he located literary intellectuals. At the other, he located scientists. What had he found between the two? A "gulf of mutual incomprehension." More basic than the hostility that he had found was a lack of understanding.

Snow discussed this separation's harmful effects on social progress, cohesion, and equity, themes later addressed by Titmuss and Sandel—and one that planners also face. Each of the three authors also addresses physical separation—again, the world of the planner. Having moved between scientists and writers for more than 30 years, Snow christened the gap between the two as the "two cultures." Early in his lecture, he spoke about his feeling that he was moving among two groups. Those in the two groups were quite similar in many ways: intelligence, race, social origin, and incomes. But while he moved easily among

the scientists and the literary intellectuals, he found that most of the others had almost ceased to communicate. This personal discovery was the beginning of his investigation, one that would lead to conclusions about the reasons for the two cultures, their negative effects, and the need to remedy the situation. "This polarization is a loss to us all," he later noted.

The intellectual chasm was not just theoretical for Snow, as he valued creative chances that he believed had often come from clashes, whether between subjects, disciplines, or cultures. And why were these clashes so important? For Snow, it was because the clashes had led to so many breakthroughs that were keys to human progress. By the end of his lecture, Snow explained what could be done to yoke the two cultures together. He called for people in every discipline to advance the legitimate human desires of all while addressing the unacceptable mismatched distribution of even the most basic goods and services. He took this notion even further four years later in his follow-up notes, which included the uplifting thought that people in both the arts and sciences can grasp "the remedial suffering of most of their fellow humans" as well as "the responsibilities, which, once they are seen, cannot be denied." Snow's two cultures are still relevant to today's issues, as are those raised by Titmuss.

Sandel, writing recently, also identifies several current issues that many planners struggle with in their daily work. His final chapter, "Naming Rights," brings many of the arguments and overriding social issues together in a final discussion, "Skyboxification."

"The more things money can buy, the fewer the occasions when people from different walks of life encounter one another. We see this when we go to a baseball game and gaze up at skyboxes, or down from them, as the case may be. The disappearance of the class-mixing experience once found at the ballpark represents a loss not only for those looking up but for those looking down."

Planners know that we have increasingly become a society in which people are less likely to encounter those who differ from themselves. Why support public schools if our children and grandchildren can purchase other options? Why support public recreation facilities if we have our own gym, swimming pool, or health club? How should we address the proliferation of gated communities? Who should own the public streets where we park? Who sets the policies? Should private companies be able to place billboards masquerading as bus shelters in public rights-of-way (even when the Americans with Disabilities Act is violated)?

As Sandel observes, "We live and work and shop and play in different places. Our children go to different schools. You might call it the skyboxification of American life. It's not good for democracy, nor is it a very satisfying way to live." Snow raised critical issues in 1959 by focusing on two cultures. Titmuss raised moral issues in 1970 about markets versus altruism. Sandel in 2012 asks if we really want a society where everything is up for sale. All ask if markets should be the only mechanisms for allocating goods, services, or even opportunities.

Yes, I would argue, a high-occupancy toll lane raises moral issues because it fundamentally differs from a high-occupancy vehicle lane. Traffic engineers may see them as much the same since they both allocate scarce highway capacity. But they allocate access to this scarce public good in different ways and for different purposes and for different people. Planners must encourage an informed public debate on such policy issues, just as we should encourage debate about the social policy concerns raised by zoning decisions or those raised by parking pricing or parking control decisions. The common zoning ordinance, including the form-based code, is social planning. As parking becomes a more sophisticated field of public policy and practice, it also becomes more a tool of social planning.

In today's fiscal environment, with shrinking public budgets, and today's ideological environment, with calls for privatization, we planners must sharpen our skills and revisit our core values. We need to be thoughtful about the large questions and the distributive effects.

41. Contracting Issues

Institute for Local Government

Question: *I'm very frustrated with our city's contracting process. There's a ton of red tape and it takes forever for vendors to go through the process then for us to make a decision. Lots of business people I know simply choose not to go through the process because it costs return. Because my own company does business with these folks, I can personally attest that they would give the city quality results at a competitive price. What am I missing here in terms of what best serves the public's and the city's interest?*

Answer: Certainly, the process a city uses to select the provider of goods and services can seem both cumbersome and time-consuming. Like so many ethical issues for public officials, the expectations play a significant role in the procurement process.

There are two aspects to these expectations:

(1) that the city will get the best deal for its money; and

(2) that the process will be fair. Let's look at each issue.

Values at stake in this dilemma

- Responsibility
- Loyalty
- Fairness

Getting the Best Deal

Getting the best deal for the city is part of your responsibility as a public official to be a prudent steward of scarce public resources. How do you determine whether your city is getting the best deal? Typically this means receiving materials or services of appropriate quality for a competitive price.

A key way to assure the public of this fact is for a city to use a competitive and comparative process that enables it to evaluate both price and quality. A risk of "sole-sourcing" is that the city has no way of knowing whether there would have been a better deal out there for the city.

This is not to say that a city should put all contracts out to bid. The questions for public officials to ask themselves, however, is whether the process the city uses to select contractors provides assurance to the public that it is receiving the best value for the dollar.

A Fair Process

Both the business community and the public expect public processes to be fair.

Originally published as Institute for Local Government (2004). "Securing Goods and Services: Contracting Issues." Institute for Local Government, California. October 2004. www.ca-ilg.org/sites/main/files/file-attachments/resources__Everyday_Ethics_Oct04_0.pdf. Reprinted with permission of the publisher.

Some elements of a fair vendor selection process include:

- Widely publicizing the opportunity to compete for the city's business;
- providing the same information to all businesses so that no one business has an advantage;
- applying the evaluation criteria consistently to all bidders; and making sure the contract is administered in such a way that the city gets the full benefit of its deal.

Red flags can go up when a city makes multiple demands for "best and final" offers after all bids have been opened and made public. According to one private sector representative, multiple calls for "best and finals" raise concerns about the fairness of the process and give the impression that the city will keep asking bidders to resubmit until the city gets the bidder it wants into the position of being the low bid.

With respect to the contract administration issue, the goal is to avoid having a would-be vendor submit an unrealistically low bid, only to propose amendments to the contract that would increase costs. This would be unfair to a vendor who would have stuck to an original, ultimately lower bid.

Avoiding Favoritism

One aspect of fairness is making sure that a would-be vendor does not have an advantage merely because of a friendship with local officials, a past history of support for someone's campaign, or a family relationship. This is where the value of personal loyalty to individuals must yield to one's responsibilities as a public official to get the best deal for the public through a fair process.

In a small privately owned business, it can be perfectly ethical and gracious to give preference to a friend or return a favor in a business relationship. So, too, are such pleasantries as being treated to a meal or receiving other niceties to create goodwill and solidify a potential business relationship. In the public sector, however, giving preference to friends is likely to be characterized as cronyism at best and corruption at worst.

What About Trust?

When confronted with charges of unethical practices, public officials were acting with anything but the public's best interests in mind. Why do the media and the public instantly gravitate toward thinking the worst of someone's intentions?

This is a fundamental distinction between personal and public ethics. As one scholar explains, personal ethics are based on face-to-face relationships with individuals. Public ethics, on the other hand, tend to involve relationships that are more removed in most communities. Most constituents simply don't know a public official well enough to form an opinion about his or her ethics.

The reality is that the public cannot know how an official sorted through all the efforts—proper and improper to influence his or her decision-making process on contracts. As a result, the media and the public tend to judge public officials' ethics by the circumstances surrounding those officials' actions. If the circumstances are such that improprieties could have occurred, the public will conclude that improprieties likely did occur.

Media coverage and the existence of those who do in fact abuse the public's trust exacerbate the public perception issue. The public is aware of instances (typically rare) in which an unscrupulous public official will steadfastly claim to have the most sterling character. Regrettably, this "bad apple" syndrome creates almost a presumption of untrustworthiness.

This is the origin of the maxim that public officials are wise to avoid even the appearance of impropriety. If the public is inclined to infer wrongdoing merely from circumstances that could have involved wrongdoing, the most reliable way to promote the public confidence is to avoid those circumstances in the first place. One scholar goes so far as to assert that, because the appearance of impropriety erodes public trust, the appearance of impropriety constitutes a breach of an official's responsibility to promote public trust in government.

About Those Contracting Processes

So, in essence, the answer to the opening question is that the city contracting process is generally not designed for speed. Instead, the process is designed to reassure the public that the process is fair and competitive. To be sure, this can result in businesses declining to participate in the process and a missed opportunity for the public to receive a product at a more competitive price.

Furthermore, some of the checks and balances in the contracting process are designed to ensure that no one individual plays too great a role in contracting decisions. These layers to the process limit any one official's ability to skew the outcome based on personal interests, as opposed to the public's interests.

Perhaps the ultimate explanation is that the public is willing to incur the costs associated with minimizing the opportunities for mischief in the contracting process, even if the process turns away some would-be contractors. The theory is that, in the long run, fair processes prevent improprieties and increase the likelihood that the public will, in fact, get the best deal over time.

Typical Steps in the Procurement Process

Step 1: Establish a need for a product or service not otherwise available to the city through internal resources.

Step 2: Determine standards or specifications for the product or service.

Step 3: Invite vendors to submit proposals to supply the product or deliver the service.

Step 4: Evaluate the proposals according to evenly applied criteria and select the winner.

Step 5: Negotiate the contract.

Step 6: Vendor performs according to contract terms.

42. Putting Public Safety in Private Hands

Dennis Compton

Make no mistake about it—the decision to privatize all or part of any public safety emergency response system is a political decision driven by several factors, the least of which sometimes is the safety of the public.

That seems like a brash statement, but it really isn't. For elected officials, making decisions about the safety and well-being of constituents should be first and foremost on their list of priorities, but that is not always the case.

Downside Potential

How many times, and for how many years, have fire chiefs and union leaders nationwide warned about the downside of profit-based (private) public safety emergency response services? Their concerns are often met with reactions like "The fire chief is just resistant to change, is not innovative and is trying to protect his/her turf," or "The union is just trying to protect jobs and the security of their union."

Neither statement is based on fact. Actually they amount to political excuses for trying to blow off the opinions and concerns of the professionals they hire to respond to and manage public safety emergencies. A perfect (and current) case-in-point is the emergency transportation component of the EMS system.

It is widely recognized that an EMS call for service requires notification, dispatch, response, extrication (where necessary), triage, treatment and transportation. This is a continuum of steps that must be taken to successfully provide critical emergency services to people who call 9-1-1.

Have you ever wondered why that last step (the ambulance ride) is the step in the continuum that is most frequently singled out for privatization? It's not complicated— there's money in it, and the people who own private ambulance companies tend to financially support local elected officials, which can affect their votes. If there wasn't money in it, private companies would not be vying for ambulance contracts within government jurisdictions.

Fire chiefs and union officials have often cautioned government officials that the privatization of emergency services can result in diminished service quality and pro-

Originally published as Dennis Compton (2014). "Putting Public Safety in Private Hands." *Firehouse*, 39(2), February 2014. Reprinted with permission of the publisher.

longed response times. They have also made clear their concern that if, for any reason, the private ambulance company suddenly decides to close, the safety of the public would be jeopardized.

In some locations, policy-makers listened and kept the entire EMS response system fire service-based.

Elsewhere, the concerns fell on deaf ears and fire chiefs and union officials were accused of exaggerating potential negative effects. However, something has happened yet again that should get the attention of elected and appointed officials—but will it?

In December 2013, First Med EMS, which operated under the names of TransMed, Life Ambulance and MedCorp, ceased operations. This company serviced more than 70 municipalities in Kentucky, North Carolina, South Carolina, Virginia, West Virginia and Ohio. The shutdown occurred without notice, leaving public officials—with the exception of the fire chief—shocked that this could happen.

Even though the officials acted surprised, they must have known that this was not the first time such an event has happened. Private companies providing fire suppression and EMS have gone under in many places, each time without warning. Of course, there is no warning, because the company does not want its creditors or contractors to know of the plans to fold for fear they might intervene.

"How Could This Happen?"

Fire chiefs and union officials have had to react immediately to this loss of service, while the policymakers act stunned and appalled at these "totally unforeseen circumstances" that have put their constituents at risk. "How could the fire chief have let this happen?" they ask.

This is an opportunity for fire service leaders to re-inform and re-educate their policymakers about the perils of private sector public safety emergency response services. In doing so, the advantages of fire service-based EMS systems can be put on full display as well.

It's not about turf or jobs; it's about the safety of the public. To some extent, the issue boils down to a simple matter of corporate mentality and the impact it has on employees and the services they provide. In a fire chief's world, when crews return from EMS calls, the chief wants to know (first and foremost) if the patient lived, while in the profit-based world the executives tend to be focused on whether the patient paid. Did he live or did he pay?

It's such a mentality that is prevalent at the very top of the system that creates big differences in organizational culture and the quality of service. The fire department clearly comes out on top every time in that comparison.

Risk of Failure

In this new year of 2014, fire service leaders should make an enhanced effort to bring the situation involving First Med EMS to light in their local political arena. Elected officials deserve to be well informed of these types of system failures and the real potential of their decisions concerning whether to privatize emergency response services.

For those who have built fully fire service–based EMS systems, be sure the policymakers know the wisdom of their decisions. And for them, as well as those who chose instead to enter into private sector contracts for service, remind them of the many times when private-sector fire and EMS response systems have closed shop, leaving communities to scramble to protect the public.

As I said previously, this could be a real opportunity for those in the fire service directly impacted by this issue—if they choose to take advantage of it.

43. Privatization of Medicare

John Geyman

This is a dangerous time for Medicare. The bill passed by the House on March 27, by a surprising bipartisan majority of 392–37—H.R. 2, the Medicare Access and CHIP Reauthorization Act of 2015—threatens to end traditional Medicare as a social insurance program that protects seniors in a single large risk pool. The Senate is set to vote on the bill in two weeks.

The timing could not be more ironical. Medicare was passed 50 years ago by overwhelming bipartisan support in Congress—by votes of 302–116 in the House and 70–24 in the Senate. Since 1965, it has provided a set of comprehensive benefits as an earned right without regard to health conditions or income, with all beneficiaries paying into the program through mandatory contributions from individuals and/or employers (National Academy of Social Insurance, 1999). For the last 50 years, Medicare has been a solid rock of coverage in a shark-infested sea of unstable and expensive private plans.

But all that can go away if Republicans (and many Democrats) recklessly pass H.R. 2 without concern for its long-term implications. There are many problems in this bill, crafted as it is to serve the agenda of politicians waving the false flag of "entitle-ment reform" and lobbyists for organized medicine, private insurers, the drug industry, and other corporate stakeholders in the medical-industrial complex. As is typical in a large legislative package that is difficult to understand, and many legislators have not read, the devil is in the details.

H.R. 2 does have one useful goal—to replace the flawed Sustainable Growth Rate (SGR) formula for setting Medicare payment rates for physicians. The SGR formula was set in 1997 in a deficit-reduction law that ties payment rates to economic growth, which since then has led to recurrent last-minute budget crises, known as the "doc fix" over cuts in physician reimbursement. There have been 17 short-term "fixes" over the last ten years, each time kicking the can down the road without resolving how to proceed.

H.R. 2 eliminates the SGR formula, and proposes different ways to pay physicians, including expanded use of capitation, accountable care organizations, bundled payments, and various ways to implement "pay for performance" incentives. These are all supposedly aimed to improve quality of care and contain costs through a "merit-based incentive payment system" (MIPS). But are all untested, unproven, and unlikely

Originally published as John Geyman (2015). "Privatization of Medicare: Urgency of the Latest Threat." *Huffington Post*, May 31, 2015. www.huffingtonpost.com/john-geyman/privatization-of-medicare_b_6978726.html. Reprinted with permission of the author and copyright owner.

to either increase quality or contain costs while adding greatly to administrative complexity. In his 2014 Health Affairs blog, Jeff Goldsmith warned us about this approach:

"With this legislation, Congress is preparing yet again to enshrine in statute another payment strategy that is both unproven and highly controversial. The proposed legislation casts in concrete an almost laughable complex and expensive clinical record-keeping regime, while preserving the very volume-enhancing features of fee-for-service payment that caused the SGR problem in the first place. The cure is actually worse, and potentially more expensive, than the disease we have now" (Goldsmith, 2014).

Among the many structural changes in this massive bill are two that, if adopted, will seriously undermine the future integrity of Medicare: (1) its limits on first-dollar supplemental Medigap insurance coverage, and (2) introduction of means testing whereby higher-income Americans would pay more for their Medicare coverage (Editorial Board, 2015).

The first will hurt the approximately 12 million of the 50 million Medicare enrollees who rely on Medigap. Based on the already disproven premise that "more skin in the game" reins in unnecessary health care, the bill would prohibit plans from covering Part B deductibles. That would transform the whole concept of comprehensive, universal coverage of seniors over 65 with a consumer-directed approach to financing that care, thereby enabling further privatization of Medicare. Medicare patients could expect to face ever-higher deductibles, unaffordable for many, who would end up forgoing necessary care. The Medicare Rights Center, a national, nonprofit organization, has this to say about H.R. 2: "[it] does not represent a fair deal for people with Medicare-expecting too much from beneficiaries in return for too little" (Medicare Rights Center, 2015).

The second big change—means testing—may seem innocuous, or even a good idea on first blush, but has the potential to unravel the large Medicare risk pool, leading to higher prices, further privatization, and fewer benefits. H.R. 2 would increase payments, permanently, that higher-income seniors would pay for their Medicare coverage, thereby establishing a precedent for future increases. But that could have detrimental impacts on the overall Medicare risk pool, thereby threatening the coverage of lower-income beneficiaries. Jacob Hacker and Theodore Marmor, who have studied the Medicare program over many years, tell us that affluent Medicare enrollees account for only about 1 or 2 percent of Medicare's total costs. But with this change, affluent seniors would likely shift over to private programs that they could easily afford, thereby breaking up the Medicare risk pool and compromising the universality of Medicare coverage. The end result of that, of course, is increasing costs of coverage by adverse selection, a downward spiral of coverage, and erosion of broad political support for Medicare (Hacker and Marmor, 2003).

Conservatives have pushed for privatization Medicare as an "entitlement program" for many years, by shifting it from a defined-benefits program to one with defined-contributions. As new Speaker of the House in 1994, Newt Gingrich famously declared that this "could solve the Medicare problem and cause it to wither on the vine" (Gingrich, 2002). Recent years have already seen continuing privatization of Medicare—including the Medicare + Choice HMOs in the 1990s (discredited by excesses of managed care), its sequel, Medicare Advantage, and the Medicare Prescription Drug, Improvement and Modernization Act of 2003 (MMA). Each of these have benefitted insurers, drug companies and other corporate stakeholders more than patients.

Republicans have attached the above two

"poison pills," plus other changes not being reported, to a goal that both parties support—eliminating the unworkable SGR formula. But H.R. 2 will continue the unraveling of traditional Medicare, and lead to higher costs that will be unaffordable for many seniors and disabled enrollees. Both parties are congratulating themselves on bipartisanship as they oversell the SGR part of the problem. It is unfortunate and misguided that Democrats are taken by this SGR ruse to transform Medicare. They are seeming to cave to the Republicans without concern for the bill's long-term implications. They need to read the bill and stand up in defense of traditional Medicare. It is inappropriate for them to congratulate themselves on a "transformative" success that is such a long-term threat to the most vulnerable among us.

H.R. 2 will go to the Senate, which returns from recess on April 13. While it is expected to pass there, there is a big risk that its poison pills will not be recognized and dealt with by legislators. It may well be acted upon quickly as the Senate decides what to do with the austere conservative budget passed by the House that would repeal the Affordable Care Act, cut Medicaid, food stamps, and other safety-net programs.

House Republicans want to convert Medicare into a voucher program, and would like to see the Senate concur. All this ties together as the biggest threat to health care for seniors and the disabled that we have yet seen. Democrats need to discover their spine!

REFERENCES

Editorial Board. (2015). "The House may be about to finally fix the 'doc fix.'" *Washington Post*, March 25, 2015.

Gingrich, N. (2002). *Entitlement Politics: Medicare and Medicaid 1995–2001*. New York, NY: Aldine de Gruyter.

Goldsmith, J. (2014). "Primum non nocere: Congress's inadequate Medicare physician payment fix." *Health Affairs*, January 24, 2014.

Hacker, J. S., and T. R. Marmor. (2003). "Medicare reform: fact, fiction, and foolishness." *Public Policy & Aging Report* 13 (4): 1, Fall 2003.

Medicare Rights Center. (2015). *Response to House Legislative Package to Repeal and Replace the Sustainable Growth Rate (SGR) Formula (H. R. 2)*. New York: Medicare Rights Center.

National Academy of Social Insurance. (1999). *Study Panel on Medicare's Larger Social Role, Final Report*. Washington, D.C.: National Academy of Social Insurance.

44. Perils of Privatization

Ann Hagedorn

One November morning in 2004, three U.S. military men boarded a small turbo-prop plane at Bagram Air Base near Kabul for a two-and-a-half-hour flight to Farah, a base in western Afghanistan. They were Lieutenant Colonel Michael McMahon, Chief Warrant Officer Travis Grogan, and Specialist Harley Miller, the only passengers on Flight 61. The flight was operated by an affiliate of Blackwater, the private military company under U.S. contract for air transport of mail, supplies, and troops.

Forty minutes after takeoff, flying far north of the customary route from Bagram to Farah, the plane crashed into the side of a mountain. McMahon, Grogan, the pilot, co-pilot, and the mechanic apparently died instantly. At the time, McMahon was the highest-ranking U.S. soldier to die in the war. Miller, though he suffered internal injuries, may have lived for as long as ten hours after the crash, but the route was so obscure that rescuers could not locate the wreckage in time to save him.

In the years afterward, investigators for a joint U.S. Army and Air Force task force and for the National Transportation Safety Board would reveal that the Flight 61 pilots had never flown the route between Bagram and Farah and, in fact, had been in Afghan-istan for only 13 days. Also, they deviated from the standard course almost immediately after leaving the ground. Further, according to investigators, Blackwater failed to follow standard precautions to track flights, failed to file a flight plan, and failed to maintain emergency communications in case of an accident. The NTSB report included a cockpit voice recording of the plane's crew, which Representative Henry Waxman read to members of Congress at an October 2007 hearing before the House Committee on Oversight and Government Reform. Parts of it depict the pilots' unprofessional behavior and their jollity as they flew through narrow canyons on their wayward route:

"You're an X-wing fighter Star Wars man," said one of the pilots.

"You are [expletive] right. This is fun," the co-pilot replied and later said, "I swear to God they wouldn't pay me if they knew how much fun this was."

Blackwater went into the annals of government contracting as one of the great disgraces of privatization. A staff report prepared for the Oversight Committee found that Blackwater billed the government $1,222 per day per guard, "equivalent to $445,000 per year; over six times more than

Originally published as Ann Hagedorn (2015). "The Perils of Privatization." *American Prospect*, 26(1), Winter 2015. Reprinted with permission of the publisher.

the cost of an equivalent U.S. soldier." Reeling from scandals, Blackwater later reorganized and changed its name to Xe, and then again to Academi, which is now part of a holding company called Constellis.

With this record, how could the company continue to get government contracts for several more years? It had cozy relationships with military brass on the ground. Its top officials and directors included Cofer Black, the former head of the CIA's counterterrorist center; Bobby Ray Inman, former head of the NSA and deputy director of the CIA; former Attorney General John Ashcroft; and Jack Quinn, former White House counsel to President Clinton and chief of staff to Al Gore.

Blackwater, however, is hardly a one-off in the abuses of privatization, though it is a useful place to start. According to enthusiasts of free market discipline, privatizing a public service—in this case, military support operations—offers efficiency and cost savings. Private companies, presumably, are under market discipline and are free of cumbersome bureaucracies and stultifying government monopolies. They are thus free to innovate. But the reality is far messier.

As Blackwater showed, many of the efficiencies are spurious, because contractors cut corners. The notion of market discipline can be short-circuited by political influence that steers contracts to favored companies despite their poor performance. Often, apparent savings are bogus because of costs that are passed along to the government. In some cases, privatizing something as necessarily public as national defense is convenient because the contractor, not the government, takes the fall when something goes wrong. This is precisely the opposite of accountability.

Moreover, efficiency in the sense of cost savings is not always the right goal in the public sector, nor does it define success. The most successful option in a military campaign may not be the quickest or the least

expensive. As the Blackwater experience showed, hiring military contractors in war zones introduces significant risks—such as deficiencies in vetting, training, and oversight, especially at the level of subcontractors—that can potentially detract from overall military effectiveness. As one military analyst noted in his study of the risks of privatizing counterinsurgency operations, "Whenever efficiency outweighs accountability, the possibility exists of efficiency undermining effectiveness of services and democratic values."

Further, the cost savings so often proclaimed by privatization advocates as the measurement of success are the immediate and apparent ones, which are short-term. But costs are frequently hidden, especially considering that for every U.S. contract there can be as many as five layers of subcontracting. If the oversight is weak, there is always the potential for abuse, waste, and corruption, resulting in human costs as well as financial.

For example, in Afghanistan in October 2009, when insurgents attacked a U.S. combat outpost purportedly protected by Afghan security guards under U.S. contract, the guards fled, and were found "huddling in their beds." Lost in the controversy over the death of Ambassador J. Christopher Stevens in the 2012 Benghazi attack was the role of private contractors. When the attack began, the subcontractors hired by a U.S.-contracted private security firm to guard the perimeter and entrance to the diplomatic compound fled, leaving the guards on the inside vulnerable.

According to a report from the Senate Armed Services Committee, there were U.S.-contracted guards in Afghanistan working directly for the local Taliban. The committee's report found that private security contractors were "tunneling U.S. taxpayers dollars to Afghan warlords and strongmen linked to murder, kidnapping, bribery as well as Taliban and other anti-

Coalition activities," including more than $12,000 a month to the salary of a Taliban supporter. And more recently, a nasty legal feud between military auditors and the big defense contracting firm KBR exposed the striking fact that the company had continued to submit bills to the U.S. government for nine months after the 2012 end of its multimillion-dollar contract to provide training in detecting improvised explosive devices.

Equally unsettling and revealing is the multibillion-dollar industry of prison privatization. The U.S. imprisons more people than any nation in the world, resulting in a potential bonanza for private prison companies whose business model depends on high incarceration rates. According to the American Civil Liberties Union, "The private prison industry has been a key player over the past two decades in driving the explosion of mass incarceration in the U.S." Between 1990 and 2009, the number of inmates in private prisons nationwide, including state and federal, has increased by more than 1,600 percent.

Studies and audits of privately held prisons in recent years show that the cost-cutting incentive threatens the quality of food, medical care, and sanitation and may even contribute to heightened violence. In 2012, a federal judge in Mississippi described the abuse and beatings at a privately operated youth correctional facility as "a picture of such horror as should be unrealized anywhere in the civilized world." In Texas, an auditor's report at a privately held juvenile facility revealed that living conditions were abhorrent, depicting the cells as "filthy, smelled of feces and urine."

In 2012, *The New York Times*, after a ten-month investigation of privately held halfway houses in New Jersey, exposed an array of horrors, ranging from sexual abuse of female inmates to lax security and a significant number of escapes, and from drug dealing and gang activity to fraudulent records of drug treatment with fabricated rehabilitation progress. And all such incidents could easily be bundled into one immense deceit: inadequate oversight, well concealed by a tangle of corporate influence and New Jersey politicians from both parties, including Governor Chris Christie. The governor, in fact, was once the lobbyist for a company operating several New Jersey halfway houses, such as one 900bed facility that was run by his close friend, former partner, and political adviser, and publicly endorsed and praised often by the governor himself. Workers at that facility told reporters that robbery, sexual assault, and violence drove inmates to "regularly ask to be returned to prison, where they feel safer." And within a day of escaping another of the company's "houses," one inmate had murdered a former girlfriend.

Privatization, in sum, is effectively a fraud. When a product is provided purely via the market, and there are no public purposes involved, market accountability can work. Consumers can compare price and quality, and give their business to the vendor offering the best product at the most attractive cost. Alternatively, when government performs a function directly, there are public forms of accountability, such as congressional hearings and GAO investigations.

But when a public function is privatized, the result is a muddled middle ground, where neither market accountability nor public accountability works well because of all the layers of intermediaries. Enthusiasts of markets claim that government is the domain of political corruption, while markets are transparent. But the actual track record of privatization shows that there can be at least as much corruption and deception in privatizing a service as in providing it directly. For all the rhetoric about public-private partnerships, our society works better when we keep public functions public and private ones private.

45. Arguments For and Risks of Privatization

Chicago Council on Global Affairs Emerging Class of 2008

While public officials may see privatization as a panacea for government ills, privatization remains highly controversial among the public. Both proponents and opponents of privatization deals are vehement in their arguments and often talk past each other, with each group focusing on only part of the issue. Proponents of privatization tend to stress the financial gains of a deal and the potential operating efficiencies of the private sector. Opponents usually stress the social implications. In fact, any privatization deal has both financial and social implications. Only by addressing both considerations—and really thinking about the core functions of governance—will the public debate do justice to the fundamental question: When is infrastructure privatization in the public interest?

The Argument for Privatization

Public authorities are increasingly turning to privatization as a public policy tool for a number of reasons, including a constrained capacity to build and maintain necessary infrastructure; budget challenges; a belief in the efficiency of the private sector; and a lack of viable alternatives. These drivers occur in a context of a demand for investments that both generate cash and protect against inflation, among buyers eager to take advantage of historically very low borrowing costs. Each of these is briefly examined below.

1. **Privatization Can Be an Effective Way to Fund Critical Infrastructure Needs.** In the global era, cities around the world are building and enhancing their social and physical infrastructures to become or remain competitive. They are also facing the daunting challenge of how to pay for the upgrades. It is hard to imagine a more vivid picture of underinvestment in essential infrastructure than the 2007 bridge collapse in Minnesota, in which an eight-lane bridge across the Mississippi River crumbled into the water during rush hour, killing 13 people and injuring scores

Originally published as The Chicago Council on Global Affairs Emerging Class of 2008 (2011). "The Pros and Cons of Privatization." *Government Finance Review*, 27(3), June 2011. Reprinted with permission of the publisher.

more. For well over a decade, the American Society of Civil Engineers (ASCE) has given U.S. infrastructure very poor grades in its Report Card for America's Infrastructure across a range of categories (American Society of Civil Engineers, 2009).

In 2009 the ASCE reported that the United States would need $2.2 trillion in investment just to maintain its existing stock of roads and bridges-not to mention new investments in transit, energy, communications, and other infrastructure that are necessary to make our lives better in the twenty-first century.

While the United States invests an average of 2.4 percent of its gross domestic product every year in infrastructure, Europe and China invest 5 percent and 9 percent, respectively (Economist, 2006). Governments in the United States—local, state, and federal—are in no position to close this gap. Public finances in many jurisdictions (e.g., California and Illinois) were in poor shape before the financial crisis; now they are worse. Governments at every level are making cuts. Taxpayers are refusing to pay more, and often voting to pay less. Privatization can be a politically expedient tool for funding infrastructure improvements.

It is also important to recognize that privatization revenues can finance investments in infrastructure and human capital that make future generations more productive. For example, if revenues from an asset are used to improve the quality of, or the access to, education (particularly for disadvantaged citizens), the economic benefits could be quite significant. Privatization can unlock capital for investments in infrastructure that promote growth, ease congestion, improve the environment, or otherwise enhance the lives of future generations.

2. **Privatization Can Provide a Source of Immediate Revenue for Strained Public Budgets.** Policymakers are increasingly turning to privatization as a way to deal with strained public finances. The demographic trends in most industrialized societies—and in some industrializing societies such as in China—will impose huge additional costs on the public sector in coming decades. Citizens around the world are generally living longer (spending much longer stretches in retirement) and, especially in industrialized countries, having fewer children. While this is a healthy trend in many ways, it also puts new stresses on the traditional mechanisms for funding old-age benefits, since the ratio of retirees receiving public benefits to workers paying for those benefits is growing steadily.

Aging societies—including America's large baby boom cohort, which has now reached retirement age—will create a more or less permanent fiscal crunch around the globe. The present financial crisis exacerbates the structural challenge within aging societies. Like the federal government, states and municipalities are reeling from increased financial claims just as their tax revenues are at cyclical lows. Privatization offers a large source of immediate revenue to help meet these budget challenges.

3. **Private Infrastructure Funds Are an Attractive Investment Vehicle for Certain Investors, Making Infrastructure Privatization Appealing to Potential Bidders.** It may strike some as a curious fact that a once little-known Australian bank is among the largest players in infrastructure privatization globally. Indeed, Macquarie Bank was a key member of the consortium that acquired the Chicago Skyway and, soon thereafter, the Indiana Toll Road. Macquarie also manages an infrastructure investment fund that holds, among other assets, Thermal Chicago, the world's largest district cooling system, which supplies steam and chilled water to approximately 100 buildings in downtown Chicago for cooling and heating under a long-term contract.

Macquarie was an early mover in infrastructure investment funds in part because of a 1992 Australian pension reform. Anticipating an increase in pension liabilities that would strain the public budget, Australia created a compulsory retirement scheme involving private investments. By 2006 Australians had more money in managed funds per capita than any other developed country (*Sydney Morning Herald*, 2006).

This, in turn, drove a creative search for places to invest pension assets, including infrastructure. Fortunately for Macquarie, the Australian government was privatizing toll roads at the same time, which allowed Macquarie to package toll roads into a bond-like investment vehicle. The long-term, stable cash flow of infrastructure (e.g., tolls for 99 years) offers the predictability of a bond with the added advantage that tolls (as well as airport landing fees, port fees, etc.) generally rise with inflation, giving investors a natural hedge against inflation. Many banks around the world have since launched similar infrastructure funds to help meet the investment requirements of aging baby boomers. Financial investors have been attracted to infrastructure-related investments by the premiums they often yield over corporate and public bonds.

4. **Historically Low Interest Rates Enable Private Firms to Make Highly Leveraged Infrastructure Investments.** Debt is cheap. While historically low bond yields make it difficult for pensioners to fund their retirement, the flip side is that borrowing costs are low, making leveraged investments in infrastructure by private firms attractive. The stable, predictable cash flow generated by infrastructure assets can generally support highly leveraged transactions.

For example, the consortium in which Macquarie participated to buy the Chicago Skyway offered the City of Chicago almost 80 percent more than the next highest bidder and several times what the city believed the asset might be worth. Macquarie funds have paid similarly large premiums over what other public investors were willing to pay for infrastructure assets elsewhere in the world. These bids are largely due to Macquarie's aggressive view of how much debt these infrastructure assets can support.

5. **Because the Private Sector Can Often Deliver Greater Efficiencies than Government, Privatization Can Result in Better Service at Lower Cost.** The present wave of privatizations can also be viewed in the context of the broader liberalization programs ushered in with Margaret Thatcher in the 1980s and to a lesser degree by Ronald Reagan in the United States. Thatcher's privatization of large state-owned corporations such as British Gas was driven by her conviction that "the imperfections of state intervention in the economic field are likely to be not merely equal to, but greater than, the imperfections of the market." Poorly run private businesses must fix themselves or perish; state-run enterprises face no such constraint (Margaret Thatcher Foundation, 1980).

Today, the United Kingdom is arguably the most market-oriented of all states when it comes to infrastructure, having sold everything from the rights to operate individual London bus lines to on-site management of concessions in hospitals and elementary schools.

Reagan similarly made privatization a theme of his presidency, describing the 1987 divestment of Conrail, a large freight railroad, for $1.575 billion as "the flagship of privatization and the first of what we hope will be many government functions returned to their rightful place in the private sector" (Reagan, 1987). While his two terms in office did see the privatization of many services through government contracting, intentions to privatize government corporations and assets gained little traction despite the creation of the high-profile Commission on Privatization (Brinkley, 1987).

Today, much empirical evidence supports the claim that private companies are generally more efficient operators than government entities (Megginson, 2009). The reasons for this are various and include management incentives tied to performance, a better capacity to fund capital investments, greater operating leverage, the introduction of proprietary technology, and the de-politicization of pricing and other operational decisions (e.g., raising tolls or cutting money-losing routes).

Broadly speaking, the public appears to have more general confidence in the efficiency of the private sector than was the case several decades ago, when the fear of private monopolies outweighed concerns about public inefficiency. However, the backlash in Chicago against its poorly executed parking meter privatization has almost certainly jaded local opinion against infrastructure privatization, at least in the short run. There is also a heightened skepticism and distrust of Wall Street, as reflected by a May 2009 Pew Research Center study showing that 67 percent of the public surveyed say that "Wall Street only cares about making money for itself." There would thus likely be skepticism of many of the financial players that would be involved in any future privatization deal as well.

6. **Privatization Can Be a Politically Expedient Solution to Public Problems.** Another advantage of the private sector, unrelated to efficiency or expertise, is that its executives do not have to run for reelection, although they do have to respond to shareholders. Private operators can do things that politicians are unwilling or unable to do, such as raise tolls or parking fees. This can actually work to the public's advantage because the price of a privatization deal reflects these additional revenues that will be recovered by the private operators.

7. **The Alternatives to Privatization are Unattractive.** Privatization decisions do not take place in a vacuum, which is a policy reality often lost in the public discourse. The long-term lease of public assets has the

potential to generate enormous public revenues. That point is obvious. The less obvious reality is that in the absence of those revenues-if a privatization deal is not done-a government must implicitly choose a different course. At bottom, this is just math. Without the large influx of cash provided by a privatization agreement, a public entity has four choices:

a. Raise Taxes. If the goal is to finance some level of spending, then whatever revenue does not come from privatization must come from somewhere else. One likely source of "somewhere else" is higher taxes, which is both politically unpopular and can have adverse economic consequences in the long run.

b. Borrow. Most governments have the capacity to issue bonds, which provide an opportunity to make investments in the present (or to pay current bills) and then spread payments over a longer term such as 30 years-even longer in some cases. Privatization revenues are another source of revenues to make such investments (or to pay current bills) and can replace or supplement public borrowing. It should be noted that privatization and public borrowing, which are seemingly dissimilar tools, have broadly similar intergenerational effects.

Both privatizing a public asset and issuing public debt provide a benefit in the present that must be paid for in the future. In the case of debt, future taxpayers must repay the bonds, with interest. In the case of privatization, future taxpayers must forgo the revenue stream that has been sold (e.g., future toll revenues). Both public tools involve spending in the present at the expense of the future; of course, both can be justified if the current spending leaves future generations better off.

c. Spend Less. Privatization effectively packages a future stream of income (e.g., tolls or parking meter revenues) into a large dollop of public income in the present. This revenue can be used to cover deficits, invest in new infrastructure, expand social services, or do anything else that governments typically do. If a government does not earn privatization revenues and is unwilling or unable to raise taxes or borrow, then this spending cannot happen. As a result, the government will have to cut deeper to balance a budget, invest less in infrastructure, or spend less on social services, and so on.

d. Manage Assets More Efficiently, Either to Stanch the Financial Bleeding or to Improve Profits. This may involve politically unattractive decisions that improve revenues (such as raising tolls) or that reduce costs (such as demanding labor concessions from public employees).

Risks of Privatization

Privatization is an extraordinarily powerful governance tool. As with any other tool, it can be used incorrectly, in the wrong circumstances, or with malevolent intentions. Privatizing public assets has implications that stretch across generations and involve billions of dollars. The following is an inventory of potential pitfalls that ought to be considered in the context of any privatization decision.

1. **Privatization Constrains Future Options.** By definition, privatization places a public asset in private control for some period of time, if not indefinitely. A privatization contract can be written to demand all kinds of performance measures-but only those that can be anticipated at the time the contract is written. A lot can change in 20 or 50 or 99 years; the public has little control over a private entity that is adhering to a contract that is valid but nonetheless outdated because it no longer reflects what the

public desires or expects. In contrast, an elected government controlling a public asset is always accountable to voters. If those citizens decide that they want something different with respect to an asset (because of changes in technology, lifestyle, demographics, or anything else), then the government is unhindered in its ability to cater to those evolving preferences.

2. **Privatization May Have Social Implications, Adversely Affecting Certain Groups.** The primary benefit of privatization lies in the efficiencies of the private sector. Profit-seeking firms have a powerful incentive to increase revenues and reduce costs. This incentive, usually a good thing, can turn out to have adverse social consequences when certain kinds of public assets are put in private hands.

First, a private operator may cut costs by taking actions that harm a vulnerable segment of society, such as low-income citizens. For example, an efficient operator will cut money-losing services (e.g., bus routes to certain neighborhoods) and purge customers who aren't profitable. The subsequent reduction in service may cut off workers from their jobs or eliminate some basic service for the most needy.

Second, private operators may act in ways that create costs that spill over into the public sector. Take the example of a privatized toll road whose operator has leeway in setting use fees. It is understood that levying tolls on highways will alter driver behavior and road usage. Transportation research has shown that, in the face of rising toll costs, drivers' route selection is highly elastic, meaning that many will modify their choice of routes when confronted by relatively small increases in fees (Swan and Belzer, 2008).

Some motorists will detour onto public roads that do not charge tolls. As drivers opt to reroute their travel, congestion levels on other roadways will increase, leading to rising costs for other drivers in the form of longer commute times and higher public costs for road maintenance and repair.

Third, making a good asset more popular, and thereby increasing revenues, may not always be in society's best interest. Consider the case of a lottery privatization. A private operator can improve the "efficiency" of the lottery by making it more popular. Revenues will go up. However, low-income citizens buy a disproportionate share of lottery tickets, so that a more popular lottery will essentially transfer income away from some of society's neediest citizens, leaving any resulting social problems for the public sector to fix.

Finally, a private operator may maximize profits by limiting competition, which was the case with the British Airport Authority (BAA), which had a disincentive to invest in expanding capacity, thereby boosting profits at the expense of airport congestion (a cost borne by weary travelers). In fact, BAA invested heavily in airport retail, creating at least the appearance of a misaligned incentive, since stranded travelers have more time to shop.

3. **Stealing from the Future?** Privatization deals typically generate huge cash windfalls in the present in exchange for revenue streams that would otherwise accrue to citizens in the future. From a public interest standpoint, we must be concerned with how any privatization proceeds are used, particularly since public budget pressures appear to be the catalyst for the sale or lease of assets in the United States (though not necessarily elsewhere in the world).

Future generations can benefit if privatization revenues are invested in things that will increase future productivity and prosperity, such as human capital and infrastructure. Or future generations can be robbed if the cash inflows—often a large lump sum—are squandered or used to pay current expenses. In that case, current citizens are paying their own bills by tapping into a revenue stream-tolls, landing fees, and parking meters for instance-that could have been used to pay bills in the future. This is essentially a transfer of wealth from future citizens to current citizens.

From a political economy standpoint, it is worth pointing out the obvious, which is that current citizens can vote and future citizens, depending on the time frame, often cannot. If one takes a long view of social welfare, a privatization deal that passes political muster today may still not be in the public interest because the people who stand to lose aren't around to be heard and counted.

4. **Privatization May Result in an Undervalued Deal.** Citizens must receive the fair market value for any public assets put in private hands. Again, this is separable from deciding whether or not a particular asset is a good candidate for privatization. A good deal demands the right price; anything less than that is simply a transfer of wealth from taxpayers to the private firm or firms involved. And again, basic political economy matters: Elected officials have an incentive to accept a "bad deal" if control over the cash inflows strengthens their own political position. Machiavellian motivations aside, public servants may also simply lack the technical and financial skills to get a fair price for taxpayers.

One relatively obvious point is that shortening the duration of a privatization deal can minimize mistakes over valuation (or any other errors, for that matter. It can also decrease the gains accrued from the deal).

5. **Private Entities May Fail to Fulfill Contractual Obligations.** A privatization contract is only as good as its monitoring and enforcement. Privatization is built upon "contractible quality," meaning that the contract explicitly specifies what is expected of the private operator in terms of quality and service levels, among other issues. Contracts do not enforce themselves. Government must devote resources to overseeing

privatization contracts and must have a strategy in place in case a private firm does not or cannot fulfill its contractual obligations.

6. **A Lack of Public Input.** A lack of public input—real or perceived—at any point in the privatization process can compromise the outcome and leave citizens deeply disaffected. In theory, any government is designed to represent the voice of its citizens; in practice, privatization may demand public input above and beyond the normal processes of government at every step in the process. Even a "good" privatization deal in a financial sense will generate public consternation and distrust if there is a lingering belief that it did not reflect the public will.

Process matters. Every step of a privatization deal must be perceived as fair, transparent, and inclusive. The ends will not justify the means, since there is no obvious metric for quantifying the success of a privatization agreement (unlike the private sector, in which a good return on investment can redeem even the sloppiest deal). If anything, a poor public process can poison a deal that makes sense in every other respect.

Conclusions

If privatization were a prescription drug, its risks would be the warnings on the side of the bottle. There is nothing about the warnings that suggests one should abstain from taking the medicine. Yet, the more powerful the medicine, the more important it is to consider side effects and improper usage. Each of these potential concerns suggests ways in which privatization can be used to advance the public interest. We can mitigate the risks and adverse effects by selecting the right kinds of assets; by writing good contracts and then monitoring them; by demanding the right price; and, perhaps most important, by developing a good process for doing all of this.

REFERENCES

American Society of Civil Engineers. (2009). *Report Card for America's Infrastructure*. Reston, VA: American Society of Civil Engineers, March 25, 2009.

Brinkley, Joel. (1987). "Reagan Appoints Privatization Unit." *New York Times*, September 4, 1987.

Economist. (2006). "The Cracks Are Showing." *Economist*, June 26, 2006.

Margaret Thatcher Foundation. (1980). "The New Conservatism." Lecture to the Bow Group. London, UK: Margaret Thatcher Foundation, August 4, 1980.

Megginson, William. (2009). "Privatization in the Developed World." Briefing to report authors, November 13, 2009.

Reagan, Ronald. (1987). "Remarks at a White House Ceremony Marking the Sale of the Consolidated Rail Corporation." Washington, D.C., April 3, 1987.

Swan, Peter, and Michael Belzer. 2010. "Empirical Evidence of Toll Road Traffic Diversion and Implications for Highway Infrastructure Privatization." *Public Works Management & Policy*. 14 (4): 351-373.

Sydney Morning Herald (2006). "Australia 'Tops' in Managed Funds." *Sydney Morning Herald*, January 23, 2006.

46. Woes and Wows of Public-Private Partnerships

Rachel Burstein and Edward Shikada

Like many agencies, San Jose, California, has been working at public-private partnerships for many years. Some have been tremendously successful, including volunteers turning around the city's Municipal Rose Garden from nearly losing accreditation with a national rose society to garnering a designation as "America's Best."

In 1928, the city council set aside 5.5 acres of a former prune orchard for a formal rose garden. Construction continued through the depression era, with the news reporting in 1932 that "a crew of 32 men has been at work preparing beds at the rose gardens. Funds to pay these men, who have been unemployed and are heads of families residing in this city, were raised by city employees donating a percentage of their salaries."

The garden opened to great fanfare and became a destination for generations, including countless weddings and high school graduations.

Over the years, budget cuts impacted its beauty as resources were insufficient to maintain the rose garden, and the rose bushes were dying for lack of regular maintenance. Neighbors volunteered to help but initially encountered concerns with liability, quality of volunteers' work, and loss of city employees' work.

To overcome these concerns, the council provided volunteers' insurance and confirmed this policy direction. With Rose Society–certified volunteers training 375 others, the Friends of the San Jose Rose Garden was formed in 2007 to assist in caring for the roses. In just a few short years, this partnership has brought the garden back to being designated "America's Best Rose Garden" by the All-America Rose Selections. This volunteer model has since been used in gardens throughout the nation.

Other partnerships have been less fruitful. One involved the relationship with a corporation that took years to recover after staff-level collaborations were found to conflict with procurement rules. Where staff believed close collaboration was allowed and a competitive procurement not necessary based on adoption of a brand as the city's standard, a subsequent investigation determined that proper steps had not been taken.

When it comes to addressing budget shortfalls and creating greater efficiencies

Originally published as Rachel Burstein and Edward Shikada (2013). "Wows and Woes of Public-Private Partnerships." *Public Management (PM) Magazine*, 95(11), December 2013. Reprinted with permission of the publisher.

in local government, however, public-private partnerships often receive acclaim as the way to go. Local governments outsource governmental services like trash pickup or parks maintenance to external providers, and others hire consultants to advise them on key policy issues.

But public-private partnerships are different than these contractual relationships. Whether it's a university that provides free consulting, a manager investigating an organizational redesign, a nonprofit that manages a street festival on a city's behalf, or a private company that provides pro bono help in prototyping and implementing a new technological system, public-private partnerships seem to offer considerable advantages over local government's typical go-it-alone approach.

On the face of things, it would appear that if a private company, a university, or a nonprofit is willing to supply labor, offer expertise, or provide in-kind donations, then city or county staff members don't have to find qualified personnel, commit money, or convince the public or management staff that the project is worthwhile. So, what's not to like about public-private partnerships?

Inherent Complexities

As anyone who's ever taken on this type of partnership knows, things aren't so simple. Even if a local government is not initially responsible for allocating money for a partnership, these relationships have significant costs. In order for them to succeed, communities must have the capacity and commitment to manage relationships for the duration of the project, and to continue successful projects if partnerships dissolve.

Both partners must have a clear alignment of interests and vision from the beginning of the project, and local government leaders must make sure that by pursuing a partnership they are not detracting from the development of internal capacity at city hall. Public-private partnerships can be an effective way of deploying existing governmental services or providing new ways of serving and engaging the public, but only if they are approached carefully and strategically.

We should note that the term "public-private partnerships" means different things to different people. Among government contractors, the term has been used to encompass all forms of nontraditional service agreements, from design-build construction to shared-risk models.

Real estate developers use the term to describe private development of publicly owned land. From some labor viewpoints, it has become a euphemism for outsourcing. Within this context, it comes as no surprise that confusion, suspicion, and ambiguity are routinely encountered in any discussion of these partnerships.

A Mixed Bag

Administrators understand that there are often significant hurdles involved in making these relationships work. In the California Civic Innovation Project's (CCIP) recent survey of city managers, county administrators, and their deputies, managers often expressed concerns about sustainability of projects, the motives of partners, the investment of local resources, and partners' influence in determining whom local government serves. (Survey results can be found at http://ccip.newamerica.net/publications/policy/the_case_for_strength ening_personal_net works_in_california_local_government.)

CCIP's report also found that few local government executives identified a public-private partnership as the most important new approach undertaken by their community in the past five years. While approximately one-third cited projects involving new ways of delivering services and more than one-fourth mentioned regional collaborations, fewer than 3 percent identified a public-private partnership as the single most important innovation in the past five years.

For many local governmental leaders, public-private partnerships are far from essential. Instead, they often represent one-off projects pursued for publicity or as a limited test case that is rarely parlayed into a more central piece of a community's core mission or function. Indeed, they might even present a conflict with that core mission.

In 2007, San Jose's city council asked staff for a report on pending partnerships and obstacles. The response was nearly a dozen initiatives that had encountered one or more policy conflicts, and as a result the council directed and received more than six months of progress reports on issues resolution. Absent this sustained council visibility, even the most worthwhile efforts might have languished in the "too-tough-to-tackle" issue pile that confronts every organization.

Partnership efforts can also encounter unexpected turbulence. For example, the San Jose city manager's office thought that a foundation for council discussion of prevailing wage rules could be laid with an objective university student team report that chronicled prior council actions on the topic. A local labor organization challenged the university team's objectivity, commissioning its own report rebutting the students' findings and reinforcing the positive impact of prevailing wage rules.

The CCIP survey also found significant variation in how respondents value different types of groups that might act as partners, with community groups ranking much higher than colleges and universities, for example. This distinction points to the value of personal relationships in these partnerships.

Community groups typically involve individuals that have long-standing involvement in community issues, or at least the potential to establish long-standing involvement. University students, and to some extent faculty too, are much more likely to only engage in a single project.

At the same time, public-private success can be found within the one-off niche. San Jose has established an ability to quickly refresh a shelf list of possible projects that is used by university and management development teams as practical exercises. While progress has been made in several areas as a result, this approach nonetheless reflects the reality that risky or time-sensitive topics won't be on the list.

Ensuring Meaningful Partnerships

While concerns are understandable, they should not deter communities from pursuing meaningful public-private partnerships with the potential to make local government more effective in responding to community needs. Determining which partnerships fit the bill and how they should be managed can be complicated, though, especially for smaller communities with more limited resources.

The good news is that there are steps that managers can take to increase the chances of success before a project even begins:

Align purposes. Addressing community need is a powerful motivation for city and county administrators. Indeed, this ranked second on a list of 10 factors for adopting local government innovations and new approaches in CCIP's study. Yet responding to community needs may not carry the same importance for a potential partner.

Even when both parties agree that serving the public is the first priority, local government staffers and partners may define community differently. Achieving clarity on the purpose of the initiative in general and for each party from the beginning can go a long way toward preventing missteps later.

This is a particularly sensitive point when it comes to business involvement. Historically, a frequent assumption underlying business involvement in public-private partnerships has been the promise of future compensated work, either through expansion of a pilot or subsequent phases of a project. Yet this motivation can run afoul of procurement rules.

A recent trend, however, shows promise of avoiding such conflicts. Many businesses have been willing to consider partnerships for other purposes—recognition, employee development, and marketing to future prospective customers, for example.

Initiate ongoing communication. Discussing purpose and goals is important, but cities and counties also need to do a better job of informing partners of the skills and capacity they bring to the relationship, and identifying areas in which their contributions will be limited from the outset. Communication, however, should not end with the partner.

Too often, local government management staff members fail to inform the public and lower-level staff of the partnership by articulating its value and responding to fears and objections from the beginning. This is particularly important when for-profit companies are involved. An early start, transparency, and a willingness to adjust proposals in response to objections are all important if the partnership is to be successful.

As noted earlier, even the term public-private partnership can be met with suspicion based on its historical connection to outsourcing. Partnerships are relationship-based and as such, require ongoing maintenance.

This is particularly important as innovative partnerships can inevitably encounter

such policy conflicts as worker wage requirements. Addressing policy exceptions is more difficult when this is the first conversation that engages stakeholders on a proposal.

Clearly define roles and responsibilities. While it is often difficult to establish an explicit road map for the roles and responsibilities for each party ahead of time, doing so can allay problems later. It might, for example, be easier to gain support for a project internally if employees understand that the new initiative will not displace them, and may, in fact, draw on their expertise and strengths.

San Jose has found that an extremely important role is that of a partnership coordinator, responsible for troubleshooting issues no matter where they lead. This provides a path and support to the team that reinforces the importance of its work, while recognizing that the group is creating a road map for others.

Establish complementary skill sets. Partnerships work best when the partner can offer something—say, knowledge of a particular technical area or an army of volunteers—that isn't present or readily accessible within city hall. At the same time, there are particular things that city or county staffers offer, and the direction of the project must be carefully monitored by local government leaders. Ensuring that there are neither overlapping skill sets or resources nor gaps in what elements are needed to make the partnership work can prevent headaches later.

This balance of skills can make or break a partnership. Competing expertise is extremely challenging, as any manager who has challenged police or fire deployment methods can attest. At the same time, implementing a successful technology project might require a minimum level of staff knowledge to bridge the gap between existing resources and state-of-the-art application.

Of course, even the best planned partnerships may not always result in success. A partner may pull out of its commitment or a mission may change. A city may face internal or external pressures that prevent the full realization of the project. Leadership and availability of resources may change the priority or scale of the partnership.

Planning for Contingencies

Because so much can change at the drop of a hat, it's important that local government leaders take the time to plan for contingencies and to evaluate the effectiveness of projects in real time. Here are tips that can help in the process:

Manageable and targeted projects. The most effective public-private partnerships are those that are targeted and time-limited, addressing a specific existing community need. Local governments should never assume continued partner support and should look for ways that a city or county can continue to support the project—whether this involves committing funding for the project in the future or in having the partner train staff to assume responsibility.

Successful partnerships are built on relationships, and building relationships takes time. Both parties to a relationship are most comfortable building on small successes rather than launching into a large, risky venture from the outset. In San Jose's case, the mayor's office is currently leading an effort to create a sustainable model for Silicon Valley workers to donate their time and talent to public sector challenges.

An early conclusion was that this effort requires the ongoing engagement and attention to managing relationships between agencies and volunteers, as well as recognizing the practical limits of volunteer time commitments.

Documentation, evaluation, and flexibility. In some cases, partnerships may be a waste of a locality's time, energy, or money. But it is often difficult to know how things will play out until after a partnership is already under way.

That's why careful documentation of internal capacity and other local government investments relative to outcomes is so important. Partners and local governments must demonstrate flexibility in response to assessments and revising or ending projects when they are not meeting stated objectives.

It is also important for local governments to allocate resources for evaluation after the conclusion of a partnership, assessing the effectiveness of the effort in meeting the objectives for the project that were identified in the beginning. Such evaluations can inform future partnerships.

Partnerships are blazing new trails for government. Such trails are most valuable when providing markers for others to follow.

Accountability and buy-in. With no contract to tie them to a city or county, partners are free to remove themselves from a project at any time. Yet local government leaders can do more to ensure partners' continued participation as well as the continued commitment of their own staff.

By committing terms to writing, publicizing the effort in the local press from the outset, and including staff commitments to partnerships in performance reviews, managers can build accountability into the process. They also gain buy-in both from employees who will be involved in the project, and from higher-ups with the power to commit resources. It is important for managers to support employees for the duration of the partnership. This means allocating enough time for employees to work on the project and providing ongoing infrastructure and support to employees involved in the partnership.

Public-private partnerships are hardly a silver bullet for addressing resource deficiencies in local government. But they can be made far more effective if local governments are careful and strategic in designing and implementing projects with third parties.

This isn't always easy; it requires awareness, resources, and commitment from the outset, but it can also result in great rewards for both local governments and partners.

47. Pros and Cons of Privatizing Government Functions

Russell Nichols

Last summer, residents of Maywood, Calif., woke up one morning to find the government as they knew it gone. After years of corruption and mismanagement, the small, blue-collar city south of Los Angeles fired almost all of its employees, dismantled its police department and contracted with a neighboring city to take over most municipal tasks. On July 1, local officials announced that Maywood had become the country's first city to be fully outsourced.

It was an unprecedented move spurred by a loss of commercial liability insurance and Workers' Compensation. As the city drowned in deficits and faced multiple lawsuits, city leaders saw outsourcing as a light at the end of a collapsing tunnel.

But it was only a mirage.

Bell, Calif., the city that Maywood officials had tapped to run its services, erupted with a pay and pension scandal, forcing several top Bell officials to resign. By September, Bell had scrapped its contract with Maywood, leaving the city to fend for itself and find new contractors for its outsourcing hopes.

The search for financial salvation is sweeping the country as local governments grapple with waning sales and property tax revenues. The economic recession has strangled budgets, forcing layoffs and the disbanding of departments. Feeling pushed to the brink of bankruptcy, cities are trying to find effective ways to make do with less. Maywood, in its outsourcing attempt, may be the most extreme example, but in California and other states in the past decade, more public officials have turned to outside sources for help in providing services at a lower cost to the state.

In theory, the idea of contracting public services to private companies to cut costs makes sense. If someone is willing to fix streets or put out fires for less money, that should be a plus for a government's bottom line. Many state and local governments have identified hundreds of millions of dollars in savings by hiring outside contractors—or a neighboring city's services—to handle tasks like trash collection, pothole repair, and water and wastewater treatment.

But according to analysts, outsourcing is by no means a perfect solution. Some agencies don't have the metrics in place to prove in advance that outsourcing a service will

Originally published as Russell Nichols (2010). "The Pros and Cons of Privatizing Government Functions." *Governing*, December 2010. Reprinted with permission of the publisher.

save money. Problems from poorly conceived contracts can create cost increases that surpass the costs of in-house services, and if there's shoddy contract oversight, a government is vulnerable to corruption and profiteering. The privatization of public services can erode accountability and transparency, and drive governments deeper into debt. "Governments at all levels are just desperate to balance their budgets, and they're grasping at privatization as a panacea," says Susan Duerksen, director of communications for In the Public Interest, a project that examines privatization and contracting. "But there's evidence that it often is a very bad deal with hidden costs and consequences when you turn over public service to a for-profit company."

Privatizing to Save Money and Time

Various governments—from small towns all the way up to federal agencies—have been sending public services to the private sector since the 1980s. The trend stems from the common belief that private companies can help governments save or make money by doing jobs faster and cheaper, or managing a public asset more efficiently.

This past March, for example, New Jersey Gov. Chris Christie created the state Privatization Task Force to review privatization opportunities within state government and identify barriers. In its research, the task force not only identified estimated annual savings from privatization totaling more than $210 million, but also found several examples of successful efforts in other states. As former mayor of Philadelphia, Pennsylvania, Gov. Ed Rendell saved $275 million by privatizing 49 city services. Chicago has privatized more than 40 city services. Since 2005, it has generated more than $3 billion in upfront payments from private-sector leases of city assets. In 2005, West Virginia

Gov. Joe Manchin worked to transform the state's Workers' Compensation Commission into a private insurance carrier, BrickStreet Insurance. That has led Workers' Compensation rates to decline about 30 percent statewide, translating to more than $150 million in annual employer savings.

"Sterile philosophical debates about 'public versus private' are often detached from the day-to-day world of public management," the New Jersey Privatization Task Force reported. "Over the last several decades, in governments at all levels throughout the world, the public sector's role has increasingly evolved from direct service provider to that of an indirect provider or broker of services; governments are relying far more on networks of public, private and nonprofit organizations to deliver services."

The report took careful note of another key factor: The states most successful in privatization created a permanent, centralized entity to manage and oversee the operation, from project analysis and vendor selection to contracting and procurement. For governments that forgo due diligence, choose ill-equipped contractors and fail to monitor progress, however, outsourcing deals can turn into costly disasters.

The Effects of Inefficient Outsourcing

No industry has gone through greater outsourcing catastrophes in the past year than government IT. Last fall, Texas cut short its seven-year contract with IBM, an $863 million deal that called for IBM to provide data center and disaster recovery services for 27 state agencies. When an audit criticized the state's Department of Information Resources for lax oversight, inadequate staffing and sloppy service, the partnership fell apart. In Virginia, the state's 10-year, $2.3 billion IT contract with Northrop Grumman to run the state's computers, servers, e-mail systems and help desk services also has been plagued by inadequate planning, cost overruns and poor service.

Technology plays such a critical role in the storage and delivery of vital data that even minor delays and deficiencies can disrupt business operations, such as car registration renewals, and unemployment and medical care services. In August, a storage area network failure in Virginia knocked two dozen state agencies' computer systems offline in another devastating blow to the state's IT outsourcing contract. A week later, the state Department of Motor Vehicles still couldn't process drivers' licenses at customer service centers because databases were down.

"The problem is that outsourcing deals are really about risk," says Adam Strichman, co-founder of Sanda Partners, an outsourcing consultancy. "You're taking the risk of the unknown and dumping that on your supplier," he says. "You're outsourcing a problem to a company that has limited control over the root cause of the problem." The only way for a public-private partnership to work, he suggests, is to drive transformation from within the agency. And that's the hard part. Red tape usually prevents governments from making significant modifications, and private companies lack the authority to enforce real changes. When such a public-private stalemate stunts a project, it helps to have an exit strategy.

Those risks extend beyond the technology world. In 2009, in the wake of an audit of economic development agreements between Niagara Falls and two developers, New York State Comptroller Thomas P. DiNapoli discovered that the projects faltered because the city failed to monitor development contracts. One of the projects, a downtown retail mall, has been vacant since 2000; the second project, which began in 1997, yielded nothing more than a rudimentary building foundation.

"Before governments hire outside contractors, it's important to examine the cost-effectiveness," says Nicole Hanks, deputy press secretary of the state comptroller's office. "More times than not, it's less expensive to use state workers instead of outside contractors."

Guidelines to a Successful Outsourcing Deal

A good outsourcing deal starts with a thorough cost-benefit analysis to see if a third party can effectively deliver services better and more cheaply than public employees. Strichman says governments should hire an outsourcing consultant who can provide an independent assessment. But even with a consultant, conflicts of interest can tarnish a golden opportunity. After all, private companies may want to provide a service efficiently and well—and often do—but governments must ride herd on implementation of the contract. As Duerksen points out, a company's motivation "is not the common good; it's profit. If they can cut corners in any way, they often do."

In that regard, the provider that offers the lowest bid might not be the best option. But with his experience in several large-scale government outsourcing deals, Strichman has seen first-hand that in a bidding war, the company that has "a liberal interpretation for the lowest price wins," which inevitably leads to strife when high expectations meet underachievement. "Anyone can bid any outsourcing deal 5 percent cheaper, but the problem is you don't know what they cut out," he says. "When price reductions appear unrealistic, there's no magic. They are unrealistic."

Even with the proper oversight channels, policies won't work if departments don't participate. In 2005, the Wisconsin Legislature passed a law that required a cost-benefit analysis be completed for any purchase of service more than $25,000. The law outlines analysis procedures and reporting requirements. Soon after, the Contract Sunshine Act was enacted, requiring all Wisconsin agencies to provide online information about state contracts in excess of $10,000.

The laws were created to promote transparency and to ensure that agencies complete an effective cost-benefit analysis prior to procurements. But compliance has been low, says Janice Mueller, state auditor for the Wisconsin Legislative Audit Bureau. "We were asked to look and see why state agencies are not consistently reporting," she says. "It's really difficult to compel compliance."

In other cases, outsourcing efforts may be stifled by union contracts or a lack of available services. Mayor Sharon McShurley in Muncie, Ind., wanted to outsource the city's fire protection services to save money. But the city ceased its cost analysis after realizing that no such private services existed in the area. "It does tie our hands as administrators trying to figure out how to balance the budget and provide services with a reduction in revenue," she says. "I like the idea of outsourcing. Competition drives prices down. We don't have the revenue that we used to have."

48. Benefits and Downsides of Privatizing Municipal Services

Stephanie Rozsa and Caitlin Geary

In a world of constrained resources, local governments of all sizes and metro types are exploring new ways to reduce costs and infuse innovation. One method, privatization—the provision of goods or services to the public by private businesses under contract by the public sector—is increasingly looked to as a viable option. Privatization is grounded in the belief that market competition can be a more efficient and cost effective way to provide services. Today, facing recessionary deficits and shrinking municipal workforces, privatization is gaining popularity. In fact, many local governments are using privatization to turn the crisis into an opportunity by restructuring government management, modernizing delivery systems and raising new revenues in order to better serve residents and support long-term growth.

Types of Privatization

Privatization allows flexibility in deciding how much to involve the private sector in the design, building, operation, financing and ownership of public facilities and services. Here are the most common types (Stone, 1997):

- Contracting out (outsourcing)—Municipalities purchase or contract for services or functions, which may or may not have been previously performed by public sector employees.
- Public-private partnership—Municipalities enter into a joint venture with one or more private companies to collaborate on any or all of the planning, funding and operation of a project.
- Competitive contract Bidding—Municipal departments or offices can bid for a city contract against private-sector companies.
- Asset Sales/lease—Municipalities sell or lease city assets to the private sector. Such assets might include land, buildings, utilities or other property.
- Vouchers—Vouchers are coupons with monetary value that can purchase services in the private marketplace.
- Government corporations—This involves the establishment of a

Originally published as Stephanie Rozsa and Caitlin Geary (2010). "Privatizing Municipal Services" in *National League of Cities Municipal Action Guide*. Washington, D.C.: National League of Cities. Reprinted with permission of the publisher.

quasi-government agency, subject to overall regulation, but that functions more as a private business. These are more common at the federal level, like the postal service, but can occur at the local level through entities like municipal enterprises and special or public authorities.

- Volunteer partnerships—These are instances in which a function is mostly conducted by volunteers, but in which the municipality provides some degree of funding, guidance, and perhaps staffing.
- Complete privatization—A complete transfer of a function to a private entity.

Potential Benefits

Unlike other funding methods, privatization allows communities the flexibility to locally determine their own growth and development. While privatization's record of success is not guaranteed, here are some considerations that will increase the likelihood of success (Kemp, 1991; Fryklund et al., 1997; National League of Cities, 2008).

Cost Savings. As citizen demand for services increases and government revenue decreases, the private sector also offers additional advantages that benefit the bottom line, including market competition; access to an agile talent pool; purchasing power; flexible resource deployment; service improvement without an increase in tax rates or user fees; significant tax benefits that can reduce net costs; and the creation of economies of scale. An economy of scale is especially important for cities too small to have sufficient staff expertise or command market power in purchasing. According to the National Center on Public Private Partnerships, governments often realize cost savings of 20 to 50 percent when the private sector is involved in service provision.

Private Sector Proficiencies. The public sector can draw on the vast knowledge of the private sector, including workplace efficiencies that reduce demands on a shrinking city workforce. In addition to abundant technical and financial expertise, the private sector usually boasts superior access to newer technologies and far more diverse funding sources. Such a partnership also introduces innovative management practices and flexible operating procedures into the public sector and allows both parties to share the construction, operations, management and financial risks.

Red Tape Reduction. Operating in the private sector often involves less bureaucracy, which leads to expeditious project completion. And as municipalities confront tax and spending limitations, outside funding offers flexibility to increasingly constrained municipal budgets.

Potential Downsides

While privatization can be an effective management and service delivery tool, it remains a complicated and controversial process. Municipal leaders should consider the following:

Conflicts of Interest. When a profit-focused private company provides public services, a conflict of interest may be created if the company attempts to cut corners or exercise policy-making authority. This issue can be addressed by bundling services, contract clarity and effective contract enforcement.

Decreased Control. Once a public asset is transferred to the private sector, municipal control and oversight is automatically reduced. And while risk is shared between sectors, it is also increased by adding a new partner into a process normally initiated by a single sector.

Citizen Dissatisfaction. If the voting public regards the private sector or the particular private partner negatively, enthusiasm for even the most well-planned partnership can be dampened. Disgruntled citizens can also jeopardize a project in progress if their concerns are ignored.

Imprecise Performance Measurement. Accurate quantitative measures tell the story of a contractor's cost and performance efficiencies. Such measures, however, are difficult for cities to produce accurately and consistently, as service indicators and cost-benefit evaluations are often not standardized.

Case Studies

Public-Private Partnerships: Baltimore

The City of Baltimore recently initiated a five-year joint venture with Ports America Chesapeake to update the Seagirt Marine Terminal. At $106 million, the investment was too expensive for the city to finance alone. The modifications will allow for cargo to be received and mobilized more efficiently. The project will create 3,000 construction jobs and 2,700 direct, indirect, or induced jobs over the course of the next three years and will generate nearly $16 million in new taxes for the state. In addition, Ports America agreed to pay more than $100 million to the state of Maryland for road, bridge and tunnel modernization.

Complete Privatization: Sandy Springs, Georgia

Following its incorporation in 2005, the City of Sandy Springs opted to contract out all government services except public safety instead of creating a new municipal bureaucracy. This model saved its citizens upwards of 30 percent in taxes in the first year alone over the rate they paid to the county before incorporation. Inspired by this model, three neighboring communities have since incorporated using the same model and contractor, and a fourth recently incorporated and is contracting out bundles of services rather than hiring one operator.

Competitive Bidding: Phoenix

Between 1979 and 1994, Phoenix institutionalized competition by inviting private sectors to bid alongside city agencies for contracts. For example, the city geographically divided itself into three sectors for waste collection purposes and put each sector out to bid on a rotating schedule, and for which firms can serve no more than one of the three sectors. To secure the integrity of that process, the city's bid is prepared by an independent auditor and submitted under the same conditions as private bids. During that period, Phoenix awarded 56 contracts in 13 municipal services by this process, with 34 contracts going to private contractors and 22 remaining with the city agencies, saving $30 million.

Action Steps

Listed below are recommended action steps gleaned from successful case studies (Fryklund et al., 1997; National League of Cities, 2008). These general recommendations should be tailored to site- and project-specific requirements.

Assessment

- Define the needs and objectives to be accomplished by the project, and confirm the availability of resources to support the project through its full life cycle.
- Perform a feasibility study, which will evaluate the potential impact of the project. If an employee cannot perform the task, hire an outside consultant with a thorough understanding of the tax laws.
- Determine the current and future

costs and savings through a pricing study or financial risk analysis. Clarify the financial standing of the public and private partners in terms of available capital and access to borrowing.

- Determine the amount of stakeholder support for the project. Encourage cross-agency and union collaboration so all affected stakeholders can lend insight and become invested in the project.
- Analyze political risk, build the coalitions necessary to support the change, and communicate clearly and frequently with the public.
- Seek assistance from the state's privatization board, commission, or council, if available.
- Examine existing labor contracts and statutory, regulatory and tax laws. Make modifications as necessary.
- Evaluate proposals using several criteria: contractor capacity, experience and reputation; net cost and cost per unit; and demands on city resources. Aim to have at least three bidders.

Negotiation

- Hire an expert to negotiate a sound legal contract. The expert may come from your city's legal and purchasing departments or an outside organization.
- Clearly detail all expectations, performance indicators, obligations, communication guidelines, risk-sharing guidelines, incentives for superlative performance and penalties for nonperformance. Have measures in place for removing the contractor for consistent nonperformance.
- Maximize contractor incentives. One method is to bundle one or more phases of the project, which include the design, construction, service pro-

vision and long-term maintenance. Another method is quarterly incentives.

- Determine the appropriate contract term period, and anticipate a contract renegotiation process for additional or modified responsibilities, fees or payments. Include an exit strategy that details measures for the transference of the service back to the public sector, if applicable.
- Minimize disruptions in service continuity by making the transition as fluid as possible.

Oversight

- Assign a municipal department familiar with or responsible for the service to perform daily contract management.
- Establish regular on-site inspections and reporting by that department or an outside party. This should include quality control reviews.
- Hire a third party to perform formal financial and operational annual audits to track compliance with all contractual provisions, performance standards and all funds collected or expended.
- Hold council hearings if major contract breeches or complaints are filed.
- Maintain open lines of communication with the public about the new service. Provide a forum for community input and complaints. Include overall satisfaction levels as part of the contractor's evaluation.

REFERENCES

Fryklund, Inge, et al. (1997). *Municipal Service Delivery: Thinking Through the Privatization Option. A Guide for Local Elected Officials.* Washington, D.C., and Illinois: National League of Cities and the Center for the Study of Ethics in the Professions, Illinois Institute of Technology.

Kemp, Roger L. (1991). *Privatization: The Provi-*

sion of Public Services by the Private Sector. Jefferson, NC: McFarland.

National League of Cities. (2008). *Legislating for Results: Motivating Contractors and Grantees to High Levels of Performance.* Washington, D.C.: NLC.

Stone, Mary N. (1997). *Perspectives on Privatization by Municipal Governments.* Washington, D.C.: National League of Cities.

49. Claims and Concerns

Nora Leech

The purpose of this chapter is to provide a description of the evolution of the public policy known as "Privatization." Privatization is a movement to deregulate private industry and transfer many government services, assets and functions to the private sector. We, as citizens of the United States, have been experiencing the growing effects of the privatization movement since the 1980s. Privatization efforts have been tried (with varying degrees of success) on federal, state and local levels. Federal efforts include Social Security/Medicare, student loans, military services and interstate highways. On the state and local level, agencies responsible for social services, transportation, mental health and public health care, corrections, and education have all seen remarkable increases in privatization activities since 1988 (U.S. General Accounting Office, 1997). On a local city and neighborhood level, efforts are prominent to privatize public libraries, parks, court services and roads/bridges.

The pace of the movement to privatize has escalated since 2008. The current economic recession and the trend in government over the years to reduce taxes have increased government budget deficits. The current recession (the largest since the Great Depression) is resulting in business failures, high unemployment, and a loss of tax revenues for federal, state and local governments.

Whether the current financial situation is directly related to the deregulation of the financial services sector is the subject of great debate. Regardless of the causes, the revenue losses have added to the drive to downsize government by privatizing functions, services and assets. Although saving money through greater efficiencies may appear to be the primary reason for such a push to downsize government at this moment, there are other forces and philosophies behind the move to privatize that have been active since the early 1970s and have gained significant momentum since the 1980s.

This is a good time to take measure of privatization's impact on our citizenry: what is working and what is not. The United States has more than 30 years of privatization efforts to evaluate. It is important to think about the lessons learned within the greater framework of this public policy debate.

The Idea

Milton Friedman, the Chicago School of Economics, stated the goals of privatization

Originally published as Nora Leech (2011). "Privatization: The Public Policy Debate." *League of Women Voters Privatization Study*, Washington, D.C. Reprinted with permission of the publisher.

as a public policy agenda to reduce the size of government, deregulate business and reduce taxes (Friedman, 1962).

Claims and Concerns

Those promoting privatization of government services, assets and functions claim that the private sector will provide increased efficiency, better quality and innovation in services. Proponents claim privatized services will provide a cost savings to those being served (public consumers of the services) as well as to the government no longer responsible for providing the services or maintaining the assets. Many suggest that the government has overextended itself into sectors that could well be covered by private, for-profit companies. Some claim that privatizing government programs like interstate highways, trains or the postal service will mean that large expenses will be taken off the government books, thus providing relief to taxpayers. Advocates believe that private firms have better incentives to control costs and respond more effectively to competition.

Those concerned with the public policy of privatization say that the private sector mandate to make a profit can endanger public safety and reduce services available to the general public (particularly in poor and rural areas). They are concerned that there will be increased costs to consumers through fees and tolls and increased costs to government through poorly written contracts. They are concerned that the private sector will increase profit margins and include expenses like high executive salaries and corporate debt loads (interest on debt) that consumers and tax payers will have to pick up. There is also a concern that private companies will lack transparency, adequate oversight and accountability.

How do individuals complain to a corporation if they feel abused by high prices when there are no or limited alternatives? There is a fear of increased corruption between government and for-profit private companies as the lines between government and business professionals become blurred. There also is a concern that privatizing strategic sectors such as ports, utilities and defense to foreign-controlled multinational corporations will put the country at risk in the event of war. There is concern that the strategy to privatize large sectors of government services and functions will result in chronic high unemployment, low wages and abusive labor practices, especially during economic downturns. There is also a concern that the privatization policies will result in growing inequality between the wealthy and poor, thereby losing the revered American middleclass.

Larger Than the United States

The privatization movement is an international movement. David Linowes, chair of the 1987 President's Commission on Privatization, explains that outside the United States, it is known as the privatization movement and involves outright divestiture of government properties. In the United States, it has meant deregulation and tax reduction (Linowes, 1987).

Outside the United States

Countries with significant state corporations are encouraged to divest these businesses to the private sector. Prominent divestitures in the news have included Russia's natural gas (Gazprom), Bolivia's municipal water system in Cochabamba and the United Kingdom's British Rail. As an incentive, lenders have been known to require that governments reduce the size of the public sector through privatization and deregulate industries engaged in international trade as conditions for loans (Labaton, 1999).

In the United States

The deregulation of the financial services industry would be a notable example in the news and examples of tax reductions would be the significant reductions in corporate taxes over the last 20 years, as well as efforts to reduce individual taxes on capital gains and inheritances. Linowes states that the tax reductions of the 1980s were intended to reduce the government influence over private sector activity.

However with today's financial downturn, the focus in the United States is increasingly on downsizing government by privatization of assets, services and functions. The loss of taxes from the economic downturn and from tax cuts are jointly adding to the deficit imbalance which is creating a political crisis. Current recommendations under consideration for privatization include roads, bridges, prisons, schools, parks, health, tax collections, postal service, Amtrak, social welfare services, public health services and Worker's Compensation, to name a few. In the United States, pressure is coming from international lenders, most recently via bond rating companies threatening to downgrade U.S. bonds. A lower bond rating generally requires paying higher interest rates to lenders. This, in turn, should increase the government deficit unless taxes can be raised or cuts can be made in other areas.

History

The Chair of President Reagan's Privatization Commission provides some background. "The Privatization movement was developed mainly in reaction to the Progressive movement of the early Twentieth Century. In the Progressive Era, while other nations were most likely to nationalize an industry, the United States was more likely to subject the industry to systematic government regulations" (Linowes, 1987).

In the 1970s, disillusioned with the Progressive Era vision, leadership in the increasingly global private sector became more active, asserting that burgeoning tax rates and government regulations of industry were inhibiting free trade. Leaders expressed their skepticism about a "planned market" where the government plays a prominent role regulating businesses. They agreed with economist Milton Freidman's broader philosophical view, that free markets were the solution to many problems—health care, product safety, banking failures and financial speculation. Linowes reminds us that the Progressive movement policies were themselves a reaction against the Social Darwinism (survival of the fittest) and laissez-faire, free market theories prevalent in the late19th century.

Though many large corporations and leading financial institutions may advocate a return to laissez-faire, free market policies, there are other perspectives on the unregulated boom/bust economies of the late 1800s. It was a time of great instability. There were multiple economic depressions including the panic of 1893, where millions of Americans lost their life savings and homes due to bank failures and foreclosures. These were times of corruption in government witnessed by the railroad scandals and banking failures. These were times of unacceptable labor conditions where men in the steel mills worked 12 hours a day, seven days a week, 363 days a year; where workers maimed at work were dismissed with no compensation for themselves or their families; and where children put in 12-hour days in textile factories and coal mines under appalling work conditions. These were times when diseases—

malaria, cholera and TB—were common due to government inaction, and times of unsafe food due to unregulated food industries. And these were times of massive business failures and unemployment (Beatty, 2008).

These unstable times were followed by the catastrophic events of World War I, the Great Depression and World War II.

At the onset of these troubled times, those advocating progressive policies began to create a much stronger role for government in the well-being of its citizens by regulating business and the economy. To protect the aged, Social Security was initiated. To protect the public health, businesses were regulated (a prime example was the meatpacking industry that disgorged offal upstream of major cities). Public education was strengthened to provide an informed citizenry and a productive workforce. Programs were established to protect labor, such as workers' compensation, and laws were passed to limit the workday and provide a minimum wage. Additionally, programs were created to help the unemployed in economic downturns.

High inflation and the banking failures in the late 1800s and early 1900s led to the creation of the Federal Reserve in 1913. Although called the Federal Reserve, the new central bank (not a government bank) was an association of private bankers with limited government input. It had the power to minimize inflation by managing the amount of currency in circulation. But banks continued to fail as depositors withdrew their savings and the country fell into the Great Depression. In 1933, President Franklin Delano Roosevelt created the Federal Deposit Insurance Commission (FDIC) to encourage depositors to trust banks. Along with the ability to control inflation, the Federal Reserve was challenged by the U.S. government to maintain "full employment," aware that policies to limit inflation carried the risk of high unemployment (Madrick, 2011).

In the 1980s, however, advocates for laissez faire, free market policies were growing increasingly influential. In September 1987, the President's Commission on Privatization was created. The Commission's purpose was "to review the appropriate division of responsibilities between the federal government and the private sector and to identify those government programs that are not 'properly' the responsibility of the federal government or that can be performed more efficiently by the private sector." The Commission in 1988 recommended a broad spectrum of government activities that could be transferred to the private sector. These included low-income housing, housing finance (Fannie Mae and Freddie Mac), federal loan programs, air traffic control, educational choice (voucher programs and charter schools), U.S. Postal service, military commissaries, prisons, federal asset sales such as Amtrak and the Naval Petroleum Reserves, Medicare, international development programs, and urban mass transit (Linowes, 1987).

Theories Supporting Privatization

Yale Law Professor Paul Starr explains that the normative theories, justifying privatization as a direction for public policy, have drawn their inspiration from several different schools of thought on what constitutes a "good society" (Starr, 1988).

"Property Rights" and "Public Choice"

The intellectual inspiration behind contemporary privatization in the United States has come from the "Public Choice" and "Property Rights" schools of thought. Prominent leaders advocating these theories include Milton Friedman of the Chicago

School of Economics and Fredrick Von Hayek, whose book, Road to Serfdom, warned of the growing welfare state.

Starr's basic assumptions include:

- Democratic political systems have inherent tendencies toward government growth and excessive budgets.
- Expenditure growth is due to self-interested coalitions of voters, politicians and bureaucrats.
- Public enterprises necessarily perform less efficiently than private enterprises.

The broader philosophical view is that government social programs and regulations, inflationary spending aside, were almost always detrimental to the efficient workings of an economy. In 1962, Milton Friedman, in his book, Capitalism and Freedom, provided an intellectual map for a reversal of the progressive policies of the nation. Friedman urged the U.S. government to eliminate Social Security, progressive income taxes, free public high schools, the minimum wage, housing and highway subsidies, and health care, even for the elderly, noting that an unregulated market place would take care of these problems. Friedman believed that if individuals were given the choice, free of government rules and regulations, of where to work, where to invest their retirement funds, where to send their children to school, where to buy their healthcare and where to rent or buy their homes, competition to supply the best goods or services would result in a greater number of cheaper and higher-quality options. He postulated that with reduced government and lower taxes, the poor would be better off, inequality would be minimized, and discrimination eliminated.

Friedman sought as well to discredit the Keynesian economic theories advocating government intervention to manage the economy during financial crises. Keynes had suggested that even if interest rates and prices fall, business may not invest because of lack of demand for their goods. Thus, he advocated for government spending to kickstart the process and stated that, with an expanding economy, the deficit resulting from the spending would quickly be replaced (Krugman and Wells, 2011).

Privatization in Practice

Professor Starr describes four types of government policies intended to bring a shift from the public sector to the private sector: attrition, transfer of assets, contracting out, and deregulation.

- Attrition. Attrition results from cessation of public programs and disengagement of government from specific kinds of responsibilities. Restriction of publicly produced services in availability or quality may lead to a shift by consumers toward privately-produced substitutes. Or, government may let the service run down by drastically reducing their budgets. An example might be the U.S. Postal Service.
- Transfer of assets. Such transfer may occur with the direct sale or lease of public land, infrastructure and enterprises. Examples might be federal and state parks, state-owned liquor stores and the proposed privatization of public libraries.
- Contracting out (public/private partnerships) or vouchers. Instead of directly producing some service, the government may finance private services, for example through contracting out or vouchers. Examples might be charter schools or prisons.
- Deregulation. Deregulation may be the result of deregulating entry into activities previously treated as public monopolies. Examples might include

utilities, water, waste management, air traffic control and ports.

These four policies vary in the degree to which they move ownership, finance and accountability out of the public sector. The spectrum runs from total privatization (as in government disengagement from some policy domain) to partial privatization (public/private partnerships or vouchers, such as for school or housing). In the case of partial privatization, the government may continue to finance but not operate services, or it may continue to own but not manage assets. Partial privatization may dilute government control and accountability without eliminating them. Examples might be detention centers for juveniles or welfare services.

What Is the Role of Government?

In rethinking the proper relationship of government, business and civil society, fundamental political and economic questions arise. What should the role of government be in protecting the environment, helping the poor, defending the nation, providing justice, ensuring democracy, protecting public health, ensuring public safety, pro-viding education, promoting a thriving economy, ensuring safe work environments and a living wage. Our country must seek a pragmatic balance between social and economic returns.

REFERENCES

Beatty, Jack. (2008). *Age of Betrayal: The Triumph of Money in America, 1865–1900*. New York: Vintage Books.

Friedman, Milton. (1962). *Capitalism and Freedom*. Chicago: University of Chicago Press, 1962.

Krugman, Paul, and Robin Wells. (2011). "The Busts Keep Getting Bigger: Why?" A Review of Jeff Madrick's Age of Greed. *New York Review of Books*, July 14, 2011, p. 28.

Labaton, Stephen. (1999). "Congress Passes Wide-ranging Bill Easing Bank Laws." *New York Times*, Nov. 5, 1999.

Linowes, David. (1987). *Privatization, Toward More Effective Government*. Washington, D.C.: President's Commission on Privatization, Sept. 1987.

Madrick, Jeff. (2011). *Age of Greed: Triumph of Finance and the Decline of America, 1970 to the Present*. New York: Knopf.

Starr, Paul. (1988). "The Meaning of Privatization," *Yale Law and Policy Review* 6 (1988): 6–41.

U.S. General Accounting Office. (1997). "Privatization: Lessons Learned by State and Local Governments." *Report to the Chairman, House Republican Task Force on Privatization*. Washington, D.C.: U.S. General Accounting Office, March 1997.

50. Local Governments Scramble for Budget Solutions

Christine Smith and Shelley Fulla

For decades, the mantra of local government has been to do more with less, which has led many counties and municipalities to limit or reduce spending in their operating budgets.

However, in a number of states the election results of 2010 have translated the public debate over the appropriate level of government spending into specific proposals to reduce the amount of state financial support for local governments.

In some states, such as Wisconsin, revenue reductions are paired with state requirements that limit or reduce the ability of local governments to independently raise revenues via property taxes. In a recent survey of local governments in the upper Midwest, Baker Tilly provides insight into the budget options that counties and municipalities are considering in response to a challenging economic situation and to proposed revenue cuts.

Public Employee Fringe Benefit Cuts and Wage Freezes Appear Most Likely

Many municipalities and counties responding to the survey reported they are more likely to pursue budget options that reduce the cost of public sector labor without cutting staff, either via fringe benefit cost reductions (3.61) or a wage freeze (3.44), as shown below.

- 57.7 percent of survey respondents indicated staff benefit cost reductions, and 60.3 percent indicated a wage freeze, were "almost a certainty" or "likely" (that is, had a better than 50/50 chance).
- 43.6 percent indicated staffing reductions were almost a certainty or likely.
- 34.7 percent of survey respondents rated budget initiatives that involve shared service with neighboring jurisdictions as having a better than 50/50 chance.
- 33.3 percent of respondents indicated that the likelihood of consolidation

Originally published as Christine Smith and Shelley Fulla (2012). "Local Governments Scramble for Budget Solutions." Baker Tilly: bakertilly.com. Reprinted with permission of the publisher and author.

of service delivery had a better than 50/50 chance.

- 29.4 percent rated "increased revenue" as either "likely" or "almost a certainty."
- 20.5 percent rated privatization/outsourcing as having a better than 50/50 chance.

On a scale of 1 to 5, with 1 indicating essentially no chance and 5 indicating almost a certainty, staff reductions (2.98), were ranked as having just under a 50/50 chance of being acted on by local governments in the survey. As a group, survey participants assessed the likelihood of both "Increase Revenues" (2.69) and "Other Shared Service Arrangements" (2.71) (i.e., joint purchasing, mutual aid) as less than 50/50. It should be noted that a majority of the respondents were from local governments in Wisconsin, where the budget debate has been particularly intense, and where public employee fringe benefits have been a focus of legislative activity.

Staff Reductions Are Anticipated

In some states, the recent recession created strong pressures for staff reductions in local government. This is particularly true in Illinois, where a significant portion of local government revenues depends on transactional taxes and fees such as sales taxes, hotel/motel taxes, and real estate transfer fees which are highly sensitive to swings in the economy. In states like Wisconsin, where more stable property tax revenues are a larger source of local government revenues, widespread layoffs have not occurred to date, although many local governments have avoided filling position vacancies to achieve budget savings. As noted, survey respondents rated "staff reductions" as having a just under 50/50 chance of being

implemented in their community when compared to a range of other budget options. However, when asked directly, more than 61 percent reported that they are anticipating at least some staff reductions in response to current budget pressures.

Staff reductions can take a number of forms, including:

- Not rehiring to fill vacant positions: This approach to staff level reductions is widespread
- Layoffs: A Reduction in Force can be targeted to a specific Department or function, or can be an across-the-board cut
- Furloughs: Labor cost reductions achieved through reducing the number of hours worked (and compensated)

Of the survey respondents anticipating reductions, the scale of anticipated position reductions is likely to involve a "few positions" across a range of pre-defined functions, with Public Works, Streets & Highways, Parks & Recreation, Administrative functions, and Public Safety all receiving roughly equal ratings.

Additional survey comments included:

- Hoping to reduce staffing through attrition
- Depends on attrition in departments as well as targeted cuts
- Two retirements anticipated in public works this year, one position will like be replaced in the utilities

Increasing Revenue Is Also Anticipated

Overall, survey respondents rated the likelihood of implementation of new revenue enhancements as less than 50/50 when compared to other budget savings options. However, when asked directly, more than half of respondents (56.6 percent) reported they anticipate increasing revenue in response to current budget pressure.

Local governments have a variety of authorized revenue tools (taxes, fees, and rates), and survey respondents reported significant differences in the likelihood of specific revenue approaches. Survey respondents reported that increased user fees (3.76) and increased grant writing (3.49) were the most likely approaches to be implemented.

Additional comments included:

- Expect increased use of special charges
- Likely to implement a recycling user fee if budget is passed
- Implemented (a new) Jail fee (room and board charges for inmates)
- Possibility of implementing an indirect cost allocation plan
- The two revenue approaches that offer the greatest opportunity for increased revenues for local governments: increased sales, hotel & wheel taxes (2.31) and exceeding levy limits via referenda (1.55) were rated least likely to be implemented.

A Majority of Local Governments Do Not Anticipate New Outsourcing Efforts

Local government organizations have engaged in both contracting and outsourcing throughout history. Almost every public sector organization with which Baker Tilly has worked either contracts for or outsources at least some services or functions. For the purposes of this research, "outsourcing" means the procurement of services under contract with an external for-profit or not-for-profit organization, whereas "contracting" represents paying for services provided by another local government.

More than two thirds (69.8 percent) of respondents answering this question indicated they are not seriously considering outsourcing additional local government services in the short term. Because of the nature of the survey, it is unknown whether the number of local governments seriously considering increased privatization/outsourcing is higher or lower than in previous years.

Survey respondents who indicated they are considering new outsourcing efforts were asked to identify specific functions that are under consideration, or to comment on the question. Respondents indicated:

- Solid Waste Collection (***)
- Currently analyzing-to be determined (***)
- Animal Control
- Considering utility meter installation & repair
- General administration
- Grass cutting
- Imaging of documents printing
- Landscaping, communication
- Nearly everything outsourceable is already out-sourced after 5+ years of levy caps in Wisconsin
- Records management
- Recycling
- Snow Plowing
- Some highway maintenance, housekeeping, campground management
- Staffing by temporary services

Note: Asterisks indicate multiple responses for the same category

Local Governments Already Outsource a Broad Range of Functions

All of the counties participating in the survey, and 86.4 percent of the municipalities, volunteered information about the single most successful outsourcing arrangement currently in place. Of the 27 municipal functions reported in the survey, the most commonly identified beneficial outsourcing arrangements were legal services, residential solid waste collection and disposal, and recycling. The small number of counties responding to the survey did not appear to strongly favor a particular function.

The two most commonly cited benefits for these arrangements included operating savings (3.79) and improved focus on core functions (3.47).

There are risks inherent to outsourcing government service delivery, and any potential initiative should be evaluated rigorously both in terms of fiscal impact and impact on service delivery. Eleven and a half percent of survey respondents indicated that they have brought some functions back in-house that were previously externally sourced. When asked why outsourcing was abandoned in these cases, survey respondents indicated:

- Difficulty contacting them on weekends to help with City events. And to cut expenses
- The contracted management team

was ineffective and ignoring the utility infrastructure
- Cost savings and qualified (internal) staff
- Needed additional work for current employees
- More cost effective (to do in-house)
- Too expensive and not enough result
- We are better able to allocate these resources and manage our preventive maintenance program at a lower cost

The Bottom Line?

Local governments face serious fiscal challenges that will require hard choices, and not all budget options are appropriate for all communities. For example, your community may be self-insured, which can limit potential fringe benefit savings opportunities. Alternatively, your organization may have already enacted significant staffing reductions in recent years, and you may wish to explore shared services or consolidation opportunities. If your organization is looking for alternatives on how to meet these challenges while preserving core services, it is important to draw on the lessons learned from similar communities.

51. Prudent Privatization

Stephen Goldsmith

Too often, political rhetoric overshadows careful analysis.

Local and state officials across the country now face urgent questions concerning how to fund infrastructure deficits and gaping budget holes. Last year, for example, New York Governor David Paterson surprised many with his announcement that he would consider leasing state assets (such as bridges and highways) to private contractors to fix the budget. This has triggered a round of arguments for and against the idea of privatization.

Most of the voices in the debate focus on the wrong issue—public ownership—while ignoring the real issue: public value.

The privatization debate is consumed by political rhetoric taking the place of careful analysis. Some on the right argue that private ownership is always more efficient (i.e., a more efficient monopoly), and some on the left claim that corporations are corrupt and that it is somehow un–American for companies to make a profit delivering public services, even if they do it better, faster, and cheaper than government.

Determining whether to sell or lease a public asset should depend on the terms of the deal itself and the uses of the proceeds. But these nuanced and difficult questions rarely surface in the public debate. This is partly because few governments, including at the federal level, have a distinct capital budget, reducing the incentive for long-term investments and encouraging financial sleight-of-hand. Furthermore, many cases show that asset sales are last-ditch attempts to fill budget gaps rather than principled efforts to provide public goods at a better price.

This motivation is understandable. City, county, and state budgets across the country are structurally out of balance as they face falling tax revenues and promises for public services that far exceed what taxpayers or the economy can bear. Over the last 10 years, state spending on education, health care, welfare, corrections, and trust-fund benefits increased 100 percent, and many states are on track to double again between 2000 and 2010. Crisis requires action, and it may be better to sell an asset than to allow a government to renege on promises or lapse into bankruptcy.

However, despite these tough conditions-or perhaps because of them-glossing over the problem by selling assets delays disaster rather than preventing it. Those who favor privatization should not support monetizing a physical asset to fill a budget hole without dealing with the underlying conditions that created the hole in the first place.

Originally published as Stephen Goldsmith (2009). "Prudent Privatization." *Government Finance Review*, 25(3), June 2009. Reprinted with permission of the publisher.

So when does private financing, owner-ship, or operation of public infrastructure make the most sense? When it is part of a broader plan to correct the poor maintenance of existing infrastructure and to build the transportation, energy, and environmental projects needed to keep our economy healthy and support our growing population.

The need for a comprehensive plan to maintain and expand our physical infra-structure is undeniable. Over a quarter of the nation's bridges are rated as structurally deficient; nearly 50 percent of the 257 water-way locks operated by the Army Corps of Engineers are functionally obsolete; airport capacity increased from 1991 to 2001 by only 1 percent while air traffic grew by 35 per-cent; and worsening urban highway con-gestion is estimated to produce an annual drain on our economy of $78 billion. In addition, water and waste-water infrastruc-ture demands are mounting; the EPA proj-ects that $277 billion in drinking water infrastructure improvements is needed over the next 20 years to comply with regulations and ensure a safe water supply.

The good news for states and localities is that they hold valuable physical assets that they can leverage to create positive local change. Monetizing these assets can play a critical role in resolving their capital and infrastructure needs.

A few principles might help guide the debate to determine when such a transac-tion makes sense, and how to structure a sale or lease to ensure the partnership is engi-neered to produce public value efficiently:

1. It rarely makes sense to sell a capital asset to fund an operational hole.

2. Success should not be measured by how much privatization has occurred but by how well government performs as a re-sult. Accountability for public and private entities is critical.

3. Management efficiencies should help offset borrowing costs. Better technology,

the benefits of shared services, or larger-scale providers often embed solutions into the financing.

4. Government should be clear about what it wants to control, such as pricing, access, and equity, and what risks it wants to shift, such as construction, operations, and financial responsibilities. But it should be flexible regarding the process used to manage the projects.

5. Always use a transparent and compet-itive process with clear evaluative terms.

6. Government as seller should be repre-sented by sophisticated and experienced advisers.

7. Consider the effect on existing work-ers; they can almost always be incorporated into the solution. The process should rec-ognize and attempt to accommodate the existing labor force if it expresses an interest in participating in a manner that increases productivity and efficiency.

Living by these principles can make or break a deal. Chicago, when arranging its Skyway transaction, handled these deal points correctly. Similarly, Indiana ap-proached the lease of its toll road in exactly the right way. The state was well advised, controlled the rates, set the terms for pave-ment quality, and, most important, invested the proceeds to fully fund the state's infra-structure deficit. Over a decade ago, how-ever, Atlanta showed how not to manage a wastewater infrastructure privatization with a process driven by politics, inaccurate base-line data, and unclear performance stan-dards. That city's leaders chose the same private partner we did when I was mayor of Indianapolis for a similarly sized trans-action. One worked and the other did not.

Government can derive enormous ben-efit from public partnerships and asset sales. However, whether to do them at all and whether they'll succeed depend greatly on the process and the purpose.

I. Privatization Glossary from the League of Women Voters

Asset Sale

An asset sale is the transfer of ownership of government assets, commercial type enterprises, or functions to the private sector. In general, the government will have no role in the financial support, management, or oversight of a sold asset. However, if the asset is sold to a company in an industry with monopolistic characteristics, the government may regulate certain aspects of the business, such as the regulation of utility rates.

Competition

Competition occurs when two or more parties independently attempt to secure the business of a customer by offering the most favorable terms. Competition in relation to government activities is usually categorized in three ways:

(1) public versus private, in which public-sector organizations compete with the private sector to conduct public-sector business;

(2) public versus public, in which public-sector organizations compete among themselves to conduct public-sector business; and

(3) private versus private, in which private-sector organizations compete among themselves to conduct public-sector business.

Contracting Out

Contracting out is the hiring of private-sector firms or nonprofit organizations to provide a good or service for the government. Under this approach, the government remains the financier and has management and policy control over the type and quality of services to be provided. Thus, the government can replace contractors that do not perform well.

Divestiture

Divestiture involves the sale of government-owned assets or commercial-type functions or enterprises. After the divestiture, the government generally has no role concerning financial support, management, regulation, or oversight.

Employee Stock Ownership Plans

Under an employee stock ownership plan (ESOP), employees take over or participate in the management of the organization that employs them by becoming shareholders of stock in that organization. In the public sector, an ESOP can be used in privatizing a service or function. Recently, for example, the Office of Personnel Management established an ESOP for its employees who perform personnel background investigations.

217

Franchising of Internal Services

Under the franchising of internal services, government agencies may provide administrative services to other government agencies on a reimbursable basis. Franchising gives agencies the opportunity to obtain administrative services from another governmental entity instead of providing them for themselves.

Franchising-External Services

In the franchise-external service technique, the government grants a concession or privilege to a private-sector entity to conduct business in a particular market or geographical area, such as concession stands, hotels, and other services provided in certain national parks. The government may regulate the service level or price, but users of the service pay the provider directly.

Government Corporations

Government corporations are separate legal entities that are created by Congress; generally with the intent of conducting revenue-producing commercial-type activities and that are generally free from certain government restrictions related to employees and acquisitions.

Government-Sponsored Enterprises

Government-sponsored enterprises (GSE) are privately owned, federally chartered financial institutions with a nationwide scope and limited lending powers that benefit from an implicit federal guarantee that enhances a GSE's ability to borrow money in the private sector. They are not agencies of the United States but serve as a means of accomplishing a public purpose defined by law.

Joint Ventures

See public-private partnership.

Leasing Arrangements

Leasing arrangements are a form of public-private partnership. Under a long-term lease, the government may lease a facility or enterprise to a private-sector entity for a specified period. Maintenance, operation, and payment terms are spelled out in the lease agreement. Under a sale-leaseback arrangement, the government sells an asset to a private-sector entity and then leases it back. Under a sale-service contract or lease-service contract, an asset sale or long-term lease is coupled with an arrangement with the purchaser to furnish services for a specified period. Leases in which the government leases a facility (e.g., a building lease) are considered a form of contracting out, rather than a public-private partnership.

Managed Competition

Under managed competition, a public-sector agency competes with private-sector firms to provide public-sector functions or services under a controlled or managed process. This process clearly defines the steps to be taken by government employees in preparing their own approach to performing an activity. The agency's proposal, which includes a bid proposal for cost-estimate, is useful to compete directly with private-sector bids.

Outsourcing

Under outsourcing, a government entity remains fully responsible for the provision of affected services and maintains control over management decisions while another entity operates the function or performs the service. This approach includes contracting out, the granting of franchises to private firms, and the use of volunteers to deliver public services.

Performance Based Organizations

Under a performance based organization (PBO), policymaking is to be separated from service operation functions by moving all policymaking responsibilities to a Presidential appointee. The service operations are moved to an organization to be headed by a chief executive officer (CEO), hired on a competitive contract for a fixed term. The CEO's contract defines expected performance and in exchange for being held accountable for achieving performance, the CEO is granted certain flexibilities for human resource management, procurement, and other administrative functions.

Privatization

The term privatization has generally been defined as any process aimed at shifting functions and responsibilities, in whole or in part, from the government to the private sector.

Public-Private Partnership

Under a public-private partnership, sometimes referred to as a joint venture, a contractual arrangement is formed between public- and private-sector partners, and can include a variety of activities involving the private sector in the development, financing, ownership, and operation of a public facility or service. It typically includes infrastructure projects and/or facilities. In such a partnership, public and private resources are pooled and their responsibilities divided so that each partner's efforts complement one another. Typically, each partner shares in income resulting from the partnership in direct proportion to the partner's investment. Such a venture, while a contractual arrangement, differs from typical service contracting in that the private-sector partner usually makes a substantial cash, at-risk, equity investment in the project, and the public sector gains access to new revenue or service delivery capacity without having to pay the private-sector partner.

Service Shedding

Divestiture through service shedding occurs when the government reduces the level of service provided or stops providing a service altogether. Private-sector businesses or nonprofit organizations may step in to provide the service if there is a market demand.

Subsidies

The government can encourage private-sector involvement in accomplishing public purposes through tax subsidies or direct subsidies, such as the funding of low-income housing and research and development tax credits.

User Fees

User fees require those who use a government service to pay some or all of the cost of the service rather than having the government pay for it through revenues generated by taxes. Charging entry fees into public parks is an example of a user fee.

Volunteer Activities

An activity in which volunteers provide all or part of a service and are organized and directed by a government entity can also be considered a form of outsourcing. Volunteer activities are conducted either through a formal agency volunteer program or through a private nonprofit service organization.

Vouchers

Vouchers are government financial subsidies given to individuals for purchasing specific goods or services from the private or public sector. The government gives individuals redeemable certificates or vouchers to purchase the service in the open market. Under this approach, the government relies on the market competition for cost control and individual citizens to seek out quality goods or services. The government's financial obligation to the recipient is limited by the amount of the voucher. A form of vouchers are grants, which can be given to state and local governments that may use the funds to buy services from the private sector.

II. Managed Competition Guidelines from Washoe County, Nevada

1. Introduction

1.1. Background

Local governments have begun utilizing performance based service delivery models to reduce costs and improve quality of their services. These models involve careful comparison of costs and benefits of services performed internally versus externally. Managed competition models have been successfully implemented in other counties and cities and have proven to instill market discipline, competitiveness, reduced costs, and improved quality into service delivery while assuming internal providers often do and can compete with external counterparts.

Over the past five years, Washoe County endured enormous strains on its operations and finances in the context of the country's economic downturns and slow recovery. While diligently struggling to deliver services, the County and its employees have suffered five years of successive and incremental budget cuts and personnel reductions. During this period, the County reduced spending by $154 million and reduced its workforce by nearly 20 percent.

The County is now at a threshold where such incremental changes are no longer sufficient. More strategic and fundamental measures must be taken. As part of a "fundamental services review," Management Partners1 recommended that Washoe County develop a managed competition process and execute it for selected services. These guidelines are a first step toward developing the managed competition process for the County.

1.2. Definition of Managed Competition

Managed competition is a structured and transparent process that gives public sector entities an opportunity to openly evaluate improvements and compare their service delivery processes, needs, costs, quality, and capabilities against those of external providers. The process gathers data, analyzes and documents service delivery, baselines performance, and establishes service levels. Managed competition is a means to analyze and make decisions about the manner in which governments deliver their services. A managed competition environment ultimately requires "in-house service units to compete with external providers."

Managed competition is a team effort leveraging the expertise, creativity, ingenuity, and resourcefulness of staff within the government entity. With established process, it unites all levels of the government entity toward continuously improving services, becoming more competitive, gaining process efficiencies, and/or saving money. It encourages staff to continually critique existing processes, policies, and practices in order to provide the best possible services. The process does not assume any predisposition as to who will eventually provide the services.

Managed competition is distinct and different from outsourcing and privatization in that the service delivery provider can remain internal or become external. A study may result in the choice of the internal provider because it delivers the most efficient processes, highest quality, and lowest costs possible. Or, the government entity may choose the external service provider because that provider has the most efficient delivery of the service(s). However, the government entity is still responsible for the services. With privatization, the government entity decides to exit entirely from the services and sells off the entity's assets related to the delivery of the services.

Effective implementation of managed competition requires staff resources and many support mechanisms to deliver integrity in the decision making processes, high quality analysis, and regular follow-on evaluation of the results. Required skills include: guidelines, policy and program planning; evaluation; continuous process improvement and workflow analysis; group process and facilitation; financial and cost analyses; risk assessment; implementation; audit; and on- going service level/performance management. Thus, internal and possible additional external resources are important factors in developing the environment to support success.

1.3. Other Definitions

The following terms are used in these guidelines:

GFOA, Managed Competition as a Service Delivery Option, http://www.gfoa.org/index.php?option=com_content&task=view&id=1557 (2006)

Throughout the rest of the guidelines, "services" will refer to one service or multiple related services.

1.3.1. Best practice—a method or technique that has consistently shown results superior to those achieved with other means, and that is used as a benchmark.

1.3.2. Services—An individual or set of closely related County processes that deliver a mandated and/or otherwise identified value to a County citizen and/or internal County customer.

1.3.3. Process—The step or set of steps used in achieving an end (in this document, the end is a service or set of services).

1.3.4. Service delivery—the implementation of and method by which a County customer receives a County service.

1.4. Purposes of Managed Competition Guidelines

The purposes of these guidelines are to set forth:

1.4.1. Goals for the managed competition process at the County.

1.4.2. Guiding principles for conducting the managed competition process.

1.4.3. Selection criteria and qualifications of services to be evaluated for managed competition.

1.4.4. High level steps for the County's managed competition process.

1.4.5. A foundation that can and will be edited as the County gains more managed competition experience and evolves its program.

2. Managed Competition

2.1. Goals

The overall goal of managed competition is to deliver competitive, sustainable, and high quality services which engender industry best practices and which can be measured and monitored to established service levels between the provider and the County. These services must ultimately satisfy the County's external and internal customers. The County's citizens and taxpayers expect the County to deliver "best value" services that are of the highest quality at the lowest cost.

The County is committed to ensuring

that best value services are delivered—but it does not necessarily have to be the actual provider.

The County managed competition process will:

2.1.1. Identify, through established criteria, County services and related processes that are high priority candidates for managed competition;

2.1.2. Support a sense of ownership of services, continuous improvement in the results achieved, and innovation in the delivery of the services.

2.1.3. Maintain or improve the quality of services provided and align that quality with customers' expectations and willingness to pay.

2.1.4. Result in competitively delivered services that are of high value and low cost while still meeting customers' needs.

2.1.5. Apply measurable, industry accepted baseline target service levels, and performance metrics for any services being studied for managed competition.

2.1.6. Consider alternative service delivery methods only if there is a better than 10 percent cost savings and if the level of services are equal to or better than existing.

2.2. Guiding Principles

The County undertakes managed competition with the following guiding principles at the forefront:

2.2.1. Efficient, Cost Effective and High Quality Services. A key goal of managed competition is to provide customers with a high quality of services at the lowest reasonable cost ethically and efficiently possible. Continuous improvement distinguishingly achieves this in a business environment through a synergy of creativity, innovation, and employee empowerment that facilitates highly competitive and sustainable service delivery.

2.2.2. Transparency and Fairness. Throughout the lifecycle of a managed competition study, the County is committed to transparency and openness. The County will maintain the highest standards of ethics and will make every effort to avoid any actual or perceived conflict of interest. The operational and competitive assessments of internal and external providers will be conducted fairly and objectively.

2.2.3. Managed Competition Is Not Outsourcing. Managed competition is commonly misperceived to be outsourcing. The intent of this managed competition process is to ensure the County is a competitive and sustainable service organization with the optimal mix of service delivery from inside and outside of the organization. The optimal mix is determined by an end to end analysis that ensures: services are delivered competitively, sustainably, and valuably; service levels are defined and understood; and performance is tracked, documented, and continually reviewed. While a result of this process may be a service being delivered from an external provider, it is not the initial goal.

Outsourcing would be a specific decision by the County to have services delivered from an external provider and should not involve any competition for services from internal resources.

2.2.4. Adequate Resources and Support. Managed competition requires staff resources and many support mechanisms to deliver integrity in the decision making processes, high quality analysis, and regular follow-on evaluation of the results. In order to provide these resources and support, the County shall take a measured and feasible approach to the managed competition process. The County shall facilitate personnel, training, consulting, continuous improvement resources, etc., as needed to support employees throughout the steps of the managed competition process.

2.2.5. Competitive Assessment and Readiness. The managed competition process must include a competitive assessment phase and, if needed, a competitive readiness phase.

• The managed competition process will first include a phase in which a team gathers and analyzes data about current delivery of services through County staff, operations, and processes.

• Additionally, the County will analyze operations according to accepted industry best practices, performance measures, and service level benchmarks to identify current performance levels and possible gaps.

• Should the County need to improve its performance, a competitive readiness phase will be available. This phase would give County operations sufficient time to develop and implement recommended improvements to align with the industry best practices and performance levels.

• The average reasonable period for the competitive readiness phase is no more than 12 months. Each managed competition study will recommend the phase length based upon findings. The timeframe will sometimes be less than 12 months and sometimes more.

2.2.6. Equitable, Fair and Consistent Request for Proposal (RFP) Process. The County will, in accordance with public policy, treat all parties consistently and equitably should the managed competition study move to a RFP and bidding stage.

• Preference will be given to bidders that sustain local jobs.

• The process will comply with all County Purchasing guidelines and policies.

• To foster a level playing field, the following factors will be fairly, objectively, and consistently applied to all providers:

• Industry accepted performance measures and metrics for the services.

• Cost calculations and comparisons based upon the above industry standards and made with verifiable data (including direct costs, indirect costs, actual wages, and/or prevailing wages).

2.2.7. Imbedded Checkpoints / Decision Steps. The managed competition process shall include checkpoints and decision steps along the course of a managed competition study. Recommended ones include, but are not limited to:

• Selection of service(s) to be part of the managed competition study. In accordance with the "Selection Criteria" section of these guidelines, the County shall, through the Strategic Planning Committee (SPC), carefully weigh the criteria when determining which services to proceed to study. The criteria include the degree of risk, legal restrictions, the marketplace of service providers, accountability, necessity, etc. The full list is itemized is the "Selection Criteria" section below.

• Post competitive assessment. After the process analysis, determine if a competitive readiness window is needed and work with the process team to improve service delivery according to recommendations.

• Embark upon RFP phase. After the process analysis and, if applicable, the competitive readiness phase, determine if services should be set out for competition. To determine this course of action, considerations should include whether or not a RFP phase will assist in achieving the goal of competitive, sustainable, high quality services.

• Provision of service. In consideration of changing a present method of service delivery, a successful bidder must show a more than 10 percent cost savings AND equal or better level of services.

• County costs include direct costs and appropriate indirect costs (including those costs that can be avoided if the services were to go to an external provider).

• External provider costs include their bid price, the County's contract administration costs, and transition costs.

• Both County and external provider costs should be netted by any estimated incremental revenue generation or cost avoidance where applicable.

• Review of performance to service level agreements and audit of results. Regardless of who provides the service, the managed competition process should result in established service level agreements and performance checkpoints between the County and the provider. The performance checkpoints and audit of services should be completed annually and include documentation in line with the County's internal audit standards and practices.

2.2.8. Possible Impacts. The managed competition process will impact services due to the inherent nature of enabling competitiveness, focusing on sustainability, delivering according to best practices, and establishing quantifiable service levels. One example might be a change in responsiveness because of new work prioritization levels. In the past, all requests may have received similar call back windows. In the future, prioritized requests may receive graduated response times. Another example could be a change in what is considered necessary now but is viewed as not cost sustainable in the future.

2.2.9. Employment Stability. The County shall continue its commitment to employment stability for its workforce and will:

• Notify employees in advance of areas planned for a managed competition study.

• Assist employees in navigating and working through the managed competition process.

• Offer tools and training to employees as needed to help with the managed competition process and with competitive readiness.

• Provide placement services for employees who voluntarily decide to separate from the County.

• Require selected vendors to first consider utilizing County employees who know the services to assist them in providing services, should a study result in an external provider.

• Negotiate impacts with affected employee associations where required by collective bargaining agreements.

2.3. Selection Criteria

The County's Strategic Planning Committee (SPC) will identify the services to become part of a managed competition study. A study may be conducted for current services (internally or externally provided) or new services. The SPC members may also receive recommendations for study area(s) from the Board of County Commissioners (BCC), the County Manager, the Organizational Effectiveness Committee, employee associations, or other avenues upon which they agree.

The following considerations shall be used when selecting services for a managed competition study:

2.3.1. Legal, Regulatory or Funding Restrictions. The County will exclude any services that have legal, regulatory, or funding guidelines which restrict the provider to be County employees. If local ordinances or laws can be changed to accommodate possible managed competition, the County may explore such actions to an extent that is reasonable and feasible.

2.3.2. Existence of Alternative Providers. There must be at least two other existing qualified external providers (aside from the County) in the marketplace for the services being considered for a managed competition study.

2.3.3. Cost Savings Potential. The services should have reasonable likelihood that managed competition will result in reduced and/or avoided costs or increased revenue where possible.

2.3.4. Service Identification and Measurement. The services must be identifiable and measurable accordingly to industry accepted performance metrics (or other performance measures developed in lieu of absent industry standards).

2.3.5. County Workforce Impacts. The County shall consider and, where required, negotiate any impacts managed competition studies may have on County employees and their workload, productivity, efficiency, etc.

2.3.6. Degree of Risk. The County shall factor in the possible degree of risk associated with services provided by an external provider through a weighted evaluation procedure. The County shall consider the impacts of risks such as defaults, breach of contract, marketplace stability, liability, potential costs of re-entry (if the County exits the service), etc.

2.3.7. Quality, Competitiveness and Sustainability. The services should have reasonable likelihood that managed competition will improve quality for the same or lower costs. The services shall be measurably competitive and financially sustainable using the chosen service delivery provider.

2.3.8. Asset Requirements. The County shall consider the extent and nature of assets needed to deliver the services through various service delivery methods. Assets can be but are not limited to financial, human/labor (knowledge/

familiarity), technological, or capital resources.

2.3.9. Control and Accountability. The County must be able to efficiently manage and control the services through the selected service delivery method. The County shall account for the responsible and appropriate use of public funds, customer satisfaction, service competitiveness, and service quality.

2.4. Steps

The high level steps for the managed competition process are:

2.4.1. Identify, through established criteria, County services that are likely and reasonable candidates for managed competition.

2.4.2. Select a service or services to be a part of a managed competition study.

2.4.3. Form a business process team with employees of the applicable area and possibly other employees affected by the applicable area for the managed competition study. The team shall include:

- Project lead.
- Project team members including but not limited to a business process champion, business process experts and administrative services representatives.
- Continuous improvement facilitator.
- Managed competition process consultant.
- Change management champion.
- If needed, other external consulting expertise—e.g., managed competition process, industry and/or process specific, performance management, etc.

2.4.4. Coordinate managed competition study with other statutory board(s) as needed.

2.4.5. Analyze County processes for selected service(s) and document the analysis of processes against best practices and baseline performance measures.

The study's analysis shall ensure that the County provider has:

- A business plan and strategy.
- Documented internal business policies and operating procedures.
- Benchmarks against industry best practices and performance measures.
- Fully allocated (burdened) service costs (costs including salary and benefits).
- Documented competitive advantages, disadvantages, gaps, recommended improvements, and next steps/options.

The study shall also contain the following (isolated from how the County may be providing the services):

- Picture of industry trends.
- Cost/benefit analysis for alternative service delivery methods.
- Pros and cons regarding different service delivery methods.
- Supported recommendation(s) for the next steps in the managed competition process.

2.4.6. Conduct a managed competition study review with the County Strategic Planning Committee. Consider options:

- Re-engineer and/or restructure internal provider operations—competitive readiness phase required.
- Retain as-is with internal provider.
- Continue with managed competition—conduct a competitive bidding process that includes the internal provider.
- Partner with another entity to share services.

- Outsource.
- Privatize.

The Strategic Planning Committee will select an option and recommend actions to be taken by the BCC or other statutory board(s) as needed.

2.4.7. Begin further implementation steps based upon the option selected.

2.4.8. Support a notification and final review period. The Strategic Planning Committee will publish the managed competition study and recommendations and then begin a 30 day final review period during which comments and/or objections may be filed. The Strategic Planning Committee will review and consider such feedback within 2 weeks after the 30 day deadline, wherein final results will be communicated.

2.4.9. Conduct RFP and bidding process (after the competitive readiness phase if applicable).

2.4.10. Select provider and complete paperwork—including a signed service level agreement with the selected provider.

2.4.11. Review provider performance according to service levels. All providers shall be subject to an initial evaluation period after signing.

2.4.12. Monitor contract and performance (annually at a minimum) according to service level agreements.

III. League of Women Voters Privatization Position

Statement of Position as Announced by National Board, June 2012

The LWVUS Board approved a new position on Privatization at its June 2012 meeting. The position is based on responses received from the 227 Leagues across the country that participated in the Privatization Study. Thanks to the many local and state Leagues and ILOs that held meetings, involved their communities, and worked to reach consensus on this important issue. Committee Chair Janis McMillen (KS) and her Committee: Diane DiIanni (TN), Carole Garrison (VA), Ann Henkener (OH), Cathy Lazarus (CA), Nora Leech (WA), Muriel Strand (CA) and Ted Volskay (SC) are to be commended for their excellent work and leadership.

Position

The League of Women Voters of the United States believes that when governmental entities consider the transfer of governmental services, assets and/or functions to the private sector, the community impact and goals of such transfers must be identified and considered. Further, the LWV believes that transparency, accountability, and preservation of the common good must be ensured.

The League believes that some government provided services could be delivered more efficiently by private entities; however, privatization is not appropriate in all circumstances. Privatization is not appropriate when the provision of services by the government is necessary to preserve the common good, to protect national or local security or to meet the needs of the most vulnerable members of society. While the League recognizes that the definition of core government services will vary by level of government and community values, services fundamental to the governance of a democratic society should not be privatized in their entirety. These services include the electoral process, justice system, military, public safety, public health, education, transportation, environmental protection and programs that protect and provide basic human needs.

The decision to privatize a public service should be made after an informed, transparent planning process and thorough analysis of the implications of privatizing service delivery. While specific criteria will vary by service and local conditions, the League believes the following considerations apply to most decisions to transfer public services, assets and functions to the private sector:

- On-going and timely communication with stakeholders and the public;
- Statement of the circumstances as they exist and what is to be gained;
- Definition of the quality, level and cost of service expected;
- Assessment of the private market; whether there are providers to assure competitive pricing and delivery; (in some cases there may not be multiple providers if a service is so specialized. i.e., high tech, airports.)
- Cost-benefit analyses evaluating short and long term costs of privatization, including the ongoing costs of contract administration and oversight;
- An understanding of the impact on customers, the broader community, environment and public employees;
- An open, competitive bidding process with clearly defined criteria to be used in selecting a contractor;
- A provision and process to ensure the services or assets will be returned to the government if a contractor fails to perform;
- A data-driven selection of private entities whose goals, purposes, and means are not incompatible with the public well-being;
- The careful negotiation and drafting of the controlling privatization contract; and
- Adequate oversight and periodic performance monitoring of the privatized services by the government

entity to ensure that the private entity is complying with all relevant laws and regulations, contract terms and conditions, and ethical standards, including public disclosure and comment.

The League believes that the enactment of state laws and issuance of regulations to control the process and delivery of privatization within a state's jurisdiction is often appropriate and desirable. Best practices for government regulation of the privatization process should include the following requirements:

- An open process that allows for citizen input and oversight in a timely manner;
- A reasonable feasibility study and project evaluation appropriate to the size and scope of the project;
- The establishment of carefully crafted criteria for selection of the private-entity (beyond the lowest cost bid);
- Additional consideration for local bidders in order to support the local economy;
- The retention of liability and responsibility with the government entity;
- Allowance for and promotion of opportunities for innovation and collaboration; and,
- Provision for employment, benefits and training plans on behalf of employees displaced as a result of privatization.

IV. International City/County Management Association Steps to Effective Privatization

November 19, 2012

Contracting with a private firm for delivery of services to residents is not guaranteed to be successful. In fact, according to the results of ICMA's recently conducted survey "Profile of Local Government Service Delivery Choices," 18 percent of local governments have brought back in house services that were previously contracted out. There are steps that local governments can take to help ensure that contracting out will be a successful delivery choice. The top seven activities reported by survey respondents that have undertaken steps to ensure success in implementing private service delivery are:

1. Identify successful uses of private alternatives in other jurisdictions
2. Propose implementation of private alternatives on a trial basis
3. Hire consultants to analyze the feasibility of private alternatives
4. Allow government departments to compete with the private sector
5. Apply private alternatives to new services
6. Apply private alternatives to growing services
7. Keep the service complaint mechanism in-house.

The last item is of particular importance. If the complaint mechanism is handled by the private firm delivering the service, the local government risks losing the ability to accurately monitor the quality of service delivery and thus loses the data necessary to hold the firm accountable.

Only 37 percent of local governments reported use of techniques to systematically evaluate private service delivery. Regular monitoring and evaluation of private service delivery is essential to ensuring that the private firm is meeting the expectations stipulated in the contract. Local governments have a responsibility to verify that the money spent on service delivery is used efficiently and effectively. Local governments that evaluate service delivery provided by a private firm show that they evaluate cost, compliance with delivery standards specified in the contract, and citizen satisfaction. The highest numbers of local governments use the following techniques:

1. Monitor citizen complaints
2. Analyze demographic and financial data
3. Conduct field observations.

Success requires effort. By taking the steps necessary to consider, implement, and evaluate private service delivery, local governments can ensure that they have made a good investment with taxpayer dollars.

About the Editors and Contributors

As of the time of their authorship

Michael **Abels** is a lecturer in the School of Public Administration at the University of Central Florida and served as city manager for cities in Florida and Ohio.

Robert **Barkin** is a Bethesda, Maryland–based freelance writer.

Greg **Beato** is a contributing editor and columnist for *Reason* magazine. His work has appeared in *The New York Times*, *The Washington Post*, *The Week*, and more than 100 other publications worldwide.

Bob **Bland** is professor and chair of the Department of Public Administration at the University of North Texas and is the author of *A Budgeting Guide for Local Government* (ICMA, 2007).

Ed **Brock** is the associate editor for *American City & County*.

John **Buntin** is staff writer with *Governing*.

Rachel **Burstein** is research associate, California Civic Innovation Project, New America Foundation, San Francisco, California.

John **Carroll** is an assistant professor for Public Administration, Huizenga School of Business and Entrepreneurship, Nova Southeastern University, Fort Lauderdale, Florida.

Craig **Chavez** is a management intern, ICMA Knowledge Center, Fullerton, California.

Chicago Council on Global Affairs Emerging Class of 2008: Olga Camargo, Piyush Chaudhari, Zach Egan, Stephen Haggerty, Joshua Hale, Minoo Javanmardian, S. Raja Krishnamoorthi, Kate Maehr, Lisa McClung, Sean Ryan, Tracey Scruggs-Yearwood, J. Jordan Shields, Roger Shores, Juliet Sorensen, Nik Theodore, Charles Wheelan, and Reza Yassari.

Dennis **Compton** a *Firehouse* contributing editor, is a speaker and the author of *Progressive Leadership Principles, Concepts and Tools* and *The When in Doubt Lead!*

Amy **Davis**, CPA, is director of finance for the City of Sandy Springs, Georgia.

Paul **Farmer** is the chief executive office of the American Planning Association.

Kevin **Fitchard** is an associate editor for *Telephony*, *American City & County*'s sister publication.

John **Flint** is city manager of Weston, Florida.

Shelley **Fulla** is project manager at Baker Tilly LLP, a full-service accounting and advisory firm.

Caitlin **Geary** is a fellow in the Economic Development Program, Center for Research and Innovation at the National League of Cities.

John **Geyman** is Professor Emeritus of Family Medicine at the University of Washington School of Medicine.

Amanda M. **Girth** is a doctoral graduate in public administration and instructor in the School of Public Affairs at American University.

231

Stephen **Goldsmith** is a former mayor of Indianapolis and the director of the Innovations in American Government Program at the Harvard Kennedy School.

Joaquin Jay **Gonzalez** III, Ph.D., is Mayor George Christopher Professor of Public Administration and Russell T. Sharpe Professor of Business at Golden Gate University. He has worked on privatization, nonprofit/NGO, and governance reform projects with the World Bank, the Institute on Governance, the Inter-American Development Bank, and Philippine Presidential Commission on Government Reorganization.

Jennifer **Grzeskowiak** is a Laguna Beach, California–based freelance writer.

Tom **Guilfoy** is director of competition at the City of Carrollton in Texas.

Ann **Hagedorn** is an award winning author of five narrative nonfiction books, her most recent being *The Invisible Soldiers: How America Outsourced Our Security*.

Cheryll **Hilvert** is director, Center for Management Strategies, ICMA, Washington, D.C.

Lawrence **Houstoun** has written extensively on business improvement districts and has published articles on destination urban parks, urban linear parks, and unexpected parks with unusual financing in the U.S. and Europe.

Institute for Local Government promotes good government at the local level with practical, impartial resources for California communities.

Jocelyn M. **Johnston** is MPA director and associate professor in the School of Public Affairs at American University.

Roger L. **Kemp**, Ph.D., ICMA-CM, is Distinguished Adjunct Professor at the Edward S. Ageno School of Business of Golden Gate University and a career city manager for 25 years in California, New Jersey, and Connecticut.

Steve **Klepper** is an administrative superintendent for the City of Corpus Christi, Texas.

Connie **Kuranko** is the director of the Walnut Creek, California–based U.S. Communities Going Green Program.

Cathy **Lazarus** is a member of the Education Study Committee on Privatization of Government Services, Assets and Functions, League of Women Voters.

Nora **Leech** is a member of the Education Study Committee on Privatization of Government Services, Assets and Functions, League of Women Voters.

Robert **Lynch** is president and chief executive officer, Americans for the Arts, Washington, D.C.

Justin **Marlowe** is co-author of "Public-Private Partnerships" in *Capital Budgeting and Finance: A Guide for Local Governments* (ICMA, 2009).

Helen S. **McIlvaine** is deputy director, Office of Housing, for the City of Alexandria, Virginia.

Monte **Mercer** is deputy executive director, North Central Texas Council of Governments, Arlington, Texas.

Henry **Mintzberg** is Cleghorn Professor of Management Studies at McGill University, Canada.

Russell **Nichols** is staff writer with Governing.

Jim **Peters** is president, Responsible Hospitality Institute, Santa Cruz, California.

Jonas **Prager** is associate professor of economics, faculty of arts and sciences, New York University, New York.

Ken **Pulskamp** is city manager, Santa Clarita, California.

Anna **Read** is project manager with the International City/County Management Association.

William **Rivenbark** is co-author of "Public-Private Partnerships" in *Capital Budgeting and Finance: A Guide for Local Governments* (ICMA, 2009).

Stephanie **Rozsa** works in the Knowledge Development Program, Center for Research and Innovation at the National League of Cities.

Alicia **Schatteman** is assistant professor in the School of Public and Global Affairs, Department of Public Administration and the Center for NGO Leadership and Development at Northern Illinois University.

Alicia **Scholer** is project manager, Responsible Hospitality Institute, Santa Cruz, California.

Katy **Singlaub** is county manager, Washoe County, Nevada.

Edward **Shikada** is assistant city manager, San Jose, California.

Christen **Smith**, Ph.D., CPRP, is president, Moro Group, LLC, Ann Arbor, Michigan.

Christine **Smith** is principal at Baker Tilly LLP, a full-service accounting and advisory firm.

Kyle **Steitz** is communications manager for SAFEbuilt, a firm that creates partnerships with communities across the country to create privatized development projects, including building department services, community planning and zoning, and code enforcement.

Muriel **Strand** is a member of the Education Study Committee on Privatization of Government Services, Assets and Functions, League of Women Voters.

David **Swindell** is director and associate professor, Center for Urban Innovation, Arizona State University, Phoenix, Arizona.

Christopher **Swope** is the project director, Information, at the Pew Center on the States and was previously *Governing*'s executive editor.

David **Taxman** is a parking and traffic planner at Desman Associates, which consulted in the Chicago privatization deal, and also with the Los Angeles parking system and the parking system in Harrisburg.

Charles **Taylor** is senior staff writer, NACo County News—The Voice of America's Counties.

A. John **Vogt** is co-author of "Public-Private Partnerships" in *Capital Budgeting and Finance: A Guide for Local Governments* (ICMA, 2009).

Ted **Volskay** is a member of the Education Study Committee on Privatization of Government Services, Assets and Functions, League of Women Voters.

Frank **Woodward** serves as assistant vice president for university advancement at Lincoln Memorial University.

Index